Teacher's Edition

WORLD ENGLISH Intro

Real People • Real Places • Real Language

Kristin Johannsen

HEINLE
CENGAGE Learning™

Australia • Brazil • Japan • Korea • Mexico • Singapore • Spain • United Kingdom • United States

World English Intro Teacher's Edition
Real People • Real Places • Real Language
Kristin Johannsen

Publisher: Sherrise Roehr

Managing Editor: Berta de Llano

Senior Development Editor: Margarita Matte

Development Editor: Michael Poor

Technology Development Manager: Debie Mirtle

Director of Global Marketing: Ian Martin

Director of US Marketing: Jim McDonough

Product Marketing Manager: Katie Kelley

Marketing Assistant: Jide Iruka

Content Project Manager: Andrea Bobotas

Senior Print Buyer: Betsy Donaghey

Cover Designer: Page 2 LLC

Cover Photo: Remi Benali/Corbis

Compositor: Nesbitt Graphics, Inc.

International Edition:
World English Intro TE ISBN 13: 978-1-4240-5112-0
World English Intro TE ISBN 10: 1-4240-5112-6

U.S. Edition:
World English Intro TE ISBN 13: 978-1-4240-6298-0
World English Intro TE ISBN 10: 1-4240-6298-5

Heinle
20 Channel Center Street
Boston, MA 02210
USA

Cengage Learning is a leading provider of customized learning solutions with office locations around the globe, including Singapore, the United Kingdom, Australia, Mexico, Brazil, and Japan. Locate your local office at:
international.cengage.com/region

Cengage Learning products are represented in Canada by Nelson Education, Ltd.

Visit Heinle online at elt.heinle.com

Visit our corporate website at www.cengage.com

Printed in Canada
1 2 3 4 5 6 7 13 12 11 10 09

CONTENTS

GETTING THERE

UNIT 6

1. How do you travel to work?

2. What other types of transportation do you use?

UNIT GOALS

Ask for and give directions
Create and use a tour route
Talk about transportation
Record a journey

62

63

> Warm-up questions stimulate students' previous knowledge and life experiences while providing teachers with useful leveling information.

> Striking photographs from around the globe introduce students to the unit theme.

> Clearly defined goals provide students with a "blueprint" that helps them visualize their learning.

> A clear and practical goal is presented, practiced and mastered every two pages in each unit.

A GOAL 1 ASK FOR AND GIVE DIRECTIONS

Vocabulary

A. Work with a partner. Locate these places on the map.

> There is a tourist office on Grand Street.

tourist office	train station	supermarket	post office	library
restaurant	hotel	park	museum	bank
art gallery	bus station	movie theater	shopping mall	

B. Read the directions and follow the red arrow.

Directions

You are in the tourist office. Cross Lincoln Avenue. Walk two blocks and cross Long Avenue. Turn left and walk two blocks. Turn right and go into the museum.

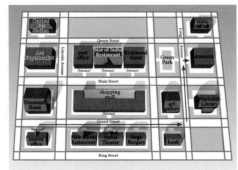

C. Follow the directions and write the destination.

1. From the tourist office walk two [...]
   Street. Walk two blocks and turn [...]
2. From Central Bus Station walk o[...]
   Street, walk two blocks, cross Lo[...]
3. From the Diamond Hotel, cross [...]
   Cross Grand Street and you are a[...]

64   Getting There

Grammar: Imperatives

Positive	Negative	Pr[...]
Turn right.	**Don't turn** left.	or [...] ac[...] be[...]

*The imperative is used for giving instructions.

A. Write the positive or negative imperative.

1. At the end of the block, _don't turn_ [...]
2. _____ (walk) for three blocks [...]
3. _____ (go) to the bank, go to [...]
4. _____ (cross) the street and t[...]
5. _____ (take a nap). It's time fo[...]

B. Use the map, and write the correct prepositions.

1. The art gallery is _____
   Avenue and Main Street.
2. The museum is _____
3. The Grand Movie Theater[...]
   Mega Burgers and the Ne[...]
4. The tourist office is _____
   Street and Lincoln Avenu[...]
5. The post office is _____
   Supermarket.

across from the

Conversation

A. A guest at the Richmond Hotel is talking to the receptionis[...]
Listen to the conversation. Where does the guest want to go[...]

Track 1-26

Hotel Guest:	Is there a <u>supermarket</u> near here?
Receptionist:	There's one <u>on the corner of Lincoln Avenue and Main Street across from the post office</u>.
Hotel Guest:	How do I get there?
Receptionist:	OK. <u>Leave the hotel and turn right. Walk one block and cross Lincoln Avenue</u>.
Hotel Guest:	Thank you very much.
Receptionist:	You're welcome.

B. Practice the conversation with a partner. Switch roles and practice it again.

C. Change the underlined words and make a new conversation.

Real Language

To ask for directions, we say, *How do I get there?*

✓ **Goal 1   Ask for and give directions**

Work with a partner. Take turns asking for and giving directions using the map on page 64.

Lesson A   65

> **Grammar** presented in the unit is practiced through a variety of activities, each designed to reinforce students' knowledge of how the language works and assure them accuracy and appropriateness in their use of English.

> **Real Language** information boxes in every unit focus students' attention on frequently used phrases and how to use them.

> Frequent **Conversation** activities motivate students to practice natural language themselves after practicing with a model dialog.

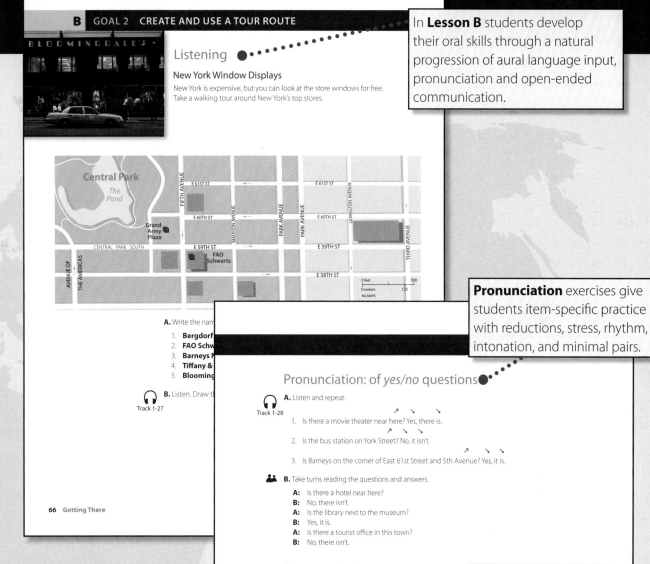

Listening

New York Window Displays

New York is expensive, but you can look at the store windows for free.
Take a walking tour around New York's top stores.

In **Lesson B** students develop their oral skills through a natural progression of aural language input, pronunciation and open-ended communication.

Central Park
The Pond

E 61ST ST   E 61ST ST

FIFTH AVENUE

MADISON AVENUE

PARK AVENUE

PARK AVENUE

LEXINGTON AVENUE

THIRD AVENUE

E 60TH ST   E 60TH ST

Grand
Army
Plaza

CENTRAL PARK SOUTH   E 59TH ST   E 59TH ST

AVENUE OF
THE AMERICAS

FAO
Schwartz

E 58TH ST

0 feet   500
0 meters   125
NG MAPS

Pronunciation exercises give students item-specific practice with reductions, stress, rhythm, intonation, and minimal pairs.

A. Write the nam

1. **Bergdorf
2. **FAO Schw
3. **Barneys
4. **Tiffany &
5. **Blooming

B. Listen. Draw t
Track 1-27

Pronunciation: of *yes/no* questions

A. Listen and repeat.
Track 1-28

1. Is there a movie theater near here? Yes, there is.
2. Is the bus station on York Street? No, it isn't.
3. Is Barneys on the corner of East 61st Street and 5th Avenue? Yes, it is.

B. Take turns reading the questions and answers.

A: Is there a hotel near here?
B: No, there isn't.
A: Is the library next to the museum?
B: Yes, it is.
A: Is there a tourist office in this town?
B: No, there isn't.

Communication

Students gain confidence and develop their speaking skills with step-by-step **Communication** activities.

Use the map on page 66. Ask for and give these directions to a partner.

1. From Barneys New York to Tiffany & Co.
2. From Bergdorf Goodman to Barneys New York.
3. From Bergdorf Goodman to Bloomingdale's.
4. From Tiffany & Co. to Bloomingdale's.

66   Getting There

✓ **Goal 2   Create and use a tour route**

Work together and write a tour route in your town.

● Language Expansion: Ground Transportation

From the Airport to Downtown
There are many ways to get downtown from the airport

Train
Take the train. Change at Midway Station. $20

Airport Shuttle Bus
Take the airport shuttle bus to your hotel. $17-$25

Subway
Take the subway direct to downtown. $2.50

Bus
Take the A100 bus to the Central Bus Station. $4.50

Taxi
Take a taxi. Approximately $60

By car
Rent a car. From $120 a day

Language Expansion sections focus on specific areas that help learners' to build language strategies and become more competent users of English.

A. Complete the chart with the names of different ground transportation.

Rental car $120
Expensive

answers questions about how much it costs to

Antarctica

Shackleton's Epic Journey—A diary

1914
August 8 Ernest Shackleton and his men leave London on their ship, *Endurance*.
1915

January 18 The *Endurance* is trapped in the ice. The men play soccer.
October 26 The *Endurance* **breaks up**. The men have to leave the *Endurance*. They camp on the ice.

Reading

A. Read the diary and follow the route on the map.

B. Choose the correct answer.

1. The journey starts in ___.
   a. Elephant Island
   b. London
   c. South Georgia
2. The *Endurance* breaks up on ___.
   a. October 26, 1914
   b. October 26, 1915
   c. October 26, 1916
3. ___ men leave Elephant Island in a small boat.
   a. Four
   b. Five
   c. Six
4. It takes ___ to sail from Elephant Island to South Georgia.
   a. one week
   b. two weeks
   c. three weeks
5. Shackleton finds help in ___.
   a. Stromness
   b. Elephant Island
   c. London

Magazine-style readings are a springboard for opinion sharing and personalization, and provide opportunities for students to use the grammar and vocabulary presented earlier in the unit.

1916
April 9 The ice begins to break up. They have to get into the small boats.
April 15 They land on Elephant Island.

Writing activities reinforce the structures, vocabulary and expressions learned in the unit.

April 24 Shackleton and five men leave Elephant Island in a small boat to find **help**. The other men stay on Elephant Island.
May 8 Shackleton lands in South Georgia.
May 19 Shackleton leaves three men with the boat. He crosses the mountains of South Georgia with two other men to find help.
May 20 They arrive in Stromness, the main town in South Georgia. They find help.

August 30 Shackleton **rescues** the men on Elephant Island.

Word Focus

rescue = save
break up = to fall to pieces
help = assistance

Writing

Write a diary about a real or imaginary journey.

June 3: We leave the airport at one o'clock. We change planes. We arrive at the hotel at eleven o'clock.
June 4: We take the subway to the museum. In the afternoon, we walk to the art gallery.

_____
_____
_____
_____
_____
_____
_____
_____
_____
_____
_____
_____
_____

✓ **Goal 4** **Record a journey**

Share your diary entry with the class.

Before You Watch

A. Study the picture. Use the words to complete the text.

A volcano is a mountain with a large hole at the top. This hole is called a _____. A volcano produces very hot, melted rock. When it is under ground, this hot, melted rock is called _____. When it leaves or comes out of the volcano, it is called _____. When the lava stays in the crater it forms a _____.
When lava leaves a volcano, we _____ erupts. We call it _____.

lava lake

eruption

crater

lava

magma

B. [covered] Read the definitions and label the pictures.

[covered] le who go to new places to learn things

[covered] ntists who study the earth (rocks and soil)

[covered] difficult trip or journey

[covered] nimal that can travel through the desert

[covered] cher at a university.

▲ rocks and soil

While You Watch

A. Watch the video. Match the sentence parts.

1. The geologists _____
2. The lava lake _____
3. Hot lava comes out of the earth _____
4. The team spends hours _____
5. It is not easy to stand near the crater _____
6. The professors are _____

a. collecting pieces of red-hot lava.
b. travel to the volcano on camels.
c. excited about studying the volcano.
d. because it is very hot.
e. is inside the crater.
f. and forms the lava lake.

B. Watch the video again and answer these questions.

1. What can geologists study at Erta Ale? _____
2. Where does the red hot lava come from? _____
3. In the early morning, what is the temperature near the crater? _____
4. How does the team feel when they return from the volcano? _____

C. What did you learn? Discuss with a partner what you see in these photos?

After You Watch

Discuss these questions with a partner.

1. Do you want to explore a volcano?
2. Why or why not?
3. How can people travel to difficult places?

Students conclude the unit by watching an authentic but carefully-graded National Geographic video clip. This application of students' newly acquired language skills is a part of the on-going unit assessment system and serves as a motivating consolidation task.

The video can be watched in class from the **Classroom DVD** or students can watch it individually on the **Student CD-ROM**.

Bonus Communication Activities that provide students with addional opportunites to develop their oral skills are provided at the back of World English Student Books 1 and Intro.

BONUS COMMUNICATION ACTIVITIES

Activity 1
Units 1 & 2

Take turns asking and answering the questions.

a. Where is the Brown family from?
b. Is it hot or cold in their country?
c. What is Mr. Brown's job?
d. Are they young or old?
e. Is Mr. Brown handsome?
f. Are the children pretty?

▲ the Brown family

Real Language

We use *I think . . .* or *Maybe . . .* when we are not sure about an answer.

I think they are from Canada.

Maybe they are from Canada.

Activity 2
Units 3 & 4

Take turns answering the questions.

a. What furniture can you see in the house?
b. Where is the furniture?
c. What electronic products can you see?
d. Where are they?
e. What personal possessions can you see?
f. Where are they?

WORLD ENGLISH ADDITIONAL SUPPORT AND PRACTICE

This **World English Teacher's Edition** is designed to make your preparation as simple as possible, allowing you to maximize actual classroom teaching time. It features page-by-page suggestions on how to teach the course, answer keys to the Student Book and Workbook, culture notes, extension activities, audio scripts of listening passages not printed in the Student Book, and video scripts.

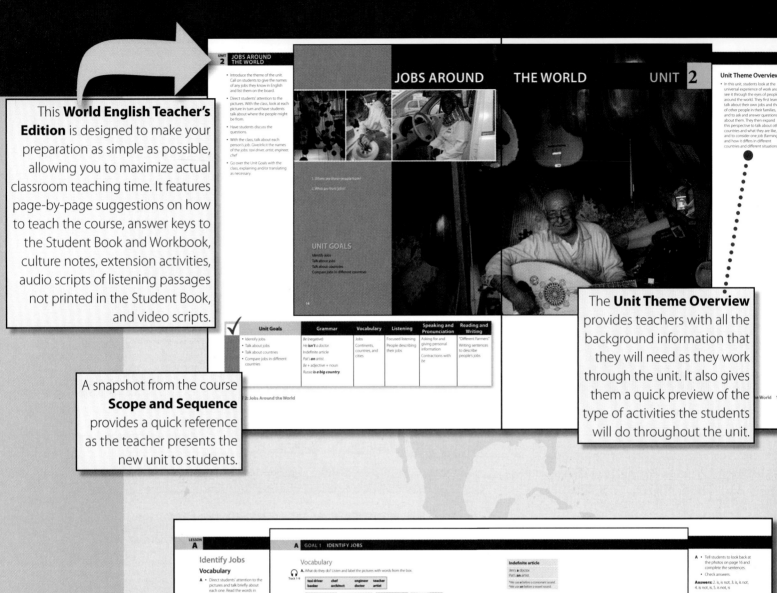

A snapshot from the course **Scope and Sequence** provides a quick reference as the teacher presents the new unit to students.

The **Unit Theme Overview** provides teachers with all the background information that they will need as they work through the unit. It also gives them a quick preview of the type of activities the students will do throughout the unit.

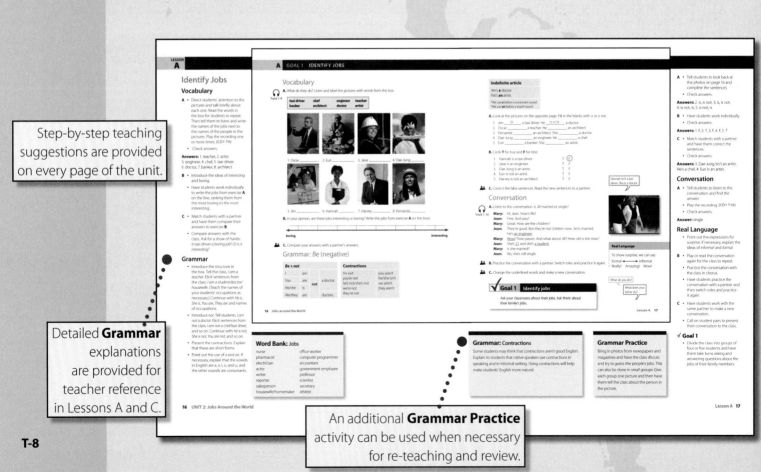

Step-by-step teaching suggestions are provided on every page of the unit.

Detailed **Grammar** explanations are provided for teacher reference in Lessons A and C.

An additional **Grammar Practice** activity can be used when necessary for re-teaching and review.

	Goals	Language Focus
UNIT 1 Friends and Family	• Describe a person	*She/He's young, with straight _____ hair.* *His/Her name is _____.*
UNIT 2 Jobs Around the World	• Asking for and giving personal information • Talking about jobs • Talking about countries	*What's your name? How old are you?* *Where are you from?*
UNIT 3 Houses and Apartments	• Describing a house	*What's in the big bedroom?* *There are two beds.*
Unit 4	• Talking about the personal possessions	*These earrings look cool.* *She already has earrings. What about these*

This Teacher's Edition provides additional Communication and Writing practice through classroom materials that can be photocopied. **Communication Activities** include information gap, group work, interview worksheets, simulations and role-plays.

UNIT 5 DAILY ACTIVITIES
Student A

Ask and answer questions to fill in the information. Are these good jobs?

Name:	Nathan	
Job:		baker
Get up:	4:00 p.m.	
Start work:	10:00 p.m.	
Have lunch:		8:15 a.m.
Finish work:	4:30 a.m.	
Go to bed:		6:30 p.m.

Student B

Ask and answer questions to fill in the information. Are these good jobs?

Name:		Amanda
Job:	radio announcer	
Get up:		2:00 a.m.
Start work:		3:00 a.m.
Have lunch:	1:45 a.m.	
Finish work:		11:30 a.m.
Go to bed:	9:00 a.m.	

	Writing Tasks	Language Focus
Unit 1 Describe Your Family	• Use *be* in a conversation. • Draw and describe family members.	*Hi, my name is Michael.* *This is Toby. He is my brother.*
Unit 2 Describe a Country	• Answer questions about yourself. • Write sentences about countries.	*No, I'm not a doctor.* *Brazil is a large country.*
Unit 3 Describe a Room	• Finish sentences about a house and an apartment. • Write sentences about a room.	*There are three bedrooms in my house.* *There is a lamp on the table.*
Unit 4 A Short Story	• Finish sentences about possessions. • Write que... • Finish sen...	*There is a watch in the purse.* *...r purse?*
Unit 5	• Write sent...	

The **Writing Program** reinforces and complements the lessons in the Student Book. Writing gives students a chance to reflect on the English they've learned and to develop an indispensable academic skill.

UNIT 5 DAILY ACTIVITIES
DAILY SCHEDULE

A. Look at Jillian's schedule.

Monday	Tuesday	Wednesday	Thursday	Friday
7:30 get up	7:30 get up	7:30 get up	7:30 get up	7:30 get up
9:00 start work	9:00 start work	9:00 start work	9:00 start work	9:00 start work
12:30 eat lunch	12:30 eat lunch	12:30 eat lunch	12:30 eat lunch	12:30 eat lunch
		3:00 finish work	3:00 finish work	
5:00 finish work		5:00 finish work		5:00 finish work
11:00 go to bed	11:00 go to bed	11:00 go to bed	11:00 go to bed	11:00 go to bed

☐ Use the words below to write sentences about Jillian's schedule.

1. get up / every morning _Jillian gets up at 7:30 every morning._
2. start work / every day _____
3. eat lunch / every day _____
4. finish work / Tuesdays and Thursdays _____
5. finish work / Mondays, Wednesdays, and Fridays _____
6. go to bed / every night _____

☐ Compare your sentences with a partner.

B. What do you do every day? Fill in the schedule with your information.

Monday	Tuesday	Wednesday	Thursday	Friday

GETTING THERE   UNIT 6

Lesson A

A. Label the pictures.

tourist office	train station	supermarket	post office	library	park
restaurant	hotel	museum	bank		

1. _____ 2. _____ 3. _____
5. _____ 6. _____
9. _____ 10. _____ 11. _____

B. Read the directions and circle the correct word in parentheses.

There's a good restaurant near my school. It's (in/on) the co... Avenue. Leave the school and (turn/get) left. Then (walk/take)... across (from/with) the park. It's (between/on) the supermark...

C. Write directions to a place near your school.

There's a/an _____ near my school. _____
_____
_____

Lesson D

A. Read the diary of a trip. Write the dates by the pictures.

The **Workbook** provides additional practice and supports the development of skills through a variety of activities.

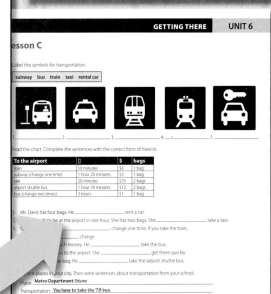

August 10 I go to Shikoku Island on a boat. Shikoku is green and beautiful.

August 13 I take the night bus to the city of Fukuoka. The bus is very cheap, so I have money for dinner in a nice restaurant.

August 15 Today is my last day. I take a shuttle bus to the airport. Goodbye to Japan!

40 Unit 6

GETTING THERE   UNIT 6

Lesson C

Label the symbols for transportation.

subway	bus	train	taxi	rental car

1. _____ 2. _____ 3. _____ 4. _____ 5. _____

Read the chart. Complete the sentences with the correct form of *have to*.

To the airport		$	bags
train	50 minutes	$6	1 bag
subway (change one time)	1 hour 20 minutes	$3	1 bag
taxi	20 minutes	$35	2 bags
airport shuttle bus	1 hour 30 minutes	$12	2 bags
bus (change two times)	3 hours	$1	1 bag

1. Mr. Davis has four bags. He _____ rent a car.
2. ...to be at the airport in one hour. She _____ take a taxi.
3. ...change one time. If you take the train, _____ change.
4. ...ch money. He _____ take the bus.
5. ...s to the airport. She _____ get there quickly.
6. ...e bag. He _____ take the airport shuttle bus.

...ee places in your city. Then write sentences about transportation from your school.

1. Place: _Metro Department Store_
   Transportation: _You have to take the 78 bus._
2. Place: _____
   Transportation: _____
3. Place: _____
   Transportation: _____
4. Place: _____
   Transportation: _____

Overview

World English uses rich, engrossing National Geographic text, photos, art, maps, and videos to involve students in learning about real people, real places, and real language.

Each unit is divided into four two-page lessons and a two-page Video Journal.

A concrete objective at the beginning of every lesson focuses students' attention on what they will be learning. At the end of the lesson, a personalization activity gives students an opportunity to apply what they've learned and lets both teachers and students check student progress.

Unit Opener

Each unit opens with a two-page spread of striking photos. These have been chosen both to illustrate the unit theme and to provide material for discussion. Before beginning the unit, teacher and students can describe the pictures, name as many things as they can in them, and make guesses about when and where the photos were taken. The two discussion questions then lead students into the topic and introduce several key vocabulary items.

In this Teacher's Edition, a Unit Theme Overview is provided to orient you to the scope of the unit and to give additional information that may be useful in discussing the unit theme. Throughout the lesson notes, For Your Information boxes contain additional facts about the topic of a listening passage, reading, or video.

Vocabulary

Lessons A and C both begin with a short activity presenting lexical items related to the unit theme. In Lesson A, the vocabulary section introduces the core words that students will need to discuss and learn about the unit topic. These are presented in context, with text or pictures to aid students in understanding. After completing the exercises in this section, students have a written record of the meanings of the words, which they can refer to later. The lesson notes in this Teacher's Edition contain a Word Bank of supplementary vocabulary that can be used in activities or taught as enrichment.

Grammar

World English features an explicit grammar syllabus, with individual grammar points tied to the unit theme. Two different grammar points are taught in Lesson A and Lesson C. They are used in the opening presentation of the lessons along with the vocabulary items and then explicitly presented in a box with examples, rules, and usage notes.

Students first do controlled practice with the structure in writing, then freer production in writing, and finally use the structure in controlled speaking practice. Every grammar point is followed by a Conversation section that gives further practice in the use of the structure.

The lesson notes in this Teacher's Edition contain a brief summary of each grammar point for teacher reference, as well an additional Grammar Practice Activity.

Conversation

Each unit contains two model conversations highlighting both the vocabulary and the grammar for the lesson. Students first listen to the conversation with their books closed and answer one general comprehension question. Next, they listen again while reading the conversation. They are then ready to practice the conversation, taking turns with both roles before making their own conversations based on the model and incorporating specified information along with their own ideas.

Listening

Lesson B starts off with a listening activity. After a warm-up to introduce the subject of the activity, students listen to a conversation, radio program, or interview multiple times, completing a series of written tasks of graded difficulty. The first time, they are asked to listen for the gist or main ideas; subsequent activities ask them to find numbers, details, or further information. A post-listening task helps students to explore and personalize what they've heard.

Audioscripts for all listening activities begin on page T-155.

Pronunciation

The pronunciation component of **World English** emphasizes stress, intonation, reductions, and other features to make learners' English more natural and comprehensible to a wide international audience. Students first learn to recognize a feature of English pronunciation and then to produce it. Examples are presented on the audio recording in the context of the unit theme. Students begin by listening, then repeat with the audio recording, and then practice freer production of the features while interacting with a partner.

If a particular pronunciation point is especially challenging for your students, it can be practiced in a number of ways. You can have the entire class repeat the items in chorus, then the two halves of the class, then rows or columns of students, and finally you can call on individual students to pronounce the items. When students practice in pairs, circulate around the room listening and correcting.

Communication

In contrast to the controlled speaking practice in the Conversation sections, the Communication activities give freer practice with the structures and vocabulary that the students have learned. These activities are designed to allow personal expression, but still within a controlled field of language, so that all students can feel confident of success. While students are doing these activities, you should circulate around the class to help with vocabulary and ideas as needed and to make note of errors and interesting responses to discuss with the class after the end of the activity.

The lesson notes in this Teacher's Edition include one Expansion Activity per unit for further discussion around the theme of the listening passage. For classes where more practice of free communication is desired, this book also contains 12 Communication Activity Worksheets, which may be photocopied, one for each unit. The activities, which require 15 to 30 minutes of class time each, reinforce the vocabulary and structures from the unit while giving students another opportunity to express their own ideas in English.

Language Expansion

The first part of Lesson C is a Language Expansion activity that is meant to broaden students' vocabulary around the unit theme by introducing a closely related group of lexical items. These are presented in context and are used immediately in writing and then speaking, giving students more options when doing the Grammar and Conversation activities that follow in Lesson C.

Reading

Lesson D is centered around a reading passage, which is followed by a Communication activity that prepares students for writing. All of the reading passages in **World English** are abridged and adapted from authentic articles in National Geographic publications. To help students read for interest and enjoyment, unfamiliar vocabulary is explained either with glosses in a Word Focus box or in a picture dictionary illustration.

The lesson notes in this Teacher's Edition include a Web search activity and a suggestion for a simple project that can be done as a follow-up for each reading passage.

Writing

The writing activities in Lesson D of **World English** flow from the subject of the reading passage and are always preceded by a Communication activity in which students discuss and explore the topic further. This generates ideas and forms a natural prewriting sequence. Writing tasks are short and simple and range from writing single sentences in the lower levels, through writing groups of sentences, on up to writing an entire paragraph.

The writing activities in the units emphasize helping students put their ideas into written form. Where a more structured approach to writing is desired, this Teacher's Edition contains a complete Writing Program, which may be photocopied. These optional writing worksheets, one for each unit, provide instruction and practice in a sequence of writing skills graded to the level of the course.

Video Journal

Each unit of **World English** concludes with an authentic National Geographic three- to four-minute video, with a voice-over that has been specially edited for language learners. The video segments recycle the themes and language of the main unit, bringing them to life in colorful locations around the globe. A Before You Watch activity presents new words that students will hear and gives information about the setting of the video. Students watch the video several times while completing While You Watch activities that ask them first to find general themes and then to locate specific information. They give their response to the video in an After You Watch activity.

Each unit concludes with a Communication activity that draws all the strands of the unit together and allows students to demonstrate what they've learned.

Special Features in the Student Book

Real Language This feature highlights high-frequency expressions from everyday language that will make students' speech sound natural and confident. To present them, point out their use in the activity and discuss other situations when they might be useful. If desired, have students work in pairs to create conversations using the expressions.

Word Focus These boxes present and explain additional vocabulary used in an activity, as well as introduce commonly used collocations.

Bonus Communication Activities At the end of student books Intro and Level 1, six activities present students with the opportunity to practice the language and structures that they have learned in a guided oral format as they discuss stunning photographs with a partner.

WORLD ENGLISH Intro

Real People • Real Places • Real Language

Martin Milner

HEINLE
CENGAGE Learning

Australia • Brazil • Japan • Korea • Mexico • Singapore • Spain • United Kingdom • United States

HEINLE
CENGAGE Learning

World English Intro
Real People • Real Places • Real Language
Martin Milner

Publisher: Sherrise Roehr

Managing Editor: Berta de Llano

Senior Development Editor: Margarita Matte

Development Editor: Michael Poor

National Geographic Editorial Liaison:
  Leila Hishmeh

Technology Development Manager:
  Debie Mirtle

Director of Global Marketing: Ian Martin

Director of US Marketing: Jim McDonough

Product Marketing Manager: Katie Kelley

Marketing Assistant: Jide Iruka

Senior Content Project Manager/Art Direction:
  Dawn Marie Elwell

Senior Print Buyer: Betsy Donaghey

Cover Photo: Remi Benali/Corbis

Compositor: Nesbitt Graphics, Inc.

Library of Congress Control Number: 2008937885

International Edition:
World English Intro ISBN 13: 978-1-4240-5014-7
World English Intro ISBN 10: 1-4240-5014-6
World English Intro + CD-ROM ISBN 13: 978-1-4240-3476-5
World English Intro + CD-ROM ISBN 10: 1-4240-3476-0

U.S. Edition:
World English Intro ISBN 13: 978-1-4240-6335-2
World English Intro ISBN 10: 1-4240-6335-3

Heinle
20 Channel Center Street
Boston, MA 02210
USA

Cengage Learning is a leading provider of customized learning solutions with office locations around the globe, including Singapore, the United Kingdom, Australia, Mexico, Brazil, and Japan. Locate your local office at:
international.cengage.com/region

Cengage Learning products are represented in Canada by Nelson Education, Ltd.

Visit Heinle online at elt.heinle.com

Visit our corporate website at www.cengage.com

Printed in Canada
1 2 3 4 5 6 7 13 12 11 10 09

CONTENTS

Nunavut, Canada
Find out how people dress to keep warm in the Arctic. *Inuit Fashion*

Heimaey, Iceland
Are children good workers? Learn about the puffin rescuers in Iceland. *A Job for Children*

San Francisco, California, United States of America
What other work do dentists do? *Zoo Dentists*

Michoacan, Mexico
Millions of monarch butterflies travel more than 2000 miles every year. *Monarch Migration*

Your World!

Camogli, Italy
See how people decorate their houses in this fishing village. *A Very Special Village*

Greve, Chianti, Italy
Do we eat too fast? Learn about the Slow Food Movement. *Slow Food*

Chiang Mai, Thailand
Why does a 12-year old boy want to become a boxing champion? *Making a Thai Boxing Champion*

Afar, Ethiopia
How do geologists learn about volcanoes? Watch a close-up expedition. *Volcano Trek*

Vanuatu
Do you think bungee jumping is dangerous? Watch boys and men jump from a high tower and hit the ground! *Land Divers of Vanuatu*

Nairobi, Kenya
Can a small white flower save lives? Yes. The pyrethrum kills the mosquito that spreads malaria. *Pyrethrum*

● = Sites of the video clips you will view in *World English Intro* .

	Unit Goals	Grammar	Vocabulary	Listening	Speaking and Pronunciation	Reading and Writing
UNIT 1	**Friends and Family** page 2 • Meet and introduce people • Identify family members • Describe people • Give personal and family information	Simple present tense: *Be* *I'm Kim.* *They're Maria and Lola.* *Be* + adjective *They're young.* *Is John single?*	Greetings and introductions Family members Adjectives	Listening for general understanding and specific information	Talking about your family tree /r/ sound	"Families around the world" Writing sentences to describe people
UNIT 2	**Jobs Around the World** page 14 • Identify jobs • Talk about jobs • Talk about countries • Compare jobs in different countries	*Be:* Negative *He isn't a doctor.* Indefinite article *Pat's an artist.* *Be* + article + adjective + noun *Russia is a big country.*	Jobs Numbers Continents, countries and cities	Focused listening People describing their jobs	Asking for and giving personal information Contractions with *be*	"Different Farmers" Writing a paragraph to describe a person's job
UNIT 3	**Houses and Apartments** page 26 • Identify rooms in a house • Describe your house • Identify household objects • Compare houses	*There is/there are* *There are three bedrooms.* *Is there a garage?* Prepositions of place: *in, on, under, next to* *Your magazine is under your bag.*	Rooms in a house Furniture and household objects	Listening for general understanding and specific details People talking about their houses	Describing your house Final *–s*	"Unusual Houses" Writing descriptions of houses
UNIT 4	**Possessions** page 38 • Identify personal possessions • Talk about personal possessions • Buy a present • Talk about special possessions	Demonstrative adjectives *Are these your books?* *That is not your bag.* Possessive nouns *It's Jim's bag.* *Have* *She has a camcorder.*	Personal possessions Electronic products	Listening for specific information People proving ownership	Talking about the personal possessions of others Differentiating short *i* and long *e* sounds	"Jewelry" Summarizing a class survey
UNIT 5	**Daily Activities** page 50 • Tell time • Ask about people's daily activities • Talk about what you do at work • Describe a job	Simple present tense: statements, negatives, questions, and short answers *They get up at 7 o'clock.* *What time do you start work?* Adverbs of frequency: *always, sometimes, never* *I never answer the phone.*	Daily activities Telling time Professional activities	Listening for general understanding and specific details Describing a photographer's work	Asking and answering questions about work activities Falling intonation on statements and information questions	"Robots at Work" Writing a job description
UNIT 6	**Getting There** page 62 • Ask for and give directions • Create and use a tour route • Talk about transportation • Record a journey	Imperatives *Turn left and walk for two blocks.* *Have to* *She has to change buses.*	City landmarks Directions Ground Transportation	Listening for specific information Radio ad for a holiday tour	Ask for and give directions *Yes/no* questions	"Shackleton's Epic Journey" Writing a travel journal

	Unit Goals	Grammar	Vocabulary	Listening	Speaking and Pronunciation	Reading and Writing
UNIT 7	**Free Time** page 74 • Identify activities that are happening now • Talk about activities that are happening now • Talk about abilities • Talk about sports	Present continuous tense *I'm not watching* television. *I'm reading.* *Can* (for ability) He **can't** play the guitar. He **can** sing.	Pastimes Games and sports	Listening for specific information Telephone conversation	Have a phone conversation *sh* and *ch* sounds	"Sports—Then and Now" Writing sentences about your abilities
UNIT 8	**Clothes I Like** page 86 • Identify and buy clothes • Say what people are wearing • Express likes and dislikes • Learn about clothes and colors	*Can/could* (for polite requests) **Can** I try on these shoes? Likes and dislikes I **love** your sweater! She **can't stand** pink.	Clothes Colors	Listening for specific details	Describing people's clothes *Could you*	"Chameleon Clothes" Writing about what people are wearing
UNIT 9	**Eating Well** page 98 • Order a meal • Plan a party • Talk about a healthy diet • Talk about food for a special occasion	*Some, any* There's **some** ice cream in the fridge. *How much/ how many* **How many** oranges do we need? **How much** chocolate do we have?	Food types Meals Count/non-count nouns	Listening for specific details Conversation to confirm a shopping list	Planning a dinner *And*	"Special Days, Special Food" Writing sentences to summarize information
UNIT 10	**Health** page 110 • Identify parts of the body to say how you feel • Ask about and describe symptoms • Identify remedies and give advice • Learn and talk about prevention	Review of simple present tense *Look* + adjective *Feel* + adjective John **looks** terrible. I **feel** sick. My back **hurts.** *Should* (for advice) You **should** take an aspirin.	Parts of the body Common illnesses Remedies	Listening for general understanding and specific details Doctor's appointments	Describing symptoms and illnesses; giving advice Word stress	"Preventing Disease" Writing a notice board
UNIT 11	**Making Plans** page 122 • Schedule specific dates • Understand and use a date book • Talk about special life events • Describe a special occasion	*Be going to* What **are** you **going to** do? We **are going to** have a party. *Would like* (for wishes) I **would like** to be a doctor.	Special plans American holidays Professions	Listening for general understanding and specific details	Talking about celebrating holidays Reduced *Be going to*	"Life's Milestones" Writing about one's plans for the future
UNIT 12	**Migrations** page 134 • Talk about moving in the past • Talk about moving dates • Talk about preparations for moving • Discuss migrations	Simple past tense We **went** to the mountains. He **moved** from San Francisco to New York.	Verbs + prepositions of movement Travel preparations	Listening for general understanding and specific details Biographies of famous immigrants	Discussing moving *-ed* sounds	"Human Migration" Writing a vacation postcard

- Introduce the words *friends* and *family*.

- Direct students' attention to the pictures. With the class, look at each picture in turn and talk about the people in them.

- Answer the questions together with the class.

Answers: Answers will vary.

- Go over the Unit Goals with the class, explaining and/or translating as necessary.

FRIENDS AND

1. Are these people friends or family?

2. Are these people young or old?

UNIT GOALS

Meet and introduce people
Identify family members
Describe people
Give personal and family information

2

Unit Goals	Grammar	Vocabulary	Listening	Speaking and Pronunciation	Reading and Writing

• Meet and introduce people
• Identify family members
• Describe people
• Give personal and family information
	Present tense: *be*
	  I'm Kim.
	  They're Maria and Lola.
	Be + adjective
	  They're young.
	  Is John single?
		Greetings and introductions
		
		Family members
		
		Adjectives
			Listening for general understanding and specific information	Talking about your family tree
				
				r sound
					"Families Around the World"
					
					Writing sentences to describe people

FAMILY

UNIT 1

Unit Theme Overview

- In this unit, students learn to introduce themselves and their families and friends. Even such a seemingly simple activity has interesting cultural variations.

- Customs for names vary greatly in different places. English speakers commonly refer to their first name (given name) and last name (family name). In Asian countries the family name is often written first. For example, in the Korean name Pak Jin-Ho, the man's family name is Pak and his given name is Jin-Ho. In Spanish-speaking countries some people use both their father's and mother's family names. For example, in the name Francisco Cruz Rios, Francisco is his given name, Cruz is his father's family name, and Rios is his mother's family name. Informally, he is Francisco Cruz. In Islamic countries, some people use their father's given name after their own given name. For example, in the Islamic name Laila Ali Al-Ayubi, Laila is her given name, Ali her father's name, and Al-Ayubi her family name.

- There are also interesting differences in terminology for family relationships. English has comparatively few terms for different relationships. For example, the word *brother* is used for both an elder brother and a younger brother (many languages have two different words). As even these simple examples show, learning a new language involves learning about other ways to see the world.

Meet and Introduce People

Vocabulary

A
- Direct students' attention to the picture on the left and talk about the people in the picture.
- Play the recording the first time and have students listen. **(CD1 T2)**
- Point out the other expressions in the box. Use drawings of faces to show that *great* and *fine* have similar meanings (☺) while *OK* and *so-so* are less happy (😐).
- Then direct students' attention to the picture on the right. Point out that students talk differently to friends (*informal*) than to people they don't know well (*formal*).
- Play the recording again several times for the class to repeat.
- Practice with the class in chorus. Then have students practice the conversation with a partner.
- Point out the other expressions in the box. Explain that we use *good morning* until 12:00 p.m., *good afternoon* until about 6:00 p.m., and *good evening* after 6:00 p.m.

B
- Tell students to stand up, walk around the room, and greet three classmates informally.

C
- Call on individual students to greet you formally.

D
- Follow the same steps in presenting the conversations for introductions: Play the recording for the class to listen only, and then play it again several times for the class to repeat. **(CD1 T3)**

E
- Have students stand up, walk around the room, and introduce themselves to three classmates.

F
- Divide the class into groups of three and have them introduce each other.
- Call on students to introduce a group member to the whole class.

Vocabulary

🎧 **A.** Listen and repeat.
Track 1-2 Greetings

🧑‍🤝‍🧑 **B.** Greet your classmates informally.

C. Greet your teacher formally.

🎧 **D.** Listen and repeat.
Track 1-3 Introductions

🧑‍🤝‍🧑 **E.** Introduce yourself to your classmates.

👥 **F.** Work in groups of three. Practice introducing each other.

4 **Friends and Family**

For Your Information: Names in the classroom

This is a good opportunity to ask students to think about what they'd like to be called in class. Many will use their given names. Some may have a nickname or short version of their name that they want to use in class. Some learners may prefer a title like *Mr.* or *Ms.* followed by a surname. In turn, you can tell students how they should address you.

Grammar: *Be*

The verb *be* may be difficult for learners whose languages do not have a similar structure. They may produce sentences such as *He John* or *She a student*. If necessary, explain to the class that every English sentence must contain a verb (a word for an action) and that *be* is a verb.

Grammar: Present tense *be*

Subject pronoun	*Be*	
I	**am**	
You	**are**	Kim.
He/She	**is**	
We	**are**	Ron and Ed.
They	**are**	Maria and Claudia.

Contractions with *be*
I'm
You're
He's
She's
We're
They're

A. Unscramble the sentences.

1. Ron. name My is _My name is Ron._____
2. Leila. is name Her _____
3. is name Mr. Aoki. His_____
4. Tim. Their Jan names are and _____
5. name Your is Yan-Ching. _____

Possessive adjectives	
My	name is Mario.
Your	name is Rachel.
His	name is Robert.
Her	name is Liujun.
Their	names are Ben and Dan.

B. Write the sentences again. Use contractions.

1. He is Ruben. _He's Ruben._____
2. I am Peter. _____
3. You are Rebecca. _____
4. They are Ashley and Jason. _____
5. We are Carol and Melissa. _____

Conversation

Track 1-5

A. Listen to the conversation. Spell Hiroshi.

Donna: Hi, Nick. How are you?
Nick: Great. And you?
Donna: Fine.
Nick: Donna, this is my friend Hiroshi.
Donna: Nice to meet you, Hir . . . sorry?
Hiroshi: It's Hiroshi. H-I-R-O-S-H-I. Nice to meet you, Donna.

B. Practice the conversation in groups of three. Switch roles and practice it again.

C. Practice the conversation again. Use your own names.

> ✓ **Goal 1**   **Meet and introduce people**
>
> Work in pairs. Find another pair and introduce each other.

Track 1-4

Word Focus

The English alphabet =
A B C D E F G H I J K L
M N O P Q R S T U V W
X Y Z

Real Language

We sometimes spell
our names for people.

Lesson A   **5**

Grammar Practice: Name circle

Sit with the class in a circle. Begin by saying, *My name is* _____. The student on your right then says, *Her/His name is* _____. *My name is* _____ OR *I'm* _____. The next student says the names of all of those that have come before (using complete sentences). If a student forgets a name, he or she begins again with *My name is*_____. Play until all students have had several turns and have learned most of the names.

Identify Family Members

- Go over the family tree with the class. Pronounce the words for family members and have students repeat them.

Listening

A • Tell students they are going to hear about a family. Have them look at the pictures.

- Play the recording. Have them point to the people as they hear about them. **(CD1 T6)**

B • Tell students to listen again and read the sentences. Have them answer *true* or *false*. **(CD1 T6)**

- Play the recording one or more times.

- Check answers.

Answers: 1. T, 2. T, 3. F, 4. T, 5. T

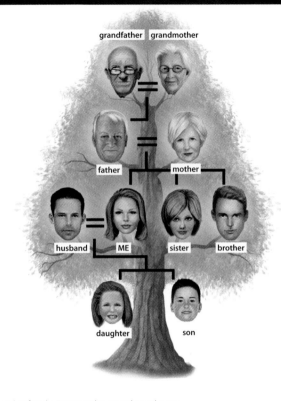

grandfather grandmother

father mother

husband ME sister brother

daughter son

Listening

A. Listen to Carlos introduce his family. Point to the people and pets.

Track 1-6

B. Listen again. Circle **T** for *true* and **F** for *false*.

Track 1-6

Carlos says:
1. This is my grandfather. His name is Pedro.   (T)   F
2. This is my sister. Her name is Karina.   T   F
3. This is my grandmother. Her name is Elena.   T   F
4. This is my father. His name is Jose Manuel.   T   F
5. These are our dogs. Their names are Lucy and Lulu.   T   F

6 Friends and Family

For Your Information: Family members

In English, the word *brother* is used to refer to both an older and a younger male sibling, and *sister* can refer to an older or younger female sibling. This may differ from your students' language. Likewise, in English *grandfather* refers to both the father's father and the mother's father, and *grandmother* refers to both the father's mother and the mother's mother. (Native speakers say, *my grandfather on my father's/mother's side.*) Be sure to clarify this for your students if necessary.

 **C.** Correct any *false* sentences. Take turns to read all the sentences to a partner.

D. Fill in the blanks in Carlos's family tree.

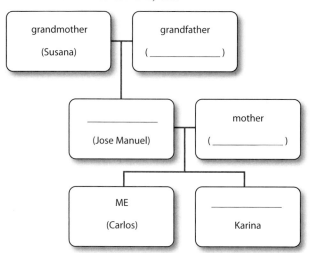

```
grandmother          grandfather
(Susana)             (_____)

_____            mother
(Jose Manuel)        (_____)

ME                   _____
(Carlos)             Karina
```

Pronunciation: The /r/ sound

A. Underline the letter *r*. Listen to the /r/ sound and repeat the word.

Track 1-7

father	Rick
mother	Rose
sister	Robert Brown
brother	Mary Brown

 **B.** Take turns reading the words to a partner.

Communication

A. Draw your own family tree.

B. Describe the family tree to a partner.

✓ **Goal 2** **Identify family members**

Bring some family photos to class. Introduce your family to your classmates.

> This is my grandmother. Her name is Aiko.

C • Tell students to listen again to correct the false statement.
  • Play the recording one or more times.
  • Check answers.

Answer: 3. This is my mother. Her name is Elena.

D • Tell students to listen again and fill in the spaces. Go over the idea of a family tree and make sure students understand the format.
  • Check answers.

Answers: Pedro, father, Elena, sister

Pronunciation

A • Tell students that /r/ has a special sound in English, and if desired explain how it differs from related sounds in their language. (In the English /r/ sound, the tip of the tongue curls back in the mouth and does not touch any other part of the mouth.)
  • Have students work individually or with a partner to find and underline all of the *r*s in the words.
  • Play the recording several times for students to repeat. **(CD1 T7)**

B • Have students take turns reading the words to each other.

Communication

A • Have students work individually to draw a simple family tree similar to the one on page 6.

B • Match students with a partner and have them take turns talking about their family trees.
  • Have students change partners and practice again.

✓ **Goal 2**
  • For homework, have students find and bring one or more family photos to class.
  • Divide the class into groups of three or four students and have them take turns showing and explaining their family photos.

Expansion Activity

With the class, draw the family tree of a celebrity students are familiar with. Then have them work with a partner to talk about the relationships in the family.

Describe People

Language Expansion

- Present the vocabulary in the pictures. Give/elicit more examples using students' names: *Who is tall? Who has curly hair?* and so on.

A • Direct students' attention to the pictures. Have students work individually to fill in the correct adjectives.

- Check answers.

Answers: 1. married, handsome, pretty 2. handsome, straight/black 3. pretty, curly 4. young, straight

B • Have students complete the sentence to describe themselves.

- Call on students to share their sentence with the class.

Grammar

- Go over the information in the box. If necessary, remind students that all sentences in English must have a verb, and *be* is a verb.

- Give/elicit more examples.

Language Expansion: Adjectives

| tall | young | married | handsome |
| short | old | single | pretty |

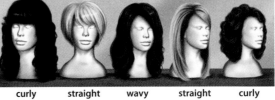

| curly | straight | wavy | straight | curly |
| black hair | gray hair | red hair | blond hair | brown hair |

A. Write adjectives to describe these people.

1. They are _____. He is _____. She is _____.
2. He is _____ with _____ hair.
3. She is _____ with _____ hair.
4. They are _____ with _____ hair.

B. Now describe yourself.
I am _____ with _____ hair.

1.

2.

3.

4.

Grammar: *Be* + adjective

Subject	*Be*	Adjective
I	am	young.
You	are	tall.
John	is	single.
Emily	is	pretty.
We	are	married.
They	are	old.

8 Friends and Family

Word Bank: More adjectives

heavy	happy
thin	sad
middle-aged	thirsty
divorced	tired
widowed	hungry

Questions with *be* and short answers

Questions			Short answers	
Are	you	married?	Yes, I am.	No, I'm not.
Is	he/she	single?	Yes, he/she is.	No, he/she isn't.
Are	they	married?	Yes, they are.	No, they're not.

A. Match the questions and the answers.

Questions
1. Is your brother tall? _b_
2. Are your brothers married? ____
3. Is Emma pretty? ____
4. Is your brother single? ____
5. Are your mother and father old? ____

Answers
a. Yes, she is.
b. No, he isn't. He's short.
c. Alan is married. Brian isn't.
d. No, they're not.
e. No, he isn't. He's married.

B. Write the questions.

1. Q: _____ ?
   A: No, she isn't. She's tall.
2. Q: _____ ?
   A: Yes, they are.
3. Q: _____ ?
   A: Yes, I am.

Conversation

A. Look at the pictures and listen to the conversation.

Track 1-8

Ana:	Who's this?
Carol:	It's my <u>brother</u>.
Ana:	What's his name?
Carol:	<u>Richard.</u>
Ana:	Is he married?
Carol:	Yes, he is.
Ana:	What a shame!

B. Practice the conversation with a partner. Switch roles and practice it again.

C. Change the underlined words and make a new conversation.

✓ **Goal 3** **Describe people**

Work with a partner. Take turns describing your classmates.

Give Personal and Family Information

Reading

- Introduce the topic of the reading. Tell students they are going to read about families in different countries.

- Have students read the article. Tell them to circle any words they don't understand.

A
- Match students with a partner and have them point to the countries on the map.
- Check answers with the class.
- Go over the article with the class and answer any questions from students about vocabulary.

B
- Have students work individually to complete the sentences.
- Check answers.

Answers: 1. mother, 2. blond, 3. son, 4. black, 5. married

C
- Have students work individually to circle the answers.
- Check answers.

Answers: 1. b, 2. a, 3. a, 4. a, 5. a

Reading

A. Look at the pictures. Show a partner where these people are from on the map.

B. Complete the sentences with words from the box.

mother	blond	son	married	black

1. June Banks is the _____ of Kevin and Kate.
2. Ian Banks has curly _____ hair.
3. Bo is the _____ of Feng and Huan.
4. Mrs. Patel has _____ hair.
5. Alisha is _____ to Ramesh.

C. Circle the correct answers.

1. Her father is Ian Banks.
   a. June
   b. Kate
2. They live in Scotland.
   a. Kevin and Kate
   b. Feng and Huan
3. His wife is Huan.
   a. Feng
   b. Bo
4. Her daughters are Alisha and Rasha.
   a. Mrs. Patel
   b. Suchir
5. Her husband is Ramesh.
   a. Alisha
   b. Rasha

Families around the World

This is the Banks family. They come from Scotland. Ian is tall with curly blond hair. His wife, June, has wavy brown hair. Ian and June have two children: a son and a young daughter. Their names are Kevin and Kate.

Meet Feng and his family. They are from China. His wife's name is Huan. They have one son. His name is Bo. He is young. He is two years old.

10   **Friends and Family**

For Your Information: Family size

An important difference in families around the world is the number of children in a family. One way to measure this is by the average number of children that women give birth to within their lifetime. This number varies widely from country to country. In Mali, in West Africa, the average woman will have 7.34 children. The countries with the lowest numbers are Singapore (1.08 children), South Korea (1.20), and Lithuania (1.20). The world average is 2.61 children.

EUROPE   A S I A

This is the Patel family. They are from India. Mrs. Patel [h]as two daughters. They are married. Their names are [A]lisha and Rasha. Their husbands are Ramesh and [S]uchir. Alisha is married to Ramesh. Rasha is married [to] Suchir. They all have black hair.

Communication

Look at the photos. Choose one photo. Describe a person to a partner. Your partner guesses who you are describing.

 He is tall with curly blond hair. He is young and handsome.

 Is it David?

Yes, it is!

1. David   2. Ayako

3. Alonso   4. Michelle

Writing

Write a description of a family member.

He is tall with curly black hair. He is single.

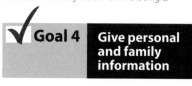

✔ **Goal 4**   **Give personal and family information**

Work with a partner. Take turns describing your family.

Communication

- With the class, review adjectives for describing people.
- Match students with a partner. Have them take turns describing the pictures and guessing the names.
- Call on a student to describe one of the people. Have the class guess the name.

Writing

- Have students work individually to choose one member of their family and write a description.
- Have students exchange papers with a partner. Ask students to mark corrections and suggestions for improvements on their partner's paper.
- If desired, have students rewrite their papers, to be collected for marking.

✔ Goal 4

- Match students with a partner and have them take turns describing people in their families.

After Reading

Match students with a partner and have them exchange information about their families, taking notes about what they hear. Then have them write sentences about their partner and his/her family.

Video Journal

Before You Watch

- Go over the pictures of animals and name them for the students.
- Then have students label the pictures.
- Check answers.

Answers: 1. male gorilla, 2. meerkats, 3. polar bear, 4. female lion, 5. male lion, 6. leopard

While You Watch

A • Tell students they are going to watch a video about animal families. Tell them to watch the video the first time and answer *true* or *false*. Go over the sentences with the class. Play the video.

- Check answers.

Answers: 1. F, 2. T, 3. T, 4. F, 5. F

E VIDEO JOURNAL *ANIMAL FAMILIES*

Before You Watch

Label the animals. Use the words in the box.

▲ East Africa

| female lion | leopard | male gorilla | meerkats | male lion | polar bear |

1. _____ 2. _____ 3. _____

4. _____ 5. _____ 6. _____

While You Watch

 A. Watch the video. Circle **T** for *true* and **F** for *false*.

1. Polar bears have big families.   T   F
2. Lions live in family groups.   T   F
3. Male lions have red hair.   T   F
4. Meerkats are big.   T   F
5. Female gorillas have gray hair on their backs.   T   F

For Your Information: Meerkat

The meerkat is a small animal that lives in the deserts of Botswana and South Africa. They live in family groups called clans. A clan usually has about 25 members, but some have more than 50. Meerkats eat insects, and they work together to find them. One meerkat watches for predators while the others dig for insects. If a predator comes close, the "guard" will bark a whistle to alert the other clan members. If everything is safe, the guard makes soft peeping sounds. Meerkats are very social animals. They groom each other's fur, and female meerkats will "babysit" for each other's young.

B • Tell students to watch the video again and complete the sentences. Have the students read the sentences. Play the video.

  • Check answers.

Answers: 1. lions, 2. long, 3. big, 4. pretty, 5. male

C • Have students watch the video again to check their answers.

After You Watch

  • Go over the names of the animals in the photos. Pronounce them for students to repeat.

A • Tell students to work individually and write the names of the animals in the correct boxes of the chart. Remind students to ask themselves, *Is the animal big or small? Does it live alone or in groups?*

B • Match students with a partner to compare their answers. Model the activity for the class. Walk around helping as needed.

  • Compare answers with the class.

Answers: rhino: big, lives alone; dolphin: small, lives in groups; ant: small, lives in groups; sloth: small, lives alone; wolf: big, lives in groups

B. Complete the sentences. Use the words in the box.

| pretty big long lions male |

1. There is one male in a family of _____.
2. A male lion has _____ hair on his neck.
3. Meerkats live in _____ groups.
4. Young meerkats are _____.
5. The _____ gorilla is the leader of the family.

C. Watch the video to check your answers.

After You Watch

▲ a rhino   ▲ a dolphin   ▲ an ant   ▲ a sloth   ▲ a wolf

A. Write the names of the animals in the correct box.

	Big	**Small**
Live in groups	lions	meerkats
Live alone	polar bears	

B. Compare your answers with a partner's answers.

A rhino is big. It lives alone. Do you agree?
Yes, I agree.
No, I don't.

Teacher Tip: Correcting writing

You can save a lot of time in marking student papers by using peer correction. Before students turn in a paper, have them exchange their work with a partner and mark any mistakes or problems they see on their partner's paper. Then have them make the corrections on their own papers before handing them in to you for marking.

- Introduce the theme of the unit. Call on students to give the names of any jobs they know in English and list them on the board.

- Direct students' attention to the pictures. With the class, look at each picture in turn and have students talk about where the people might be from.

- Have students discuss the questions.

- With the class, talk about each person's job. Give/elicit the names of the jobs: *taxi driver, artist, engineer, chef*

- Go over the Unit Goals with the class, explaining and/or translating as necessary.

JOBS AROUND

1. Where are these people from?

2. What are their jobs?

UNIT GOALS

Identify jobs
Talk about jobs
Talk about countries
Compare jobs in different countries

14

Unit Goals	Grammar	Vocabulary	Listening	Speaking and Pronunciation	Reading and Writing
• Identify jobs • Talk about jobs • Talk about countries • Compare jobs in different countries	*Be* (negative) He **isn't** a doctor. Indefinite article *Pat's **an** artist.* *Be* + adjective + noun *Russia **is a big country**.*	Jobs Continents, countries, and cities	Focused listening People describing their jobs	Asking for and giving personal information Contractions with *be*	"Different Farmers" Writing sentences to describe people's jobs

THE WORLD

Unit Theme Overview

- In this unit, students look at the universal experience of work and see it through the eyes of people around the world. They first learn to talk about their own jobs and those of other people in their families, and to ask and answer questions about them. They then expand this perspective to talk about other countries and what they are like, and to consider one job (farming) and how it differs in different countries and different situations.

Identify Jobs

Vocabulary

A • Direct students' attention to the pictures and talk briefly about each one. Read the words in the box for students to repeat. Then tell them to listen and write the names of the jobs next to the names of the people in the pictures. Play the recording one or more times. **(CD1 T9)**

• Check answers.

Answers: 1. teacher, 2. artist, 3. engineer, 4. chef, 5. taxi driver, 6. doctor, 7. banker, 8. architect

B • Introduce the ideas of *interesting* and *boring*.

• Have students work individually to write the jobs from exercise **A** on the line, ranking them from the most boring to the most interesting.

C • Match students with a partner and have them compare their answers to exercise **B**.

• Compare answers with the class. Ask for a show of hands: *Is* taxi driver *a boring job? Or is it interesting?*

Grammar

• Introduce the structure in the box. Tell the class, *I am a teacher*. Elicit sentences from the class: *I am a student/doctor/housewife*. (Teach the names of your students' occupations as necessary.) Continue with *He is, She is, You are, They are* and names of occupations.

• Introduce *not*. Tell students, *I am not a doctor*. Elicit sentences from the class: *I am not a chef/taxi driver*, and so on. Continue with *He is not, She is not, You are not*, and so on.

• Present the contractions. Explain that these are short forms.

• Point out the use of *a* and *an*. If necessary, explain that the vowels in English are a, e, i, o, and u, and other sounds are consonants.

Vocabulary

A. What do they do? Listen and label the pictures with words from the box.

Track 1-9

taxi driver	chef	engineer	teacher
banker	architect	doctor	artist

1. Oscar _____ 2. Eun _____ 3. Jane _____ 4. Dae-Jung _____

5. Jim _____ 6. Hannah _____ 7. Harvey _____ 8. Fernanda _____

B. In your opinion, are these jobs interesting or boring? Write the jobs from exercise **A** on the lines.

boring ←——————————————————→ interesting

C. Compare your answers with a partner's answers.

Grammar: *Be* (negative)

Be + not			
I	am		
You	are	not	a doctor.
He/she	is		
We/they	are		doctors.

Contractions	
I'm not	you aren't
you're not	he/she isn't
he's not/she's not	we aren't
we're not	they aren't
they're not	

Word Bank: Jobs

nurse	office worker
pharmacist	computer programmer
electrician	accountant
actor	government employee
writer	professor
reporter	scientist
salesperson	secretary
housewife/homemaker	athlete

Indefinite article

Jim's **a** doctor.
Pat's **an** artist.

*We use **a** before a consonant sound.
*We use **an** before a vowel sound.

A. Look at the pictures on the opposite page. Fill in the blanks with *is* or *is not*.

1. Jim _____is_____ a taxi driver. He __is not__ a doctor.
2. Oscar _____ a teacher. He _____ an architect.
3. Fernanda _____ an architect. She _____ a doctor.
4. Dae-Jung _____ an engineer. He _____ a chef.
5. Eun _____ a banker. She _____ an artist.

B. Circle **T** for *true* and **F** for *false*.

1. Hannah is a taxi driver.   T   (F)
2. Jane is an engineer.   T   F
3. Dae-Jung is an artist.   T   F
4. Eun is not an artist.   T   F
5. Harvey is not an architect.   T   F

 **C.** Correct the false sentences. Read the new sentences to a partner.

Conversation

> Hannah isn't a taxi driver. She is a doctor.

A. Listen to the conversation. Is Jill married or single?

Track 1-10

Mary:	Hi, Jean. How's life?
Jean:	Fine. And you?
Mary:	Great. How are the children?
Jean:	They're good. But they're not children now. Jim's married. He's <u>an engineer</u>.
Mary:	<u>Wow</u>! Time passes. And what about Jill? How old is she now?
Jean:	She's <u>21</u> and she's <u>a student</u>.
Mary:	Is she married?
Jean:	No, she's still single.

 **B.** Practice the conversation with a partner. Switch roles and practice it again.

 **C.** Change the underlined words and make a new conversation.

Real Language

To show surprise, we can say:
formal ⟵⟶ informal
Really!   Amazing!   Wow!

> What do you do?
>
> What does your father do?

✓ **Goal 1**   **Identify jobs**

Ask your classmates about their jobs. Ask them about their family's jobs.

Lesson A   17

Grammar: Contractions

Some students may think that contractions aren't good English. Explain to students that native speakers use contractions in speaking and in informal writing. Using contractions will help make students' English more natural.

Grammar Practice

Bring in photos from newspapers and magazines and have the class discuss and try to guess the people's jobs. This can also be done in small groups: Give each group one picture and then have them tell the class about the person in the picture.

A • Tell students to look back at the photos on page 16 and complete the sentences.

• Check answers.

Answers: 2. is, is not, 3. is, is not, 4. is not, is, 5. is not, is

B • Have students work individually.

• Check answers.

Answers: 1. F, 2. T, 3. F, 4. F, 5. T

C • Match students with a partner and have them correct the sentences.

• Check answers.

Answers: 3. Dae-Jung isn't an artist. He's a chef. 4. Eun is an artist.

Conversation

A • Tell students to listen to the conversation and find the answer.

• Play the recording. **(CD1 T10)**

• Check answers.

Answer: single

Real Language

• Point out the expressions for surprise. If necessary, explain the ideas of *informal* and *formal*.

B • Play or read the conversation again for the class to repeat.

• Practice the conversation with the class in chorus.

• Have students practice the conversation with a partner and then switch roles and practice it again.

C • Have students work with the same partner to make a new conversation.

• Call on student pairs to present their conversation to the class.

✓ **Goal 1**

• Divide the class into groups of four or five students and have them take turns asking and answering questions about the jobs of their family members.

LESSON
B

Talk about Jobs

Listening

A • Have students look at the pictures. Tell them to try to guess each person's job.

• Play the recording. Have students check their answers. **(CD1 T11)**

B • Tell students they are going to hear the people talking again about their jobs. **(CD1 T11)**

• Play the recording one or more times.

• Check answers.

Answers: Michelle: 35 years old, artist, yes; Carlos: 43 years old, taxi driver, no; Salim: 34, architect, yes

C • Present or review numbers in English. Tell students to listen as you read the numbers aloud.

• Read the numbers again and have students repeat after you.

• …nts with a partner …em take turns … numbers in English.

Real Language

• Point out the questions and answers about age.

• Match students with a partner and have them take turns guessing the age of their classmates.

D • Match students with a partner and have them talk about each person.

• Call on students to tell the class about one of the people.

B GOAL 2 TALK ABOUT JOBS

Listening

Track 1-11

A. Look at the pictures. Guess the people's jobs. Listen and check your guesses.

▲ Michelle

▲ Carlos

▲ Salim

Track 1-11

B. Listen again. Fill in the blanks in the chart.

	Michelle	Carlos	Salim
How old is he/she?			
What is his/her job?			
Is his/her job interesting?			

C. Work with a partner. Take turns reading the numbers in English.

Numbers	**10** ten	**20** twenty	**30** thirty
1 one	**11** eleven	**21** twenty-one	**40** forty
2 two	**12** twelve	**22** twenty-two	**50** fifty
3 three	**13** thirteen	**23** twenty-three	**60** sixty
4 four	**14** fourteen	**24** twenty-four	**70** seventy
5 five	**15** fifteen	**25** twenty-five	**80** eighty
6 six	**16** sixteen	**26** twenty-six	**90** ninety
7 seven	**17** seventeen	**27** twenty-seven	**100** one hundred
8 eight	**18** eighteen	**28** twenty-eight	**101** one hundred and one
9 nine	**19** nineteen	**29** twenty-nine	

Real Language

To ask about someone's age, we say: *How old is he/she?*
The answer is: *She's/He's 28 years old.*

D. Now tell a partner about the people in exercise **B**.

18 Jobs around the World

For Your Information: How old are you?

This can be a sensitive question in English-speaking cultures. Traditionally, women wanted to appear younger than they really were, and many women did not like to tell their age. This is slowly changing, but in general it's not polite for a young person to ask an older person's age in social conversation. You may need to explain this to your students if ages and age differences are commonly discussed in their culture.

Pronunciation: Contractions with *be*

A. Listen and circle what you hear.

Track 1-12

1. (I am)	I'm	
2. I am not	I'm not	
3. you are	you're	
4. you are not	you aren't	you're not
5. she is	she's	
6. she is not	she isn't	she's not
7. we are	we're	
8. we are not	we're not	we aren't
9. they are	they're	
10. they are not	they're not	they aren't

 B. Take turns reading the phrases in exercise **A**. Point to the phrases as a partner reads them.

Communication

Read the questions and answer them for yourself. Then ask two classmates the questions. Write their answers.

Questions	Me	Classmate 1	Classmate 2
What is your name?			
What is your job?			
Is it interesting?			

✓ **Goal 2** **Talk about jobs**

Tell a partner about the people you interviewed.

Ivan is 27 years old and he's a computer technician.

His job is interesting.

Pronunciation

A • Pronounce each set of phrases for students to listen to.

• Tell students to listen to the recording and circle the phrase they hear.

• Play the recording one or more times. **(CD1 T12)**

• Check answers.

Answers: 2. I'm not, 3. you are, 4. you aren't, 5. she is, 6. she's not, 7. we are, 8. we are not, 9. they're, 10. they're not

B • Match students with a partner. Tell one student in each pair to choose and read one phrase in each set. Their partner should point to the phrase they hear.

• Have students switch roles and practice again.

Communication

• Have students work individually to complete the column for Me.

• Have students stand up, with their books and pens, and walk around the class to talk to two classmates.

✓ **Goal 2**

• Match students with a partner and have them talk about what they learned about their classmates.

Expansion Activity

Have each student make up a new identity with a new name and job (give help as needed with names of jobs). Then have them draw a chart on a piece of paper like the one in the Communication activity and repeat the steps of the activity to talk about their "new" name and job.

Talk about Countries

Language Expansion

- Introduce the words *country*, *city*, and *capital* by giving examples.

- Pronounce the names of the countries and cities on the map and have students repeat them.

- Present the names of neighboring countries and countries that are currently in the news. Write them on the board.

- Go over the words for climate. Ask, *Is our country/city wet/hot/cold/dry?* Elicit, *Yes, it is./No, it isn't.*

- Have students work individually to guess the name of each country.

- Check answers.

Answers: 2. the United Kingdom, 3. Brazil, 4. Chile, 5. Mexico

Grammar

- Present the information in the box. Introduce the term *adjective* and elicit examples the students have learned: *old/young, interesting/boring, hot/cold,* and so forth. Point out the placement of the adjective before the noun.

Language Expansion: Countries and Cities

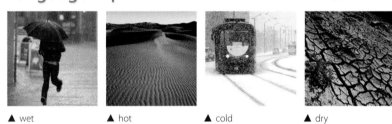

▲ wet   ▲ hot   ▲ cold   ▲ dry

Guess the country.

1. It's in Asia. It's big. It's cold. __China__
2. It's in Europe. It's small. It's wet. _____
3. It's in South America. It's big. It's hot. _____
4. It's in South America. It's small. The capital is Santiago. _____
5. It's in North America. It's hot. _____

Grammar: *Be* + adjective + noun

Statement	Question	Answer
Africa is a big continent.	Is the United Kingdom (UK) a big country?	No, it isn't. It's a small country.
Egypt is a hot, dry country.	Is the United States a big country?	Yes, it is.

Word Focus

We say **the** United Kingdom and **the** United States.

20   Jobs around the World

Word Bank: Countries

Europe: Spain, Italy, France, Germany
Asia: India, Thailand, the Philippines, Indonesia
Africa: Morocco, South Africa, Nigeria, Kenya
South America: Colombia, Peru, Venezuela, Ecuador
Central America: Guatemala, Honduras, Nicaragua, El Salvador
North America: Canada

Grammar: *Be* + adjective

In contrast to some other languages, English requires a verb (such as *be*) to be used with adjectives and adjective + noun. Emphasize to your students that every sentence in English needs a verb, and *be* is a verb.

A. Unscramble the sentences.

1. China Is a country? big _____
2. big The is a country. United States _____
3. is a Russia country. cold _____
4. Is hot Egypt a country? _____
5. country. small Japan is a _____

B. Answer the questions.

1. Is Mexico a cold country? _No, it isn't. It's a hot country._
2. Is Chile a big country? _____
3. Is Japan a hot country? _____
4. Is the UK a small country? _____
5. Is Egypt a wet country? _____

Conversation

 A. Listen to the conversation. Where is Mohamed from?

Track 1-13

Alan:	Where do you come from, <u>Mohamed</u>?
Mohamed:	I'm from <u>Cairo</u>.
Alan:	<u>Cairo</u> is in <u>Egypt</u>, right?
Mohamed:	Yes.
Alan:	So, tell me about <u>Egypt, Mohamed</u>.
Mohamed:	Well, it's in <u>Africa—North Africa</u>.
Alan:	Is it a <u>hot</u> country?
Mohamed:	Yes, it's <u>very hot</u>.

 **B.** Practice the conversation with a partner. Switch roles and practice it again.

C. Change the underlined words and make a new conversation.

✔ **Goal 3**   **Talk about countries**

Talk to a partner. Describe some countries in your region of the world.

Grammar Practice

Have students work individually to write a description of a country like the ones in the Language Expansion activity. Divide the class into groups of four or five students and have them take turns reading their descriptions for the other group members to guess.

A • Have students work individually to write the sentences.
• Check answers.

Answers: 1. Is China a big country? 2. The United States is a big country. 3. Russia is a cold country. 4. Is Egypt a hot country? 5. Japan is a small country.

B • Have students work individually to write the answers.
• Have students practice asking and answering the questions with a partner.
• Check answers.

Answers: 2. No, it isn't. It's a small country. 3. No, it isn't. It's a cold country. 4. Yes, it is. 5. No, it isn't. It's a dry country.

Conversation

A • Have students listen to the conversation to answer the question.
• Play the recording. **(CD1 T13)**
• Check answers.

Answer: Egypt

B • Play or read the conversation again for the class to repeat.
• Practice the conversation with the class in chorus.
• Have students practice the conversation with a partner and then switch roles and practice it again.

C • Have students work with the same partner to make a new conversation.
• Call on student pairs to present their conversation to the class.

✔ Goal 3

• Introduce the idea of region—a part of the world. With the class, list other countries in their region and list them on the board.
• Model the activity for the class. Choose one of the countries and talk about its size, climate, and capital city.
• Match students with a partner and have them talk about the countries on the board.

Compare Jobs in Different Countries

Reading

A • Match students with a partner and have them look at the pictures and describe them together.

• Compare answers with the class.

B • Have students read the article to complete the sentences. Tell them to circle any words in the article that they don't understand.

• Check answers.

Answers: 1. Chile, 2. farmer, 3. grapes, 4. North America and Europe, 5. Namibia, 6. millet and maize, 7. brothers

• Go over the article with the class, answering any questions from the students about vocabulary.

C • Have students work individually to answer the questions, giving short answers.

• Check answers.

Answers: 1. No, it isn't. 2. Yes, it is. 3. Yes, they are. 4. Yes, they are. 5. No, it isn't.

Reading

👥 **A.** Look at the pictures. Describe the people to a partner.

📖 **B.** Complete the sentences. Use the words in the box.

grapes	millet and maize	Chile
farmer	Europe	Africa
brothers		

1. Elena is from _____.
2. She is a _____.
3. She grows _____.
4. Her wine goes to _____.
5. Solomon and Abraham are from
   _____.
6. They grow _____.
7. They are _____.

C. Answer the questions.

1. Is it wet in Chile in the summer?
   _____

2. Is Elena's wine good?
   _____

3. Are Solomon and Abraham brothers?
   _____

4. Are they good farmers?
   _____

5. Is it cold in Namibia?
   _____

☐ The Southern Hemisphere

Different Farmers

Elena is from Chile, and she is a farmer. She grows grapes and makes wine. The weather in Chile is good for grapes. In summer it is hot and dry, and in winter it is cold and wet. Her wine is very good. It goes to North America and Europe.

CHILE

For Your Information: Chile and Namibia

Chile is a very diverse country in South America. Its long shape (2,700 miles/over 4,300 kilometers) gives it a wide variety of climates—from the world's driest desert in the north, to a warm, sunny climate in the middle, to snow and glaciers in the south. Chile produces a third of all the copper in the world, and Chilean wine has become world-famous. Chile is now the fifth-largest exporter of wine in the world.

Namibia is located in southern Africa on the Atlantic coast. It has a very small population and is the second most sparsely populated country in the world. Tourism and mining are important to Namibia's economy, but about half of the population are farmers. The Kalahari Desert is the most famous geographical feature of Namibia.

▲ maize

▲ millet

NAMIBIA

Solomon and Abraham are brothers. They are from Namibia in Africa. They are farmers. They grow millet and maize for their family. The weather in Namibia is good for millet. It is hot and dry. Solomon and Abraham are good farmers.

Communication

👥 Look at the pictures. Discuss the following questions with a partner.

1. Where are these people from?
2. What do they do?
3. Are they old or young?
4. Are their jobs interesting?

▲ Aastik

▲ Henry

Writing

Read about Aastik.

> Aastik is from Nepal. He is a farmer but his farm is very small. He grows rice. His rice does not go to other countries. It is for his family.

Write a similar paragraph about Henry. Use these words: United States, big, wheat, Asia.

_____

_____

_____

 Goal 4 | **Compare jobs in different countries**

Talk to a partner about farmers in your country. What do they grow? What is the weather like? Are their jobs interesting or boring?

Communication

- Match students with a partner and tell them they are going to look at pictures of farmers from two other countries.
- Have them work together to make guesses about the pictures.
- Compare answers with the class.

Writing

- Have students work individually to complete the paragraph about the second picture in the Communication activity. Tell them to use the model for Aastik.
- Have students exchange papers with a partner. Ask students to mark corrections and suggestions for improvements on their partner's paper.
- If desired, have students rewrite their papers, to be collected for marking.

☑ Goal 4

- Have students work together to talk about farmers in their country.

After Reading

Have students write a paragraph similar to the one in the Writing activity about a farmer in their own country.

Video Journal

Before You Watch

- Match students with a partner and have them answer the questions.
- Compare answers with the class.

Answers: 1. They rescue pufflings. 2. They are young. 3. Yes, it is.

While You Watch

A • Tell students to watch the video the first time and label the pictures. Go over the photos with the class. Play the video.

- Check answers.

Answers: 1. Puffins leave the cliffs. 2. Puffin patrols look for lost puffins. 3. Children find lost puffins. 4. Puffins get lost.

Before You Watch

Work with a partner. Look at the picture. Answer these questions.

1. What do these children do?
2. Are they old or young?
3. Is their job interesting?

While You Watch

A. Watch the video. Label the pictures below.

> Puffin patrols look for lost puffins.
> Puffins get lost.
> Children find lost puffins.
> Puffins leave the cliffs.

sky
cliffs
sea
beach
box

▲ a puffin

Word Focus

exciting= interesting, fun
crash into= run into; hit

For Your Information: Icelandic puffins

One of the world's largest colonies of puffins lives in Iceland. Of the 8 to 10 million puffins that live there, as many as 3 million breed there.

The Westmann Islands in Iceland are an important breeding site. Puffins are allowed to be harvested but they are also saved. Puffins have been an important source of food for people living on the islands. However, Icelanders have been careful not to decimate the population. In fact, a "Puffin Patrol" helps pufflings get to sea when they get lost.

In the early 1900s, the puffin was nearly made extinct in the Westmann Islands because of harvesting. Besides being hunted for food, they were also hunted for their down, which was exported. A ban was placed for 30 years and it was only lifted once the colonies recuperated. Icelanders know they must be careful with their puffin colonies.

B. Watch the video again. Circle **T** for *true* and **F** for *false*.

1. Puffin patrols look for bird nests.   T   F
2. There are puffin nests in the cliffs.   T   F
3. All the puffins fly out to sea.   T   F
4. Some puffins get lost in town.   T   F
5. Puffin patrols rescue pufflings.   T   F

C. Complete the sentences with the words or phrases in the box. Watch the video again to check your answers.

look for   rescue   leave   throw   get lost

1. Some puffins _____ in town.
2. The pufflings _____ the cliffs.
3. The children _____ the pufflings out to sea.
4. The puffin patrols _____ the lost pufflings in parking lots.
5. The children's job is to _____ the puffins.

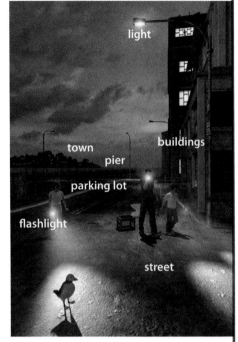

▲ A puffin patrol looks for and rescues lost pufflings.

After You Watch

Work with a partner. Take turns describing the job of the puffin patrols.

Word Focus

ALL PUFFINS   some puffins

Video Journal   25

B • Tell students to watch the video again and answer *true* or *false*. Go over the statements with the class. Play the video.

• Check answers.

Answers: 1. F, 2. T, 3. T, 4. T, 5. T

C • Tell students to complete the sentences.

• Have students watch the video again to check their answers.

Answers: 1. get lost, 2. leave, 3. throw, 4. look for, 5. rescue

After You Watch

• Elicit information of what the puffin patrol does. Ask students to refer to the pictures for their ideas.

• Match students with a partner and have them take turns describing the job of the puffin patrol.

Teacher Tip: Starting and ending group and pair work

To make group and pair work go smoothly, it's helpful to use clear signals for beginning and ending the task. Some ideas:

• Write starting and ending times on the board (Group work starts: 10:15. Group work ends: 10:25.)

• Tell your students that group work ends when you clap your hands three times.

• Train your students that when they see you raise your hand, they should also raise their hands and stop talking. The room will fall silent without you interrupting.

- Introduce the theme of the unit. Ask students, *Do you have a house? Do you have an apartment?*

- Direct students' attention to the pictures. With the class, look at each picture in turn and have students talk about each living space and where it might be. Talk about how the houses are similar to or different from houses in the students' country.

- Have students work together to answer the questions.

- Go over the Unit Goals with the class, explaining and/or translating as necessary.

HOUSES AND

1. Where are these houses?

2. Are these houses like your house?

UNIT GOALS

Identify rooms in a house
Describe your house
Identify household objects
Compare houses

26

Unit Goals	Grammar	Vocabulary	Listening	Speaking and Pronunciation	Reading and Writing
• Identify rooms in a house • Describe your house • Identify household objects • Compare houses	*There is/ there are* **There are** *three bedrooms.* **Is there** *a garage?* Prepositions of place: *in, on, under, next to* *Your magazine is* **under** *your bag.*	Rooms in a house Furniture and household objects	Listening for general understanding and specific details People talking about their houses	Describing your house Final -s	"Unusual Houses" Writing descriptions of houses

APARTMENTS

UNIT 3

Unit Theme Overview

- The houses and apartments we live in are an expression of our culture and our identity, and they also show many similarities because of the shared human experience around the world. In this unit, students learn to talk about the common features of houses and apartments and also examine some unusual houses in different parts of the world. They begin by learning the names of rooms and parts of a house/apartment and practice describing their own and other houses. They learn vocabulary for furniture and common household appliances and talk about where these things are located. Finally, they learn about houses in different parts of the world and how they are decorated.

27

Identify Rooms in a House

Vocabulary

A • Have students look at the picture. Go over the names of the parts of the house, and pronounce them for students to repeat. Ask students which rooms are in their house or apartment.

• Have students work individually to label the rooms in the apartment.

• Check answers.

Answers: 1. bathroom, 2. bedroom, 3. kitchen, 4. dining room, 5. living room

B • Have students work individually to look at the picture and complete the sentences.

• Check answers.

Answers: 1. downstairs, 2. garage, 3. bedrooms, 4. fireplace, living room

Grammar

• Introduce the structure. Say, *What's in our classroom? There is a teacher/window/clock*, and so forth. (Point to the items.) *There are 10 desks/two computers*, and so forth. Elicit more answers from the class.

• Go over the information on how to make questions and short answers in the boxes.

Vocabulary

A. Label the rooms in the apartment.

1. _____
2. _____
3. _____
4. _____
5. _____

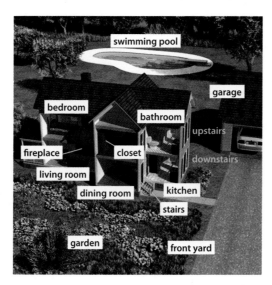

swimming pool
garage
bedroom
bathroom
upstairs
fireplace
closet
downstairs
living room
dining room
kitchen
stairs
garden
front yard

B. Complete the sentences about the house in the picture. Use the words in the box.

garage downstairs living room fireplace bedrooms

1. The kitchen is _____.
2. The _____ is in the backyard.
3. The _____ are upstairs.
4. The _____ is in the _____.

Grammar: *There is/there are*

Statement	Questions	Answers
There is a garage.	**Is there** a closet?	Yes, there is. No, there isn't.
There are three bedrooms upstairs.	**Are there** two bathrooms?	Yes, there are. No, there aren't.

*The contraction of *there is* = *there's*.

Word Bank: House/apartment parts

hall
attic
garage
family room
home office
patio

balcony
carport
utility room
pantry
basement
courtyard

Grammar: *There is/there are*

There is/there are is used to talk about the existence of items in a particular place. These sentences must include an indication of quantity (*There are 10/many/some books on the table*) and a reference (explicit or understood) to a place. *There is/There are* is not used with proper nouns.

Plural nouns

1 house	2 houses
1 bedroom	2 bedrooms

*Add an -s at the end of the word to make it plural.

A. Complete the sentences with the correct form: *there is* or *there are*.

1. _____ a big kitchen.
2. _____ three bathrooms.
3. _____ a yard?
4. Is there a closet? Yes, _____.
5. Is there a garage? No, _____.

B. Unscramble the sentences.

1. a is big There garage _____.
2. isn't There closet a _____.
3. a swimming Is there pool _____?
4. there two Are bathrooms _____?
5. garages are There two _____.

Conversation

Track 1-14

A. Listen to the conversation. Is there a garage?

Realtor: What about this <u>apartment</u>?
Client: Is it a big apartment?
Realtor: Yes, there are <u>three bedrooms</u>.
Client: And <u>bathrooms</u>?
Realtor: There is just one bathroom.
Client: Is there a <u>garden</u>?
Realtor: No, there isn't. But there's a garage.

Luxury Apartment — 1st floor

- Big kitchen/ dining room
- Living room
- 3 bedrooms
- 1 bathroom

 B. Practice the conversation with a partner. Switch roles and practice it again.

 C. Change the underlined words and make a new conversation.

✓ **Goal 1** Identify rooms in a house

Work with a partner. Draw a simple floor plan like the apartment on page 28. Tell your partner the names of the rooms.

Real Language

What about is a useful and simple way to ask for someone's opinion.

- Point out that regular nouns can be made plural by adding -*s*.

A • Have students work individually to complete the sentences.
- Check answers.

Answers: 1. There is, 2. There are, 3. Is there, 4. there is, 5. there isn't

B • Have students work individually to write the sentences.
- Check answers.

Answers: 1. There is a big garage. 2. There isn't a closet. 3. Is there a swimming pool? 4. Are there two bathrooms? 5. There are two garages.

Conversation

A • Have students read the apartment ad. If necessary, explain that *luxury* means very good and expensive, and a *realtor* is a person who sells houses and apartments. Tell students to listen and answer the question.
- Play the recording. **(CD1 T14)**
- Check answers.

Answer: yes

B • Play or read the conversation again for the class to repeat.
- Practice the conversation with the class in chorus.
- Have students practice the conversation with a partner and then switch roles and practice it again.

C • Have students work with the same partner to make a new conversation.
- Call on student pairs to present their conversation to the class.

✓ Goal 1

- Have students work in pairs to draw a floor plan for a small house or apartment and name the rooms in it.
- Combine student pairs into groups of four and have them take turns showing and explaining their floor plans.

Grammar Practice: *There is/there are*

Have students work with a partner to ask and answer questions about their houses/apartments. Model the activity for students: Ask, *Is there a living room in your apartment?* (*Yes, there is/No, there isn't.*) Call on students to tell the class one thing they learned about their partner's house or apartment.

Describe Your House

Listening

A • Tell students they are going to hear five people talking about their houses. They should write the correct name by each house. Pronounce the names for the students.

• Play the recording one or more times. **(CD1 T15)**

• Check answers.

Answers: 1. Katsuro, 2. Betty, 3. Liling, 4. Joe, 5. Ramon

Listening

🎧 Track 1-15 **A.** Listen to each person describe his or her house. Match the names to the pictures.

| Betty | Joe | Katsuro | Ramon | Liling |

1._____

2._____

3._____

4._____

5._____

For Your Information: How many bedrooms?

In some countries, houses do not have bedrooms—rooms that are used only for sleeping. For example, in a traditional Korean house, people sleep on mats that are put away in the closet during the day. Floor cushions and low tables are brought out and the "bedroom" becomes a "living room."

B. Listen again. Circle **T** for *true* and **F** for *false*.

1. There is one bedroom in Betty's house.   T   F
2. There are four bedrooms in Joe's house.   T   F
3. There is a fireplace in Katsuro's house.   T   F
4. There are five bedrooms in Ramon's house.   T   F
5. There is a yard in Liling's house.   T   F

Pronunciation: *Final -s*

Track 1-16

A. Listen and check the correct column.

	Ends in /s/ sound	Ends in /z/ sound	Ends in /iz/ sound
gardens			
apartments			
garages			
bathrooms			
kitchens			
houses			
windows			

Track 1-16

B. Listen again and repeat the words.

Communication

  Work with a partner. Take turns describing these houses.

> There is one bedroom in this house.

✓ **Goal 2** **Describe your house**

Describe your house to the class.

Lesson B   **31**

Expansion Activity

Have students work with a partner to choose a famous person and imagine a description of their house. Walk around helping as needed. When all student pairs are ready, have them present their descriptions to the class: *My name is Bill Gates. In my house, there are . . .*

B • Tell students to listen again to answer *true* or *false*.

• Play the recording one or more times. **(CD1 T15)**

• Check answers.

Answers: 1. T, 2. F, 3. T, 4. F, 5. F

Pronunciation

• Remind students that in English, plural nouns are formed by adding -*s* at the end (with a few exceptions). Tell them that the -*s* has different pronunciations.

A • Go over the three different sounds. Tell students to listen to the recording and mark the sound they hear.

• Play the recording several times. **(CD1 T16)**

• Check answers.

Answers: /s/ sound: apartments, bathrooms; /z/ sound: gardens, kitchens, windows; /iz/ sound: garages, houses

B • Play the recording again one or more times for students to repeat the words. **(CD1 T16)**

Communication

• Match students with a partner and have each student describe one of the houses. Tell them to use their own ideas about what is inside each house.

• Call on student pairs to tell the class one sentence.

☑ **Goal 2**

• Tell students they are going to describe their house or apartment to the class. Give them a minute to think about what they will say, but don't allow them to write their descriptions.

• Call on each student to describe his or her house to the class. For larger classes, divide students into groups of four or five and have them tell their group about their house.

Identify Household Objects

Language Expansion

- Go over the names of the items. Pronounce them for students to repeat.

- Have students work individually to list the items in the chart. Explain that for some items, more than one place may be correct.

- Compare answers with the class and draw a chart on the board.

Possible answers: Kitchen: refrigerator, microwave, table, chair; Dining room: table, chair; Living room: sofa, armchair, coffee table, bookcase, lamp, TV; Bedroom: bed, bookcase, lamp, TV

Grammar

- Have students look at the pictures and introduce the prepositions of place. Demonstrate with other objects in the classroom and with exercise **A**.

Language Expansion: Furniture and household objects

▲ sofa   ▲ bed   ▲ armchair   ▲ refrigerator

▲ table   ▲ chair   ▲ bookcase   ▲ microwave

▲ coffee table   ▲ lamp   ▲ stove   ▲ TV

In which rooms do you usually find the furniture and household objects above?

Kitchen	Dining room	Living room	Bedroom
stove			

Grammar: Prepositions of place

▲ in   ▲ on   ▲ under   ▲ next to

32 Houses and Apartments

Word Bank: Household items

window	night/bedside table
picture	desk
poster	dresser
rug	toilet
carpet	sink
mirror	bathtub
floor	shower
ceiling	door

A. Look at the pictures. Complete the sentences with *in*, *on*, *under*, or *next to*.

1. There's a TV _____ the bedroom.
2. There's a boy _____ the swimming pool.
3. There are three books _____ the table.
4. The stove is _____ the refrigerator.
5. The dog is _____ the table.

B. What can you see in the pictures? Take turns describing them.

> There is a sofa and a coffee table.

Conversation

A. Listen to the conversation. Where is Tracey's magazine?

Track 1-17

Tracey: Where is my <u>magazine</u>?
Kevin: Is it in the <u>bedroom</u>?
Tracey: No, it isn't. And it's not on the <u>kitchen table</u>.
Kevin: Here it is! It's under your <u>bag</u>.

B. Practice the conversation with a partner. Switch roles and practice it again.

C. Change the underlined words and make a new conversation.

✓ **Goal 3** **Identify household objects**

Work with a partner. Take turns describing a room in your house.

Lesson C   **33**

A • Have students work individually to fill in the prepositions.
• Check answers.

Answers: 1. in, 2. in, 3. on, 4. next to, 5. under

B • Match students with a partner and have them make as many sentences as possible about each picture.
• Call on each student to share a sentence with the class.

Conversation

A • Have students close their books. Write the question on the board: *Where is Tracey's magazine?*
• Play the recording. **(CD1 T17)**
• Check answers.

Answer: under her bag

B • Play or read the conversation again for the class to repeat.
• Practice the conversation with the class in chorus.
• Have students practice the conversation with a partner and then switch roles and practice it again.

C • Have students work with the same partner to make a new conversation.
• Call on student pairs to present their conversation to the class.

✓ **Goal 3**
• Have students work with the same partner to describe one room in their house or apartment.
• Call on students to tell the class one interesting thing they heard about their partner's house or apartment.

Grammar: Prepositions of place

Prepositions are words that express relationships between two things. These can be relationships of time (*I work <u>on</u> Saturday*), place (*The book is <u>on</u> the table*), or abstract relationships (*I read an article <u>on</u> Japan*).

Grammar Practice: Prepositions of place

Have students demonstrate sentences you say with prepositions of place: *The pen is on the book/in the book/next to the book/under the book.* Use objects that all students have with them, such as their textbook, dictionary, keys, wallet, and so forth.

Then divide the class into pairs or groups and have them take turns saying sentences for the other students to demonstrate.

Compare Houses

Reading

A • Match students with a partner and have them guess where each house is.

• Compare guesses with the class, but do not give them the locations of the houses.

B • Tell students to read the article and find the answers to the questions. Tell them to circle any words they don't understand.

• Check answers.

Answers: 1. no, 2. yes, 3. no, 4. yes, 5. no

• Go over the article with the class and answer any questions from the students about vocabulary.

• Talk about living in these houses. What's good about them? What's bad about them?

Reading

 A. Look at the pictures. Where do you think the houses are?

B. Read and answer the questions.

1. Is there a bathroom in the tree house? _____

2. Is it hot in an igloo? _____
3. How many rooms are in the igloo? _____

4. Are there a lot of rooms in Dar Al Hajar? _____

5. Are there bedrooms in the Crooked House? _____

▲ an Irian Jaya treehouse

Unusual Houses

The Kombai people of Irian Jaya live in tree houses. The houses are high in the trees. There is only one room in the house. It is the kitchen, the living room, the dining room, and the bedroom.

Abraham Niaqu is from Quebec in Canada. He is making a snow house called an *igloo*. There is only one room in an igloo. It is not cold in an igloo. In fact, it is quite hot.

For Your Information: Unusual houses

Kombai: The Kombai people in Indonesia live in tree houses 30 to 80 feet (9 to 25 meters) above the ground. They move from place to place and build new houses every few years. They live by hunting and gathering food.

Igloo: This is the word for a house in the language of the Inuit people of the Arctic. They are made from blocks of snow. When the outside temperature is a low as – 4 degrees Fahrenheit (– 20 degrees Celsius), the inside temperature can be as warm as 61 Fahrenheit (16 degrees Celsius) because the snow keeps body heat in.

Dar al Hajar is a palace near the city of Sanaa. It is a seven-story building with 35 rooms, many halls and stairways, and a courtyard with three fountains. The palace has been built and rebuilt many times, and no one is certain how old the current building is.

The *Crooked House* is located in the city of Sopot, Poland. It contains restaurants, shops, and bars. It is three stories tall and was opened in 2004.

This house is called Dar Al Hajar. It is in Yemen. It is a big house and there are a lot of rooms in the house. It is hot in Yemen, but it is not hot inside the house.

This house is called the Crooked House. However, it is not a house. Nobody lives in it. It is a shop—a very special shop! The architect, Szotynscy Zaleski, got the idea from a children's book. It is very unusual.

Writing

A. Look at this plan of a house. Complete the paragraph.

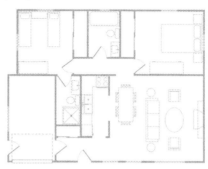

This is a plan of a house. There is a small kitchen. In the kitchen there is a _____, and a refrigerator. The kitchen is next to the _____ room. In the dining room there is a table with six chairs. The living room is _____ the dining room. There is a sofa and two armchairs in the living room. There are two _____ in the house—one big bedroom and a small bedroom. There is a _____ in the big bedroom.

B. Now write about your house.

In my house there is . . .

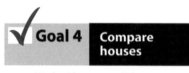

✓ **Goal 4**   **Compare houses**

Work with a partner. Take turns. Compare your own house with the houses in the reading.

There is one bedroom in the tree house. There are three bedrooms in my house.

Lesson D   **35**

Writing

A • Have students work individually to complete the paragraph about the house.

• Check answers.

Answers: stove, dining, next to, bedrooms, bed

B • Have students write about their own house or apartment, following the model in exercise **A**

• Have students exchange papers with a partner. Ask students to mark corrections and suggestions for improvements on their partner's paper.

• If desired, have students rewrite their papers, to be collected for marking.

✓ **Goal 4**

• Have students work with a partner to compare their house with those pictured. Walk around helping with vocabulary as needed.

After Reading

Have students write about an imaginary house that they would like to live in. Then have them read their work to a small group or to the class.

Video Journal

Before You Watch

A • Have students look at the map and identify the location of Camogli. Then have them work individually to complete the summary.

• Check answers.

Answers: village, Sea, fishermen, artists, paint, art

B • Match students with a partner. Have them repeat the parts of the house after you.

• Have them identify other parts of the house in the picture.

• Tell them to say which parts of the house are the same as in their house or apartment.

C • Match students with a partner. Have them look at the pictures and say which is real.

Answers: Picture on the left is real.

Before You Watch

A. Complete the video summary. Use the words in the box.

| fishermen | artists | village | paint | Sea | art |

Video summary

Camogli is a small town or _____ in Italy. Camogli is next to the Mediterranean _____. Many people in Camogli are _____. Their job is to catch fish. There are also _____ in Camogli. They _____ houses and buildings. Their _____ is called *trompe l'oeil*. It is very special. The paintings are very realistic. They make things look real, but they are not.

B. Look at the picture. Study the different parts of the house. Tell a partner which parts of the house are the same as your house or apartment.

There are three windows.

My house has . . .

C. Discuss the pictures with a partner. Which is real? Which is the *trompe l'oeil*?

36   Houses and Apartments

For Your Information: Trompe l'oeil

Trompe l'oeil is an art technique which means "trick the eye" in French. It depicts very realistic imagery which seems to be in three dimensions and creates an optical illusion when viewed. This technique has been used by artists dating back to the ancient Greeks. Many artists have used it in murals and Renaissance painters used it in ceiling paintings. Artists use the technique to challenge the boundaries between image and reality.

While You Watch

A. Watch the video. Match the parts of the sentences.

1. Artists use *trompe l'oeil* to make___
2. People like to paint their houses ___
3. The fishermen painted their houses ___
4. Raffaella and Carlo are ___
5. You can see the houses of Camogli ___

a. with bright colors.
b. artists.
c. things look real
d. from the sea.
e. with *trompe l'oeil* art.

B. Watch the video again. Circle **T** for *true* and **F** for *false*.

1. Camogli Is a large city. T F
2. In Camogli people paint their houses in bright colors. T F
3. The houses in Camogli are very special. T F
4. All the artists in Italy use *trompe l'oeil* technique. T F
5. Only fishermen paint their houses with *trompe l'oeil* art. T F

▲ This wall is a *trompe l'oeil* painting.

After You Watch

Work with a partner. Take turns describing the changes you would make to your house with *trompe l'oeil*.

I want to add two balconies.

While You Watch

A • Tell students to watch the video the first time and match the columns. Play the video.

• Check answers.

Answers: 1. c, 2. e, 3. a, 4. b, 5. d

B • Tell students to watch the video again and answer *true* or *false*. Have the students read the statements. Play the video.

• Check answers.

Answers: 1. F, 2. T, 3. T, 4. F, 5. F

After You Watch

• Match students with a partner. Have them take turns describing what things they would add to their house with *trompe l'oeil*.

• Compare answers with the class.

Teacher Tip: Encouraging use of English

A common challenge in monolingual classes is motivating students to use only English in group work. Here are some approaches to consider:

• Explain the rationale for using only English. Tell students, *We learn to speak English by speaking English.* If appropriate, tell students about your own language-learning experiences.

• Establish a clear policy. For example, you might tell students, *It's OK to ask questions in your native language, but for all other things we use only English.*

• Set an example for the students. Use only English for instructions and classroom management.

- Direct students' attention to the pictures. With the class, look at each picture in turn and have students name things they see in each one.

- Introduce the term *possessions*—things that we own.

- Have students work with a partner to discuss the questions.

- Compare answers with the class.

- Go over the Unit Goals with the class, explaining and/or translating as necessary.

POSSESSIONS

1. Do you have any of these things?

2. What is your favorite personal possession?

UNIT GOALS

Identify personal possessions
Talk about personal possessions
Buy a present
Talk about special possessions

38

Unit Goals	Grammar	Vocabulary	Listening	Speaking and Pronunciation	Reading and Writing

• Identify personal possessions
• Talk about personal possessions
• Buy a present
• Talk about special possessions
	Demonstrative adjectives
	  *Are **these** your books?*
	  That *is not your bag.*
	Possessive nouns
	  *It's **Jim's** bag.*
	Have
	  *She **has** a camcorder.*
		Personal possessions
		Electronic products
			Listening for specific information
			People proving ownership
				Talking about the personal possessions of others
				Short *i* and long *e* sounds
					"Jewelry"
					Summarizing a class survey

Unit Theme Overview

- However young or old we are, or rich or poor, we all have certain possessions that mean a lot to us— either because they are important in our daily lives for their usefulness or because they hold important meanings. In this unit, students look at both kinds of possessions, both the useful and the significant, and examine them in a more global context. Students begin by learning the names of objects that are used in daily life. They talk about common electronic products and discuss buying a present for someone. Finally, they learn about possessions that have special meaning to people in different cultures and talk about their own important possessions.

39

Identify Personal Possessions

Vocabulary

A • Pronounce the words in the box for students to repeat.

• Have students complete the captions for the pictures.

• Check answers.

Answers: 1. book, 2. notebook, 3. dictionary, 4. bag, 5. pen, 6. watch, 7. handbag, 8. wallet, 9. ring, 10. necklace, 11. glasses, 12. keys

B • Divide the class into pairs. Assign each student a role, student A or student B, and tell them to look at their picture. Go over the example with the class.

• Have students talk to their partner about differences in the pictures.

• Compare answers with the class.

Vocabulary

A. Complete the names of the objects in the pictures. Use the words in the box.

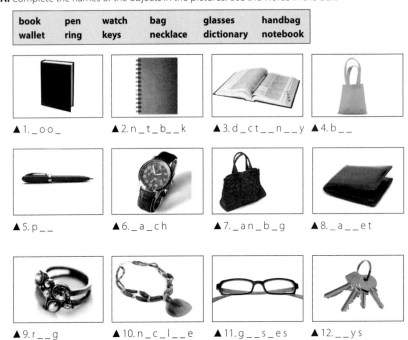

book	pen	watch	bag	glasses	handbag
wallet	ring	keys	necklace	dictionary	notebook

▲ 1. _ o o _   ▲ 2. n _ t _ b _ _ k   ▲ 3. d _ c t _ _ n _ _ y   ▲ 4. b _ _

▲ 5. p _ _   ▲ 6. _ a _ c h   ▲ 7. _ a n _ b _ g   ▲ 8. _ a _ _ e t

▲ 9. r _ _ g   ▲ 10. n _ c _ l _ _ e   ▲ 11. g _ _ s _ e s   ▲ 12. _ _ y s

> There are glasses in my picture.

> There are no glasses in my picture, but there's a cell phone.

B. Take turns. Find the differences between the two pictures.

STUDENT A

STUDENT B

40   Possessions

Word Bank: Possessions

money

pencil

key ring (car key/ house key)

bracelet

earrings

ID card

driver's license

business card

appointment book

PDA (personal digital assistant)

address book

Grammar: Demonstrative pronouns

In English, *this/these* refer to things close to the speaker, while *that/those* refer to things far from the speaker. This pattern can cause difficulty for students whose languages make different types of divisions, such as near the speaker versus near the listener, or three different degrees of distance rather than two.

Grammar: Demonstrative adjectives

	Singular	Plural	Possessive nouns
Near ☞	**This** is your bag.	Are **these** your books?	It's Jim**'s** bag.
Far ☞	**That** is not your bag.	**Those** are not my pens.	

A. Match the questions and the answers. There is more than one right answer.

Question	Answer
1. Is this your pen? ____	a. Yes, they are.
2. Are those your keys? ____	b. No, it isn't. It's Peter's.
3. Are these your glasses? ____	c. Yes, it is.
4. Is that your dictionary? ____	d. No, they aren't. They're Angie's.

B. Look at the pictures. Use the cues to write questions.

1. (far) _Are those your glasses?_
2. (far) _____
3. (near) _____
4. (near) _____
5. (far) _____

Conversation

Track 1-18

A. Listen to the conversation. What is in the bag?

Andrea: Is this your bag?
Jennifer: No, *that's* my bag
Andrea: Maybe it's Jim's.
Jennifer: Let's look inside. There's a <u>book, a dictionary, a pen, a wallet</u> …
Andrea: A <u>wallet</u>? Look inside.
Jennifer: Right, it's Jim's bag.

B. Practice the conversation with a partner. Switch roles and practice it again.

C. Change the underlined words and make a new conversation.

✓ **Goal 1** **Identify personal possessions**

Describe the contents of your bag to a partner.

1.
2.
3.
4.
5.

Grammar

- Introduce the demonstrative adjectives. Elicit more examples from students.
- Go over the demonstrative adjectives in the chart.
- Introduce how to form possessive nouns. Elicit more examples from the class.

A • Have students work individually to match the columns.
- Check answers.

Answers: 1. b/c; 2. a/d; 3. a/d, 4. b/c

B • Have students work individually to write questions about the possessions.
- Check answers.

Answers: 2. Is that your book? 3. Is this your house? 4. Are these your dogs? 5. Is that your book bag?

Conversation

A • Have students close their books. Write the question on the board: *What is in the bag?*
- Play the recording. **(CD1 T18)**
- Check answers.

Answers: a book, a dictionary, a pen, and a wallet

B • Play or read the conversation again for the class to repeat.
- Practice the conversation with the class in chorus.
- Have students practice the conversation with a partner and then switch roles and practice it again.

C • Have students work with the same partner to make a new conversation.
- Call on student pairs to present their conversation to the class.

✓ Goal 1

- Have students work with the same partner to talk about what's in their bags.
- Call on students to tell the class what's in their bags and discuss any interesting/unusual answers.

Grammar Practice:
Possessive nouns

Have each student come up and put one of their possessions on your desk (such as a key, ring, or watch). Hold each one up and ask the class, *What's this?/What are these?* Have students answer, *That's Aisha's dictionary/Those are Toshi's keys.* Give each possession back to its owner as it is identified.

Talk about Personal Possessions

Listening

A • Direct students' attention to the photos, and ask where the people might be. Explain if necessary that the guard is looking for dangerous things in people's bags.

• Tell students they are going to hear two people talking about what's in their bags. They should answer *true* or *false*. Have them read the sentences.

• Play the recording one or more times. **(CD1 T19)**

• Check answers.

Answers: 1. F, 2. T, 3. T, 4. F

B • Tell students to listen again to the conversations and answer the questions.

• Play the recording one or more times. **(CD1 T19)**

• Check answers.

Answers: 1. A notebook, a dictionary, and a *World English* book, 2. a wallet, 3. a cell phone

C • With the class, make a list on the board of what Gill and Lee have in their bags.

• Match students with a partner and have them ask and answer the questions together.

▲ Gill

▲ Lee

Listening

Track 1-19

A. Listen. Circle **T** for *true* and **F** for *false*.

1. There is cell phone in Gill's bag.	T	F
2. There is a dictionary in Gill's bag.	T	F
3. There is a cell phone in Lee's bag.	T	F
4. There is a notebook in Lee's bag.	T	F

Track 1-19

B. Listen again. Answer the questions.

1. What does Gill have in her bag that Lee doesn't have in his bag? _____
2. What does Gill have in her bag that Lee has in his bag? _____
3. What does Lee have in his bag that Gill doesn't have in her bag? _____

C. Work with a partner. Take turns. Ask and answer the questions.

1. What does Gill have in her bag that you don't have in your bag?
2. What does Gill have in her bag that you have in your bag?
3. What does Lee have in his bag that you don't have in your bag?
4. What does Lee have in his bag that you have in your bag?

For Your Information: Security checks

Common sites for security checks include airports, train stations, government buildings, museums, and sports facilities.

Pronunciation: Short *i* and long *e* sound

 Track 1-20
A. Listen and check the boxes.

	long *e* sound	short *i* sound
this		
these		
heat		
hit		
his		
he's		
sheep		
ship		

▲ sheep

▲ ship

 Track 1-20
B. Listen again and repeat the words.

Communication

1. Write the name of an object on a small piece of paper. Give the paper to your teacher.
2. Your teacher mixes the papers and gives you someone else's paper
3. Find the owner.

> Excuse me, is this your watch?

> No it isn't. I think it's Ling's.

> Yes, it is. Thanks a lot.

✔ **Goal 2** **Talk about personal possessions**

Ask a partner about what is in his/her bag

> Is there a pencil in your bag?

Pronunciation

- Explain to the class that in English, the words *ship* and *sheep* have two different sounds. Pronounce them for the class. Tell them that the sound in *sheep* is called long /e/ and the sound in *ship* is called short /i/.

A • Tell students to listen to the recording and mark the sound they hear. Play the recording several times. **(CD1 T20)**
- Check answers.

Answers: long /e/ sound: these, heat, he's, sheep; short /i/ sound: this, hit, his, ship

B • Play the recording again several times for students to repeat. Walk around listening for good pronunciation. **(CD1 T20)**

Communication

- Have students choose a possession and write its name on a piece of paper. You can also ask students to draw a small picture of the object.
- Collect the papers and redistribute one to each student.
- Go over the sample conversation with the class. Then have all students get up and walk around the class asking and answering questions to find the owner of the object. Tell them to sit down when they are finished.

✔ Goal 2

- Match students with a partner. Tell each student to ask their partner three questions about what's in his or her bag.

Expansion Activity

As a follow-up to the Goal 2 activity, have students change partners and ask questions about what is in their partner's living room, kitchen, and so on.

Buy a Present

Language Expansion

A • Introduce the items on the Web page. Ask which ones students can name.

• Pronounce the items in the box for students to repeat. Then have students work individually to label the items on the page.

• Check answers.

Answers: CD player, car audio, MP3 player, laptop, electronic dictionary, cell phone, touch phone, DVD player, camcorder

B • Have students work individually to complete the sentences.

• Check answers.

Answers: 2. cell phone, touch phone, 3. Computer, 4. Audio

Language Expansion: Electronic products

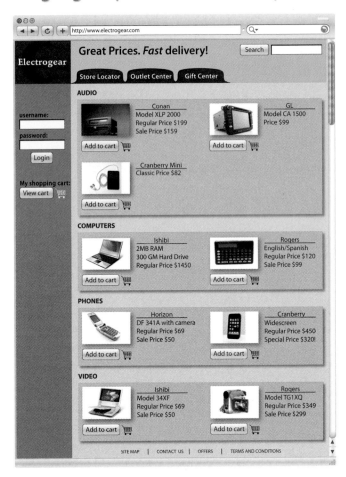

A. Label the items on the Web page. Use the words in the box.

CD player	DVD player	cell phone	laptop	electronic dictionary
camcorder	touch phone	MP3 player	car audio	

B. Read the Web page. Complete the sentences.

1. The camcorder is in the _Video_ section.
2. The _____ and the _____ are in the Phones section.
3. The electronic dictionary is in the _____ section.
4. The MP3 player is in the _____ section.

44 Possessions

Word Bank: Electronics

desktop computer	keyboard
wireless	speakers
GPS	printer
digital camera	router
flash drive	server
memory card	headphones

Grammar: *Have*

Statements	Negative
I/you/we/they **have** a laptop. He/she **has** a camcorder.	I/you/we/they **don't have** a CD player. He/she **doesn't have** a DVD player.
Yes/no questions	**Short answers**
Do I/you/we/they **have** an MP3 player? **Does** he/she **have** a cell phone?	Yes, I/you/we/they **do**. No, I/you/we/they **don't**. Yes, he/she **does**. No, he/she **doesn't**.

A. Complete the sentences with *have* or *has*.

1. Jim _____has_____ a new laptop.
2. Do you _____ a touch phone?
3. I don't _____ a cell phone.
4. Does Chen _____ a DVD player?
5. Alan _____ a camcorder.

B. Write questions with *have*.

1. you/cell phone? _Do you have a cell phone?_
2. Alison/big house? _____
3. you/my keys? _____
4. Aki/a laptop? _____
5. Mario and Linda/an apartment? _____

Conversation

Track 1-21

A. Sun-Hee and Hana are buying a present for Sun-Hee's brother. Listen to the conversation. What do they buy?

Sun-Hee:	Look at these new products!
Hana:	Wow, these <u>cameras</u> look cool. And cheap!
Sun-Hee:	My brother already has a good <u>camera</u>.
Hana:	Does he have <u>a touch phone</u>?
Sun-Hee:	No he doesn't. Let's get <u>a touch phone</u>!

 B. Practice the conversation with a partner. Switch roles and practice it again.

 C. Change the underlined words and make a new conversation.

 **Goal 3   Buy a present**

Work with a partner. Practice buying a present for a friend. Use the conversation and the Web site for ideas.

Real Language

We use *Wow! Cool!* to show interest. Both are informal.

Lesson C   45

Grammar: *Have*

Have is both a lexical verb (a verb for an action, event, or state) and an auxiliary verb. In this unit, it is taught in its basic lexical meaning: to express possession.

Grammar Practice: *Have*

Have students list the items pictured on page 44 on a sheet of paper. Then match them with a partner and have them interview each other to find out which items their partner has (*Do you have a cell phone? Yes, I do./No, I don't.*). Tell them to write down their partner's answers. Then have them change partners and tell them what they found out about their first partner (*She has a CD player. She doesn't have a touch phone.*).

Grammar

- Present the information in the box.
- Give/elicit more examples.
- Go over how the negative is formed.

A • Have students work individually to complete the sentences.
- Check answers.

Answers: 2. have, 3. have, 4. have, 5. has

B • Have students work individually to write the questions.
- Check answers.

Answers: 2. Does Alison have a big house? 3. Do you have my keys? 4. Does Aki have a laptop? 5. Do Mario and Linda have an apartment?

Conversation

A • Have students close their books. Write the question on the board: *What do they buy?*
- Play the recording. **(CD1 T21)**
- Check answers.

Answer: a touch phone

B • Play or read the conversation again for the class to repeat.
- Practice the conversation with the class in chorus.
- Have students practice the conversation with a partner and then switch roles and practice it again.

C • Have students work with the same partner to make a new conversation.
- Call on student pairs to present their conversation to the class.

☑ Goal 3

- Match students with a partner. Have them choose a friend to buy a present for and then role-play a conversation.
- Call on student pairs to present their conversation to the class.

Talk about Special Possessions

Reading

A • Introduce the topic of the reading. Talk briefly about jewelry, giving examples that students are wearing (*Mari has a ring. Estela has earrings.*).

• Match students with a partner and have them give their opinions. Then compare opinions with the class.

B • Have students read the article to answer *true* or *false*. Tell them to circle any words they don't understand.

• Check answers.

Answers: 1. T, 2. F, 3. T, 4. F, 5. T

• Go over the article with the class and answer any questions from the students about vocabulary.

C • Have students read the article again to find the information.

• Check answers.

Answers: 1. Djibouti, 2. 300 years, 3. Kiev, 4. silver

Reading

A. These people are wearing traditional jewelry. Some people say they are beautiful. Other people say they are not beautiful and think they are ugly. Discuss your opinions with a partner.

B. Read the sentences. Circle **T** for *true* and **F** for *false*.

1. Aisha's father is an important man. T F
2. Her jewelry is not made from gold. T F
3. The earrings are very old. T F
4. The necklaces come from Europe. T F
5. The bracelets are made of silver T F

C. Read and answer the questions.

1. Where does Aisha come from?

_____

2. How old are the necklace and pendants?

_____

3. Where do the earrings come from?

_____

4. What is the Viking jewelry made of ?

_____

☐ Jewelry

Jewelry is beautiful. In every country and in every age, people have jewelry.

Aisha comes from Djibouti. Her father is an important man. She has a lot of jewelry. It is made from gold.

These are earrings. They are from Kiev and are 1,500 years old. They are large and very beautiful.

For Your Information

Djibouti is a small country with a population of only 500,000 people that is located on the Red Sea in the Horn of Africa. Most of its people live in Djibouti City, the capital, which is a free trade port. The other people are nomadic herders.

The *Concepción* was a Spanish ship that sank on September 20, 1683, near the Pacific island of Saipan. An underwater excavation of the wreck, begun in 1987, recovered more than 1,300 pieces of exquisite gold jewelry.

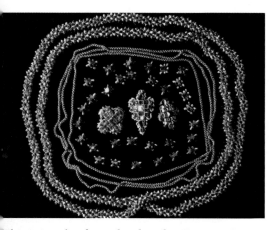

This is jewelry from the ship the *Concepción*. It is about 300 years old. There are two beautiful necklaces and three pendants. We think they come from Asia, but we are not sure.

This is Viking jewelry from Norway. It is made of silver. It is about 1,000 years old. There are chains and bracelets.

Communication

👥 Work with a partner to complete the chart.

1. Fill in the first column with your information.
2. Fill in the second column with your partner's information.
3. Fill in the third column about your partner's best friend.

Do you have a CD player? | Yes, I do. | No, I don't.

Do you have ...	Me	My partner	My partner's best friend
a CD player?			
a laptop computer?			
an electronic dictionary?			
a necklace?			
earrings?			
an MP3 player?			

Does he/she have earrings? | Yes, he/she does. | No, he/she doesn't.

Writing

Write about your partner. Use the information in the chart.

My partner has a CD player, a laptop computer, and a video camcorder. She doesn't have an electronic dictionary, a calculator, or an MP3 player.

✓ **Goal 4** | **Talk about special possessions**

Work with a partner. Tell your partner about a special possession. What is it? Where is it from? Is it old or new?

Communication

- Have students complete the first column by writing *yes* or *no*.
- Match students with a partner and have them complete the second column by asking questions and writing the answers.
- Have each student choose a friend and then exchange information by asking and answering questions to complete the third column.

Writing

- Have students write sentences about their partners, referring back to the chart in the Communication activity.
- Have students exchange papers with a partner. Ask students to mark corrections and suggestions for improvements on their partner's paper.
- If desired, have students rewrite their papers, to be collected for marking.

✓ **Goal 4**

- Match students with a partner and have them talk about their important possessions.
- Compare answers with the class.

After Reading

Talk with the class about different items of jewelry (ring, necklace, earrings, etc.) and why people wear them. Which ones do students wear? Why?

Video Journal

Before You Watch

- Introduce the idea of an archeologist by directing students' attention to the pictures. Pronounce the vocabulary for the activity and have the class repeat it. Then have students work with a partner to talk about which things archeologists are interested in.

- Compare answers with the class.

Before You Watch

Work with a partner. Decide which of these things are interesting to archeologists.

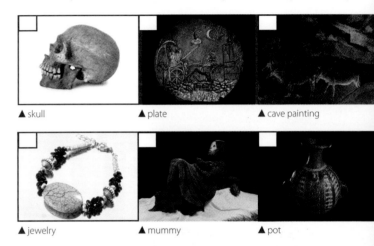

▲ skull   ▲ plate   ▲ cave painting

▲ jewelry   ▲ mummy   ▲ pot

48   Possessions

For Your Information: The Maya civilization

The Maya civilization flourished in Mexico and Central America from 2000 BC to about 900 AD, and Mayan people still live in the same area. It was one of the most advanced civilizations of its time, with highly developed sciences and systems of writing and architecture that still amaze people in the 21st century. They raised food in irrigated fields connected by a system of canals and built very complex cities with palaces, temples, pyramids, astronomical observatories, and ball courts for sports.

While You Watch

 A. Watch the video. Check the pictures that you see on page 48.

 B. Watch again and complete the sentences from the video using the words in the box.

paintings   interesting   skulls   old   slow

1. They are looking for _____ things.
2. Archeologists also study human remains, like these _____.
3. It is _____ work.
4. Archeologists study _____ in caves.
5. Sometimes the work is dangerous, but it is always _____.

After You Watch

A. Match the tools to the job. There can be more than one right answer.

TOOLS

a. broom   b. ruler   c. brush   d. hammer

1. architect ___
2. artist ___
3. archeologist ___

 B. Compare your answers with a partner's answers.

While You Watch

A • Tell students to watch the video the first time and check the items that are in the video. Play the video.
  • Check answers.

Answers: jewelry, pot, plate, painting, skull

B • Tell students to watch the video again and complete the sentences. Have the students read the statements. Play the video.
  • Check answers.

Answers: 1. old, 2. skulls, 3. slow, 4. paintings, 5. interesting

After You Watch

A • Have students work individually to match the tools and occupations.

B • Match students with a partner and have them compare answers.
  • Compare answers with the class.

Answers: Answers will vary.

Teacher Tip: Errors in spoken English

Giving immediate corrections to students during group and pair work is not very effective. Students are too involved in the activity and won't retain the correct form. Instead:

• Make notes on errors frequently heard during the activity and give a mini-lesson after the activity contrasting the error and the correct form.
• Listen to different groups in rotation, write down important errors, and give the list to the group members to correct.
• Note sentences with errors during the activity and write them on the board. Together, the class identifies the errors and corrects them.

For all of these activities, it's best NOT to include the name of the student who made the error. Students generally recognize their own sentences even without names.

- Direct students' attention to the pictures. With the class, look at each picture in turn and have students say which things they do every day.

- Ask the class to tell you other things they do every day. Help with vocabulary as needed. Compile a list on the board.

- Have students work with a partner to ask and answer the questions about daily activities.

- Go over the Unit Goals with the class, explaining and/or translating as necessary.

DAILY ACTIVITIES

1. Which of these things do you do every day?

2. What other things do you do every day?

UNIT GOALS

Tell time
Talk about people's daily activities
Talk about what you do at work
Describe a job

50

	Unit Goals	Grammar	Vocabulary	Listening	Speaking and Pronunciation	Reading and Writing
✔	• Tell time • Talk about people's daily activities • Talk about what you do at work • Describe a job	Simple present tense—statements, negatives, questions, and short answers *They **get up** at seven o'clock.* *What time **do** you **start** work?* Time expressions Adverbs of frequency: *always, sometimes, never* *I **never** answer the phone.*	Telling time Daily activities Work activities	Listening for general understanding and specific details Describing a photographer's work	Asking and answering questions about work activities Falling intonation on statements and information questions	"Robots at Work" Writing a job description

UNIT 5

Unit Theme Overview

• Around the world, many daily activities are nearly universal. We all get up, get dressed, prepare for the day, and start our day's work—at home or in an office, outdoors or at school. At the end of the day, we eat dinner and relax, alone or with family and friends. In this unit, students acquire vocabulary for daily routines and learn to use the simple present tense to talk about them. They begin by learning to tell time in English, and move on to talk about their usual activities at different times of the day. They ask and answer questions about their work activities. In the reading and video, they consider other kinds of work in other places.

Tell Time

Vocabulary

- Have students focus on the activities shown in the pictures.
- Draw students' attention to the clocks. Pronounce the times for students to repeat.
- Go over the times on the clocks again. Point out that there are two different ways to say some times (*six thirty, half past six*). Review numbers 1 to 60 if necessary.
- Draw a clock face on the board and draw the hands in at various times. Ask, *What time is it?* and have the class tell you. Then have students come up to the board and draw in the hands and ask the class, *What time is it?*

A • Have students write the times on the clocks.
- Check answers.

Answers: 2. It's twelve thirty/half past twelve. 3. It's four fifteen/a quarter after four. 4. It's two forty-five/a quarter to three. 5. It's ten thirty/half past ten.

B • Present the activities in the pictures. Read the phrases for students to repeat.
- Have students complete the sentences with times. Compare answers with the class.

Answers: Answers will vary.

Grammar

- Go over the chart with the class. Give/elicit more examples. First, talk about yourself (*I get up at seven o'clock.*). Have students tell what time they get up. Then introduce -*s* with *he* and *she*. Point out that some verbs take an -*es*. Ask the class about classmates: *What time does Ali get up? (He gets up at 8:00.)*
- Introduce negatives in a similar way.
- Present the questions with *What time . . .* and have students ask each other questions about the activities they learned in the Vocabulary section.

Vocabulary

▲ get up ▲ take a shower ▲ start work ▲ finish work ▲ six o'clock ▲ six thirty, half past six

▲ take a nap ▲ go to bed ▲ have lunch ▲ have dinner ▲ six fifteen, a quarter after six ▲ five forty-five, a quarter to six

A. What time is it? Write the time.

1. It's five o'clock   2. _____   3. _____   4. _____   5. _____

B. Complete the sentences with your own information.

1. I get up at _____ .   4. I finish work at _____ .
2. I take a shower at _____ .   5. I go to bed at _____ .
3. I start work at _____ .

Grammar: Simple present tense—statements and negatives

Statement	Negative	What time . . . ?
I/you/we/they **get up** at seven o'clock. He/she **gets up** at seven thirty.	I/you/we/they **don't go** to work on Saturday. He/she **doesn't go** to bed at nine thirty.	What time **do** I/you/we/they **start** work? What time **does** he/she **start** work?
*The simple present tense is used for actions that we do every day.		

52 Daily Activities

Word Bank: Daily activities

make/cook lunch/dinner

take care of my children/parents

clean the house

take a bath/shower

take public transportation to work/school

start/finish class

go to work

Grammar: Simple present tense

The simple present tense is used to talk about regular and habitual events, as presented in this unit (*I start work at nine o'clock.*). It is also used for general states (*I live in Caracas.*) and facts that are always true (*Water freezes at 32 degrees Fahrenheit / 0 degrees Celsius.*).

Time expressions with the simple present tense

every day/morning/afternoon/evening
at three o'clock
in the morning/the afternoon/the evening
on Sunday

A. Complete the sentences. Use the verbs in parentheses.

1. Alan _gets up_____ (get up) at eight o'clock.
2. I _____ (start) work at seven thirty in the evening.
3. We _____ (not take a nap) in the afternoon.
4. Wendy and Kate _____ (not have lunch) at one o'clock.
5. Dae-Ho _____ (finish) work at two o'clock every day.

B. Unscramble the sentences.

1. take a nap/I/in the afternoon _I take a nap in the afternoon_____ .
2. does not/at eight o'clock/Helen/start work _____ .
3. at one thirty/have lunch/We _____ .
4. morning/I/every/take a shower _____ .
5. work/finishes/at five o'clock/Paul _____ .

Conversation

Track 1-22

A. Listen to the conversation. What time does Mariana go to bed Sunday through Thursday?

Abel:	What time do you get up?
Mariana:	I get up at seven thirty Monday through Friday.
Abel:	And on the weekend?
Mariana:	I get up at about ten o'clock.
Abel:	And what time do you go to bed?
Mariana:	Sunday through Thursday, at about eleven o'clock, but on the weekend . . . late!

B. Practice the conversation with a partner. Switch roles and practice it again.

What time does your mother get up?

She gets up at six thirty.

C. Practice the conversation again. Use your own information.

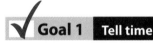

✓ **Goal 1**   **Tell time**

Work with a partner. Ask and answer time questions about a friend or relative.

Grammar Practice: Simple present tense

Have students write as many sentences as they can about things they do regularly.
(*I take a shower in the morning. I eat lunch at work.*)
Then match them with a partner and have them take turns reading their sentences. The listener should cross out any sentence that's the same on his/her own list and write down any sentence that's different. Then they should write sentences about the things their partner does that are different (*He goes to bed late.*).

- Go over the time expressions used with the simple present tense.

A • Have students work individually to complete each sentence with the correct present tense form of each verb.
   • Check answers.

Answers: 2. start, 3. don't take a nap, 4. don't have lunch, 5. finishes

B • Have students work individually to write the sentences.
   • Check answers.

Answers: 2. Helen does not start work at eight o'clock. 3. We have lunch at one thirty. 4. I take a shower every morning. 5. Paul finishes work at five o'clock.

Conversation

A • Have students close their books. Write the question on the board: *What time does Mariana go to bed Sunday through Thursday?*
   • Play the recording. **(CD1 T22)**
   • Check answers.

Answer: eleven o'clock

B • Play or read the conversation again for the class to repeat.
   • Practice the conversation with the class in chorus.
   • Have students practice the conversation with a partner and then switch roles and practice it again.

C • Have students work with the same partner to make a new conversation.
   • Call on student pairs to present their conversation to the class.

✓ **Goal 1**
   • Match students with a partner, and tell each student to choose a friend or family member to talk about. Have students ask and answer questions about the person's daily routine.
   • Call on student pairs to present a question and answer to the class.

Talk about People's Daily Activities

Listening

A • Tell students they are going to hear an interview with a man. Have them look at the pictures and try to guess the man's job.

• Play the recording one or more times. **(CD1 T23)**

• Check answers.

Answer: photographer

B • Tell students to listen again to answer the questions.

• Play the recording one or more times. **(CD1 T23)**

• Check answers.

Answers: 1. photographer, 2. 6:00 a.m., 3. 12:00 (noon), 4. in the evening/ at 8:00 p.m.

C • Draw student's attention to the date book. Pronounce the days of the week for students to repeat.

• Ask students what day of the week it is. With the class, elicit activities that students do on specific days of the week.

• Match students with a partner and have them take turns asking and answering questions about their daily activities. Remind them to provide the day of the week and time.

▲ Joel Sartore at work   ▲ photograph by Joel Sartore   ▲ photograph by Joel Sartore

Listening

 Track 1-23 **A.** Look at the photos. What is Joel's job? Listen to the interview and check your answer.

 Track 1-23 **B.** Listen again and answer the questions.

1. What is Joel's job? _____
2. What time does he get up? _____
3. What time does he take a nap? _____
4. What time does he take photos? _____

Word Focus

take a photo = use a camera

What do you do on Monday?

I go to class at 8 o'clock.

C. Work with a partner. Take turns asking and answering questions about what you do every day.

54 Daily Activities

For Your Information: Working hours

In the United States and Canada, the most typical hours for office workers are 9:00 a.m. to 5:00 p.m. Elementary, middle, and high schools normally have classes from about 8:00 a.m. to 3:00 p.m., although teachers stay at school much later than that. Universities have classes from about 7:30 a.m. until 9:00 p.m. If a factory operates with three shifts, these are typically 8:00 a.m. to 4:00 p.m. (first shift), 4:00 p.m. to midnight (second shift), and midnight to 8:00 a.m. (third shift—a slang expression for this is "graveyard shift," because everything is dark and quiet!).

Pronunciation: Falling intonation on statements and information questions

Track 1-24

A. Listen and repeat.

1. What time do you get up? I get up at six o'clock.

2. What time do they have lunch? They have lunch at one thirty.

3. What time does Bill go to bed? He goes to bed at eleven o'clock.

B. Take turns reading the following questions and answers to a partner.

1. What time does Salma start work? She starts work at eight thirty.
2. What time do they get up? They get up at a quarter to seven.
3. What time do you finish work? I finish work at six o'clock.

Communication

1. Write two more questions.
2. Answer all the questions.
3. Ask two classmates the questions.

Alison gets up at eight o'clock.

She has breakfast at nine thirty.

What time do you . . .	Me	Classmate 1	Classmate 2
1. get up?			
2. have breakfast?			
3. start work?			
4. _____			
5. _____			

 Goal 2 **Talk about people's daily activities**

Tell a partner about your classmates' activities.

Lesson B **55**

Expansion Activity

Talk with the class about people who work at night. Make a list of jobs that are done at night (for example, *police officer, taxi driver, doctor, nurse, singer, factory worker, bus driver, truck driver*, etc.). Choose several jobs and with the class work out the person's daily schedule. For example, a nurse: *She starts work at eleven o'clock in the evening, she eats lunch at four o'clock in the morning . . .* Ask, *Is this a good job? Why, or why not?*

Pronunciation

- Introduce the idea of intonation—the way our voices rise and fall when we speak. Demonstrate with your hand. Tell students that every language has its own special intonation. Explain that practicing intonation will make students' English sound more natural.

A • Tell students to listen to the intonation in the sentences. Play the recording. Show the intonation pattern with your hand. **(CD1 T24)**

- Play the recording again several times for students to repeat.

B • If desired, read through the sentences with the class and have them mark the intonation by drawing arrows above the sentences.

- Have students practice reading the questions and answers with a partner. Walk around checking for good intonation.

- Call on student pairs to read a question and answer to the class.

Communication

- Have each student complete the chart with two more questions and then write their answers to all of the questions.

- Tell students to stand up with their book and pen and move around the room to ask two other classmates for information about their daily activities. Have them sit down when they are finished.

☑ Goal 2

- Match students with a new partner—NOT one of the students they talked to in the Communication activity.

- Have them tell their new partner what they learned about their classmates.

- With the class, discuss any interesting or surprising answers.

Talk about What You Do at Work

Language Expansion

- Go over the activities in the pictures and say the expressions for students to repeat.
- If your learners are younger, you may want to add or substitute the "student activities" listed in the Word Bank box.

A • Have students work individually to categorize their activities in the chart.
- Compare answers with the class.

Answers: Answers will vary.

B • Have students work individually to list more things they do at work/school. Help with vocabulary as needed.
- Match students with a partner and have them take turns telling about their activities.
- Compare answers with the class.

Grammar

- Go over the information in the box. Ask students questions about everyday activities and elicit short answers from them. Then help them form questions and ask other students.
- Introduce the adverbs of frequency.
- Elicit information from students about their activities. Ask them to use adverbs of frequency to describe their activities.

Language Expansion: Work Activities

▲ check emails   ▲ meet clients   ▲ go to meetings   ▲ travel

▲ talk to people on the phone   ▲ make photocopies   ▲ go to the bank   ▲ fill out forms

A. Write the activities in the correct column.

Things I do every day.	Things I do every week.	Things I don't do.
I check my emails.		

B. What other things do you do at work? Make a list. Then tell a partner.

Grammar: Simple present tense—questions and answers

Question	Short answer
Do I/you/we/they **meet** clients every day?	Yes, I/you/we/they **do**. No, I/you/we/they **don't**.
Does he/she **meet** clients every day?	Yes, he/she **does**. No, he/she **doesn't**.

Adverbs of frequency

I **always** check my emails.	100%
I **sometimes** meet clients.	50%
I **never** answer the phone.	0%

Word Bank: Student activities

go to class	go to the library
take notes	do projects
take a quiz/test	do homework
write reports	talk to teachers

Grammar: Adverbs of frequency

This lesson introduces *always*, *sometimes*, and *never*. Other common adverbs of frequency include *usually*, *often*, and *occasionally*. All of these adverbs precede the verb, except when the verb is *be*.

> I *never* get up early.
> I am *never* on time for class.

A. Match the questions and the answers.

Questions	Answers
1. Do you meet clients every day? __	a. Yes, they do.
2. Does Alan meet clients every day? __	b. No she doesn't. She goes every week.
3. Do Chris and Helen travel a lot? __	c. No, I don't. I never meet clients.
4. Does Hilary go to the bank every day? __	d. Yes, I do.
5. Do you go to meetings every day? __	e. Yes, he does.

B. Write about your work. Complete the sentences using *always*, *sometimes*, *never*.

1. I _____ check my emails at nine o'clock.
2. I _____ go to meetings on Mondays.
3. I _____ make photocopies.
4. I _____ go to the bank.
5. I _____ fill out forms.

Conversation

 Track 1-25

A. Listen to the conversation. What does Brenda do at work?

Yoshi:	Tell me about your work.
Brenda:	Well, I'm a <u>personal assistant at a travel agency</u>.
Yoshi:	What do you do at work?
Brenda:	Oh, I <u>check my boss's emails. I make photocopies. I go to the bank</u>. It's not very interesting.
Yoshi:	Do you travel?
Brenda:	Sometimes. <u>I go to meetings with my boss, like to Rio and Singapore</u>.
Yoshi:	Not interesting! It sounds fantastic to me.

 B. Practice the conversation with a partner. Switch roles and practice it again.

 C. Change the underlined words and make a new conversation.

 Goal 3   **Talk about what you do at work**

Talk to a partner about what you do at work.

Word Focus

boss = your superior, the person at the top

Real Language

We can use *like* to give examples.

Lesson C   57

Grammar Practice: Adverbs of frequency

Tell students to take a piece of paper and write a list of eight activities on it (for example, *get up early, eat breakfast*, etc.). Have them write their names on the top of the paper. Collect the papers and redistribute one to each student. Next to each activity, students should write a true sentence about themselves for the activity, using an adverb of frequency where possible and adding any other information they want (for example, *eat breakfast: I never eat breakfast at home*). Have them write their names. Collect the papers again, give them back to the original student, and have each student choose one interesting sentence from the paper to share with the class (*Joseph never eats breakfast at home.*).

A • Have students work individually to match the columns.
• Check answers.

Answers: 1. c, 2. e, 3. a, 4. b, 5. d

B • Have students work individually to fill in the adverbs of frequency. (If your students are young and do not have jobs, dictate other activities for them to substitute.)
• Compare answers with the class

Conversation

A • Have students close their books. Write the question on the board: *What does Brenda do at work?*
• Play the recording. **(CD1 T25)**
• Check answers.

Answers: she checks email, makes photocopies, goes to the bank, and travels

Real Language

• Point out that *like* is often used to give examples in informal conversations. Provide an example. Say, *I do things like going to the library and attending concerts.*

B • Play or read the conversation again for the class to repeat.
• Practice the conversation with the class in chorus.
• Have students practice the conversation with a partner and then switch roles and practice it again.

C • Have students work with the same partner to make a new conversation.
• Call on student pairs to present their conversation to the class.

✓ Goal 3

• Match students with a partner and have them take turns telling each other about their work (or school) activities.

Describe a Job

Reading

- Introduce the topic of the reading. Tell students that robots are machines that do work like people.

A • Introduce the jobs in the pictures. Elicit information about the jobs that students know.

- Have students work in pairs to discuss the questions about the pictures.

- Compare answers with the class.

B • Have students read the article to mark the statements *true* or *false*. Tell them to circle any words they don't understand.

- Check answers.

Answers: 1. F, 2. F, 3. F, 4. T, 5. T

- Go over the article with the class, answering any questions from the students about vocabulary.

▲ dentist

astronaut ▶

Reading

 A. Work with a partner to answer these questions.

What do these people do at work? What are their working hours? Can a robot do their work?

B. Read. Circle **T** for *true* or **F** for *false*.

1. Robots have long holidays. T F
2. Robots finish work at five o'clock. T F
3. Working under the sea is a problem for robots. T F
4. The police use robots. T F
5. There are robots in outer space. T F

58 Daily Activities

Robots at Work

Job Description
Working Hours: 24 hours a day, every day
Salary: $0
Holidays: None
Duties: Welding cars

What a job! It's not a job description for a person. It's a job description for a robot. Robots don't eat, they don't take naps, and they don't go to bed. They work 24 hours a day— every day. They are very useful.

▲ A robot welds a car in a Japanese car factory.

For Your Information: Robots

The English word *robot* comes from the Czech word *robot*, which means "worker." In 1923, a Czech science fiction writer named Karel Capek wrote a book in which machines take over the world and embed circuits in people's brains to make them work like machines. He called these people robots.

This robot works under the sea. It is dangerous for people but it is not a problem for a robot.

A policeman's work is sometimes dangerous. This is a bomb squad. They use robots to look for bombs.

It is expensive and dangerous to send a man to outer space, but it is easy work for this robot.

Writing

Read this job description, and then write a job description for yourself or for a friend.

> **Job Description:** Personal Assistant
> **Working Hours:** 9:00 a.m. to 5:00 p.m., Monday to Friday
> **Holidays:** Public holidays + 10 vacation days per year
> **Duties:** Answer the phone. Make photocopies. Write emails. Meet clients.

Communication

Ask your classmates about the job description they wrote.

What hours do you (or does your friend) work?

What holidays do you (or does your friend) have?

What do you (or does your friend) do at work?

✓ Goal 4 | Describe a job

Tell a partner about a job you want to do.

Writing

- Go over the job description with the class. Explain that holidays are days when we don't work, and duties are activities at a job.
- Have students work individually to write a description of their own job or the job of a friend or family member. Walk around helping with vocabulary as needed.

Communication

- Divide the class into groups of three or four students and have them take turns asking and answering questions about the job descriptions.
- With the class, talk about any interesting or unusual jobs.
- Write a list of all the jobs on the board

✓ Goal 4

- Match students with a partner and have them talk about a job they want—one of the jobs listed on the board or another job. Write these sentences and expressions on the board to help them:

  I want to be a _____ .

  It's a _____ *job.*

- Compare answers with the class.

After Reading

Talk about movies and TV programs with robots in them. What do the robots do?

Video Journal

Before You Watch

A • Talk about the word *routine*. Ask, *Do you have a routine? Do you do the same thing every day?*

• Match students with a partner and have them discuss the questions about the people in the pictures.

B • Have students read the video summary and label the pictures with the words in blue.

• Compare answers with the class.

Answers: 1. elephant, 2. sea lion, 3. black jaguar, 4. toothache, 5. teeth, 6. molars, 7. mouth

E VIDEO JOURNAL   *ZOO DENTISTS*

Before You Watch

A. Look at the pictures. Which of these jobs is difficult? Which of these jobs is routine?

▲ A dentist treats a patient in her office.   ▲ Dentists treat a tiger at the zoo.

B. Read the Video Summary. Use the words in blue to label the pictures.

Word Focus

routine = something you do every day

Video Summary

Two dentists go to the San Francisco Zoo to treat animals. Their first patient is a **sea lion** named Artie. Artie eats 20 pounds of fish a day. His **teeth** are fine. Then they examine an **elephant** named Sue. They check teeth and **molars** in her **mouth** and her tusks. Their last patient is a very difficult patient. She is a **black jaguar** with a **toothache**. Sandy's teeth are very bad and she needs surgery. The dentists have a very hard day.

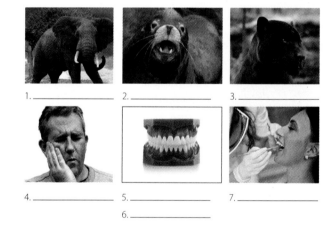

1. _____   2. _____   3. _____

4. _____   5. _____   7. _____

6. _____

For Your Information: Root canal

The root canal is the space inside the root of a tooth. There can be one or two main canals in each root. This space is filled with a loose tissue called dental pulp. When an adult tooth has reached its final size and shape (about one to two years after eruption into the mouth) its original function as a connective tissue is over and it becomes a sensory organ.

Root canal is a common term for a dental operation where the dental pulp is cleaned out and the space is disinfected and then filled.

While You Watch

A. Watch the video. Check the activities that you see.
- ☐ take an X-ray
- ☐ examine a patient
- ☐ clean teeth
- ☐ check gums
- ☐ anesthetize a patient
- ☐ perform surgery

B. Watch again. Complete the sentences. Use *always*, *sometimes*, or *never*.
1. Dr. Sarah de Sanz _____ treats human patients.
2. Dr. Brown's animal patients are _____ dangerous.
3. Animals_____ have dental problems.
4. Most dentists_____ treat animals.
5. Humans and animals _____ need good teeth.

After You Watch

👥 Ask two classmates these questions about their personal routines.

	Classmate 1	Classmate 2
1. Do you get up at the same time every day?		
2. Do you have the same breakfast every day?		
3. Do you go to work at the same time every day?		
4. Do you do the same things at work every day?		
5. Do you go to bed at the same time every day?		

Video Journal 61

While You Watch

A • Tell students to watch the video the first time and check the activities in the video. Have the students read the activities. Play the video.
- Check answers.

Answers: examine a patient, take an X-ray, anesthetize a patient, perform surgery

B • Tell students to watch the video again and complete the sentences. Play the video.
- Check answers.

Answers: 1. always, 2. never, 3. sometimes, 4. never, 5. always

After You Watch

- Have students stand up with book and pen and walk around the room to interview two classmates and write their answers.
- Compare answers with the class.

Teacher Tip: Helping groups finish at the same time

A common situation in group work is that one group completes the task long before the others—or long after. Here are some approaches you can take with a group that finishes too quickly:
- Check to be sure they have understood the task and completed all parts correctly.
- Give them additional questions.

- Have the group prepare a written report of their ideas, answers, etc.

With a group that finishes too slowly:
- Tell them to omit parts of the task.
- Take over briefly as discussion leader to help them move along.
- Set a time limit. Tell them, *I'll ask for your answers in five minutes.*

- Direct students' attention to the pictures. With the class, look at each picture in turn and talk about the kinds of transportation pictured.

- Have students tell the class how they travel to work or to school.

- With the class, list other kinds of transportation, such as bicycle, boat, bus, taxi, tram, and so forth.

- Have students work with a partner to ask and answer the questions

- Go over the Unit Goals with the class, explaining and/or translating as necessary.

GETTING THERE

1. How do you travel to work?

2. What other types of transportation do you use?

UNIT GOALS

Ask for and give directions
Create and use a tour route
Talk about transportation
Record a journey

62

Unit Goals	Grammar	Vocabulary	Listening	Speaking and Pronunciation	Reading and Writing
• Ask for and give directions • Create and use a tour route • Talk about transportation • Record a journey	Imperatives **Turn** left and **walk** for two blocks. Have to/has to She **has to** change buses.	Places downtown Directions Ground transportation	Listening for specific information Sight-seeing tour description	Ask for and give directions Information question intonation	"Shackleton's Epic Journey—A diary" Writing a travel diary or journal

UNIT 6

Unit Theme Overview

- Transportation is an increasingly important issue around the world, as people confront the impact of burning fossil fuels on the global climate. With the increasing price of gasoline, driving a car has become more expensive, and people in some countries are beginning to question the future of auto-based transportation systems—at the same time as more and more people in developing countries are finally able to afford their first car. One thing is certain: We will need to find better, more efficient ways to move greater numbers of people in the future.

- In this unit, students look at different ways of "getting there," and learn language they will need to get directions to the places they want to go. They begin by learning to ask for and give directions to common places needed by visitors to a city, and they practice describing more complicated routes. They consider different means of transportation to get to a destination. Finally, they learn to talk about a longer trip.

63

Ask For and Give Directions

Vocabulary

A • Introduce the vocabulary items. Ask the class to give you examples and/or the location of these places in their city.

• Have students work with a partner to talk about the location of each place on the city map.

• Call on students to tell where each place is.

B • Go over the directions with the students and have them follow the arrow on the map.

C • Have students work individually to follow the directions on the map and write the correct place.

• Check answers.

Answers: 2. National Library, 3. bank

Vocabulary

A. Work with a partner. Locate these places on the map.

There is a tourist office on Grand Street.

tourist office	train station	supermarket	post office	library
restaurant	hotel	park	museum	bank
art gallery	bus station	movie theater	shopping mall	

B. Read the directions and follow the red arrow.

Directions

You are in the tourist office. Cross Lincoln Avenue. Walk two blocks and cross Long Avenue. Turn left and walk two blocks. Turn right and go into the museum.

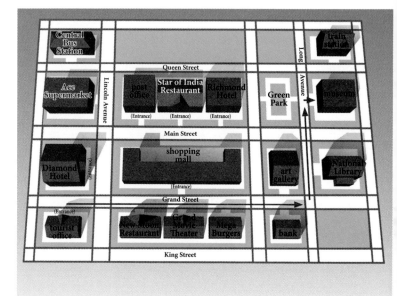

C. Follow the directions and write the destination.

1. From the tourist office walk two blocks up Lincoln Avenue. Turn right on Main Street. Walk two blocks and turn left into <u>Green Park</u> .
2. From Central Bus Station walk one block down Lincoln Avenue, turn left on Main Street, walk two blocks, cross Long Avenue, and you are at the _____ _____ .
3. From the Diamond Hotel, cross Lincoln Avenue, walk two blocks to the art gallery. Cross Grand Street and you are at the _____ .

Word Bank: Places in cities

city hall	newsstand
court house	bus stop
drugstore	subway station
church	traffic light
temple	parking lot
mosque	parking garage
department store	office building

Grammar: Imperatives

The imperative is the base form of the verb. It is used for giving instructions and also for giving orders and commands. It is considered very direct and in polite conversation is softened with *please*.

Sit down. (direct command)
Please sit down. (polite request)

Grammar: Imperatives

Positive	Negative	Prepositions of place
Turn right.	**Don't turn** left.	on the corner of across from between

*The imperative is used for giving instructions.

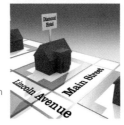

▶ The Diamond Hotel is **on the corner of** Lincoln Avenue and Grand Street.

A. Write the positive or negative imperative.

1. At the end of the block, ___*don't turn*___ (turn) right, turn left.
2. _____ (walk) for three blocks and then turn right.
3. _____ (go) to the bank, go to the post office.
4. _____ (cross) the street and turn left.
5. _____ (take a nap). It's time for lunch.

▶ The art gallery is **across from** the library.

B. Use the map, and write the correct prepositions.

1. The art gallery is _____ Long Avenue and Main Street.
2. The museum is _____ Green Park.
3. The Grand Movie Theater is _____ Mega Burgers and the New Moon Restaurant.
4. The tourist office is _____ Grand Street and Lincoln Avenue.
5. The post office is _____ the Ace Supermarket.

▶ There is a restaurant **between** the post office and the Richmond Hotel.

Conversation

A. A guest at the Richmond Hotel is talking to the receptionist. Listen to the conversation. Where does the guest want to go?

Track 1-26

Hotel Guest:	Is there a <u>supermarket</u> near here?
Receptionist:	There's one <u>on the corner of Lincoln Avenue and Main Street across from the post office</u>.
Hotel Guest:	How do I get there?
Receptionist:	OK. <u>Leave the hotel and turn right. Walk one block and cross Lincoln Avenue</u>.
Hotel Guest:	Thank you very much.
Receptionist:	You're welcome.

B. Practice the conversation with a partner. Switch roles and practice it again.

C. Change the underlined words and make a new conversation.

Real Language

To ask for directions, we say, *How do I get there?*

✓ **Goal 1**   **Ask for and give directions**

Work with a partner. Take turns asking for and giving directions using the map on page 64.

Lesson A **65**

Grammar Practice: Imperatives

Simon Says is an old American children's game. Tell students they should listen and follow your directions, but only if you say *Simon says* first. Have the class stand up. Say, *Simon says look at the window.* All should look at the window. *Simon says close your book.* All should close their books. Say, *Pick up your bag.* They should **not** pick up their bags because you didn't say *Simon says*—anyone who does must sit down. Continue giving directions at a quick pace using the vocabulary from the lesson and other items. Then ask students to come up to the front and give directions. The last student who is standing is the winner.

Grammar

- Go over the forms of the imperative. Explain that we use the imperative to tell people to do things.
- Go over the prepositions of place. Give/elicit more examples from the class, using places near the school.

A • Have students complete the sentences with imperatives.
- Check answers.

Answers: 2. Walk, 3. Don't go, 4. Cross, 5. Don't take a nap

B • Have students complete the sentences with prepositions.
- Check answers.

Answers: 1. on the corner of, 2. across from, 3. between, 4. on the corner of, 5. across from

Conversation

A • Have students close their books. Write the question on the board: *Where does the guest want to go?*
- Play the recording. **(CD1 T26)**
- Check answers.

Answers: to a supermarket

B • Play or read the conversation again for the class to repeat.
- Practice the conversation with the class in chorus.
- Have students practice the conversation with a partner and then switch roles and practice it again.

C • Have students work with the same partner to make a new conversation.
- Call on student pairs to present their conversation to the class.

✓ Goal 1

- Match students with a partner and have them take turns choosing a place on the map and asking for directions to another place.
- Call on student pairs to present a conversation to the class.

Create and Use a Tour Route

Listening

- Ask students about the most famous stores in their city and in other cities. Tell them they are going to hear about a walking tour of famous stores in New York City.

A
- Have students look at the map. Read the names of the streets to them.
- Tell them to write the names of the stores on the map.
- Check answers.
- Draw a map on the board and fill in the names.

B
- Tell students to listen to the recording and mark the tour on the map with arrows.
- Play the recording one or more times. **(CD1 T27)**
- Check answers.
- Mark an arrow on the map you have drawn on the board.

Listening

New York Window Displays

New York is expensive, but you can look at the store windows for free. Take a walking tour around New York's top stores.

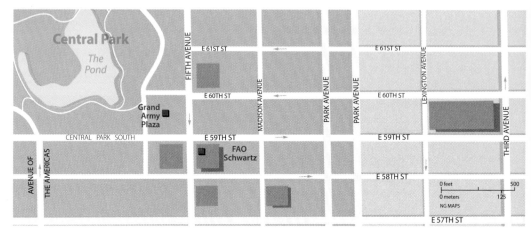

A. Write the names of the stores on the map.

1. **Bergdorf Goodman** is on East 58th Street, across from the Grand Army Plaza.
2. **FAO Schwartz** is on the corner of East 58th Street and 5th Avenue.
3. **Barneys New York** is on the corner of East 61st Street and 5th Avenue.
4. **Tiffany & Co.** is on East 57th Street and 5th Avenue.
5. **Bloomingdale's** is on the corner of East 60th Street and Lexington Avenue.

B. Listen. Draw the route on the map.
Track 1-27

For Your Information: New York stores

Bergdorf Goodman is a luxury department store. It was the first store to sell fashionable women's clothes that were ready to wear (not made by a tailor) in 1914.

FAO Schwarz is a famous toy store that was founded in 1862. It is known for unusual and expensive toys.

Barneys New York is a luxury department store that began in 1923. It was one of the first stores to advertise on the radio.

Tiffany & Co. was founded in 1837 and sells diamonds, jewelry, and silverware. The company now has 137 stores worldwide.

Bloomingdale's is a department store that began in 1861 when two brothers started selling women's clothes in a small shop.

Pronunciation: of *yes/no* questions

A. Listen and repeat.

Track 1-28

1. Is there a movie theater near here? Yes, there is.
2. Is the bus station on York Street? No, it isn't.
3. Is Barneys on the corner of East 61st Street and 5th Avenue? Yes, it is.

B. Take turns reading the questions and answers.

A: Is there a hotel near here?
B: No, there isn't.
A: Is the library next to the museum?
B: Yes, it is.
A: Is there a tourist office in this town?
B: No, there isn't.

Communication

Use the map on page 66. Ask for and give these directions to a partner.

1. From Barneys New York to Tiffany & Co.
2. From Bergdorf Goodman to Barneys New York.
3. From Bergdorf Goodman to Bloomingdale's.
4. From Tiffany & Co. to Bloomingdale's.

✓ **Goal 2** **Create and use a tour route**

Work together and write a tour route in your town.

Pronunciation

- Review the idea of intonation— the rise and fall of our voices while speaking. Remind students that practicing intonation will help make their English sound more natural.

A • Tell students to listen to the intonation in the questions and answers. Play the recording. Use your hand to emphasize the rising and falling. **(CD1 T28)**

- Play the recording again several times for students to repeat.

B • Read through the questions and answers with the class. Have them mark the intonation with arrows.

- Match students with a partner and have them practice reading the questions and answers. Walk around checking for correct intonation.

- Call on student pairs to read a question and answer to the class.

Communication

- Match students with a partner and have them take turns giving directions between the pairs of places listed.

- Ask student pairs to present directions to the class.

✓ **Goal 2**

- Have students work in pairs to choose three or four interesting places in their city and prepare directions for a walking tour that connects them.

- Call on student pairs to present their tours to the class.

Expansion Activity

With the class, make a list of four or five places near the school. Have students work in pairs to practice giving directions to each place.

Talk about Transportation

Language Expansion

- Ask students if they have ever been to an airport. How do people travel to and from the airport?

- Go over the information in the illustration, and talk about the different kinds of transportation. Are they fast or slow? Cheap or expensive?

A • Have students work individually to complete the chart.

- Check answers.

Answers: subway, bus, airport shuttle bus, train, taxi, rental car

B • Match students with a partner and have them take turns asking and answering questions about the different kinds of transportation.

Language Expansion: Ground Transportation

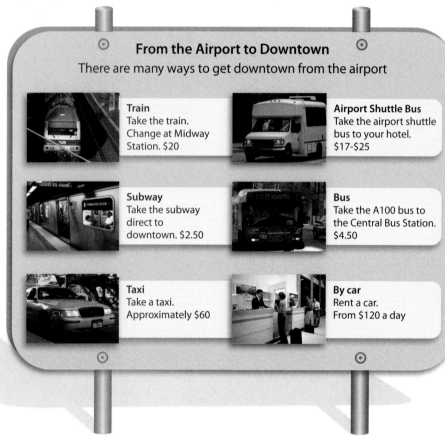

From the Airport to Downtown

There are many ways to get downtown from the airport

Train
Take the train. Change at Midway Station. $20

Airport Shuttle Bus
Take the airport shuttle bus to your hotel. $17-$25

Subway
Take the subway direct to downtown. $2.50

Bus
Take the A100 bus to the Central Bus Station. $4.50

Taxi
Take a taxi. Approximately $60

By car
Rent a car. From $120 a day

A. Complete the chart with the names of different ground transportation.

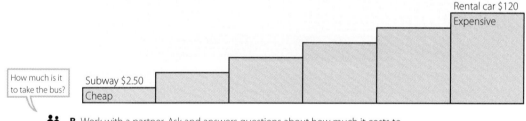

Rental car $120
Expensive

How much is it to take the bus?

Subway $2.50
Cheap

B. Work with a partner. Ask and answers questions about how much it costs to travel from the airport.

Word Bank: Using transportation

ticket	subway station
fare	stop
schedule	bus stop
line	transfer

Grammar: *Have to*

Have to is one way to express obligation in English. It is more common and less formal than *must* and is used in all tenses. *Don't/doesn't have to* expresses a lack of necessity.
We have to hand in our homework.
We don't have to hand in our notebooks (our teacher doesn't check them).

Grammar: *Have to*

Statement	Question	Short answer
I/you/we/they **have to** take a taxi.	**Do** I/you/we/they **have to** change trains?	Yes, I/you/we/they **do**. No, I/you/we/they **don't**.
He/she **has to** change buses.	**Does** he/she **have to** take a taxi?	Yes, he/she **does**. No, he/she **doesn't**.

***Have to** is used to show obligation.

A. Complete the sentences with the correct form of *have to*.

1. You __have to__ take a bus.
2. We _____ take the subway.
3. She _____ take a taxi.
4. They _____ go to the bank
5. Susan _____ check her emails.

B. Write questions using *have to*.

1. __Do we have to__ (we) change trains
2. _____ (I) take a train?
3. _____ (they) go to the meeting?
4. _____ (you) change trains?
5. _____ (Bill) cross the street?

Conversation

A. Listen to the conversation. What time does the plane leave?

Track 1-29

Tourist:	Excuse me, how do I get to the airport?
Assistant:	You can take <u>the subway</u>, but you have to change <u>trains</u>. It takes about an hour.
Tourist:	Oh! But I have to get there by two thirty. And I have four bags!
Assistant:	Two thirty! In half an hour? OK, you have to take <u>a taxi</u>! And quickly!

 B. Practice the conversation with a partner. Switch roles and practice it again.

C. Change the underlined words and make a new conversation.

✓ Goal 3   Talk about transportation

Take turns giving directions from one place to another in your town.
Say what transportation you have to take.

Grammar

- Tell the class, *We have some rules in our school. You have to go to class every day, You have to take a test every month*, and so forth. Elicit more examples.
- Go over the information in the box on the formation of sentences with *have to*.

A • Have students work individually to complete the sentences.
- Check answers.

Answers: 2. have to, 3. has to, 4. have to, 5. has to

B • Have students work individually to complete the questions.
- Check answers.

Answers: 2. Do I have to, 3. Do they have to, 4. Do you have to, 5. Does Bill have to

Conversation

A • Have students close their books. Write the question on the board: *What time does the plane leave?*
- Play the recording. **(CD1 T29)**
- Check answers.

Answer: two thirty

B • Play or read the conversation again for the class to repeat.
- Practice the conversation with the class in chorus.
- Have students practice the conversation with a partner and then switch roles and practice it again.

C • Have students work with the same partner to make a new conversation.
- Call on student pairs to present their conversation to the class.

☑ Goal 3

- Match students with a partner and have them take turns talking about how to get to places in town using different kinds of transportation.

Grammar Practice: *Have to*

What are the rules in your class? Have students work with a partner to write as many rules as they can with *have to* and *don't have to*. (For example, *We have to speak English with our partners.*) Call on student pairs to read their lists to the class and discuss any interesting "rules" you hear.

Record a Journey

Reading

- Introduce the topic of the reading. Elicit examples of what people write in a diary. Have students look at the map and the pictures and talk about the places in them. Are they hot or cold? Is traveling easy or difficult there?

A • Have students read the diary and find the places mentioned on the map.
- Go over the article with the class, answering any questions from the students about vocabulary.

B • Have students answer the questions, referring back to the diary as needed. Point out that they need to think about the information in the diary. Some of the answers are not given directly.
- Check answers.

Answers: 1. b, 2. b, 3. c, 4. b, 5. a

Reading

📖 **A.** Read the diary and follow the route on the map.

B. Choose the correct answer.

1. The journey starts in __.
   a. Elephant Island
   b. London
   c. South Georgia
2. The *Endurance* breaks up on ___.
   a. October 26, 1914
   b. October 26, 1915
   c. October 26, 1916
3. __ men leave Elephant Island on a small boat.
   a. Four
   b. Five
   c. Six
4. It takes __ to sail from Elephant Island to South Georgia.
   a. one week
   b. two weeks
   c. three weeks
5. Shackleton finds help in ___.
   a. Stromness
   b. Elephant Island
   c. London

☐ Antarctica

Shackleton's Epic Journey—A diary

1914
August 8 Ernest Shackleton and his men leave London on their ship, *Endurance*.

1915

January 18 The *Endurance* is trapped in the ice. The men play soccer.
October 26 The *Endurance* **breaks up**. The men have to leave the *Endurance*. They camp on the ice.

For Your Information: Ernest Shackleton

Ernest Shackleton was born in 1874 and participated in several of the first expeditions to Antarctica. In 1914, he set out with a group of men to try to cross the continent of Antarctica. However, the *Endurance*, was caught in the ice and crushed. For four months, the crew camped on floating ice, until the men were forced to sail in open boats for five days to reach an uninhabited island far from any shipping routes. Shackleton took the strongest of the lifeboats and sailed to the island of South Georgia. The trip took more than two weeks, in appalling conditions, and they were unable to land near the settlement. Instead, Shackleton and two of the men hiked through the snowy, mountainous interior of the island to reach the settlement. Shackleton immediately sent out a ship to rescue the men from Elephant Island, but the first three attempts couldn't get through the ice. Finally, the fourth attempt was successful. Shackleton brought all of his men safely home, and he is regarded as one of the great heroes of exploration.

1916

April 9 The ice begins to break up. They have to get into the small boats.

April 15 They land on Elephant Island.

April 24 Shackleton and five men leave Elephant Island in a small boat to find **help**. The other men stay on Elephant Island.

May 8 Shackleton lands in South Georgia.

May 19 Shackleton leaves three men with the boat. He crosses the mountains of South Georgia with two other men to find help.

May 20 They arrive in Stromness, the main town in South Georgia. They find help.

August 30 Shackleton **rescues** the men on Elephant Island.

Word Focus

rescue = save
break up = to fall to pieces
help = assistance

Writing

Write a diary about a real or imaginary journey.

> June 3: We leave the airport at one o'clock. We change planes. We arrive at the hotel at eleven o'clock.
> June 4: We take the subway to the museum. In the afternoon, we walk to the art gallery.

_____

_____

_____

_____

_____

_____

_____

_____

_____

_____

_____

_____

_____

_____

_____

✓ **Goal 4** **Record a journey**

Share your diary entry with the class.

Writing

- Go over the diary with the class. Explain that a journey is a long trip.

- Have students work individually to write their own travel diaries. Tell them the trip can be one they really took or an imaginary trip.

- Have students exchange papers with a partner. Ask students to mark corrections and suggestions for improvements on their partner's paper.

- If desired, have students rewrite their papers, to be collected for marking.

☑ Goal 4

- Call on students to read their papers to the class or have them read them to a small group.

After Reading

Tell students to work with a partner to make a list of 10 things that they would take with them on a trip to Antarctica. Compare lists with the class.

Video Journal

Before You Watch

A • Have students look at the illustration and repeat with you the words related to a volcano.

• Have students work individually to complete the text.

Answers: crater, magma, lava, lava lake, eruption

B • Have students read the definitions individually.

• Have students repeat the words with you.

• Match students with a partner and have them label the pictures.

Answers: camel, geologists, professor, trek, explorers

Before You Watch

A. Study the picture. Use the words to complete the text.

A volcano is a mountain with a large hole at the top. This hole is called a _____. A volcano produces very hot, melted rock. When it is under ground, this hot, melted rock is called _____. When it leaves or comes out of the volcano, it is called _____. When the lava stays in the crater it forms a _____.

When lava leaves a volcano, we say the volcano erupts. We call it an _____.

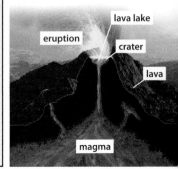

B. Work with a partner. Read the definitions and label the pictures.

explorers = people who go to new places to learn things

geologists = scientists who study the earth (rocks and soil)

trek = a long and difficult trip or journey

camel = a large animal that can travel through the desert

professor = a teacher at a university.

▲ rocks and soil

For Your Information: Volcanoes

Scientists study volcanoes to try to establish when they will erupt and thus prevent disaster. But most eruptions are unpredictable, and they can be devastating for the surrounding populations.

Volcanoes are commonly found at plate boundaries where the friction of the plates melts the rock. Many of the worlds' volcanoes are found in the Pacific. This area is called the Ring of Fire. It encompasses the west coast of South America, Mexico, and California and the east coast of Asia.

The eruption of Vesuvius (in the Mediterranean) in 79 AD is one of the most famous. It buried several Roman cities, including Pompeii. Other famous eruptions are those of Krakatau in Indonesia, Mt. St. Helens in Washington State, and Mauna Loa in Hawaii.

While You Watch

 A. Watch the video. Match the sentence parts.

1. The geologists _____
2. The lava lake _____
3. Hot lava comes out of the earth _____
4. The team spends hours _____
5. It is not easy to stand near the crater _____
6. The professors are _____

a. collecting pieces of red-hot lava.
b. travel to the volcano on camels.
c. excited about studying the volcano.
d. because it is very hot.
e. is inside the crater.
f. and forms the lava lake.

 B. Watch the video again and answer these questions.

1. What can geologists study at Erta Ale? _____
2. Where does the red hot lava come from? _____
3. In the early morning, what is the temperature near the crater? _____
4. How does the team feel when they return from the volcano? _____

C. What did you learn? Discuss with a partner what you see in these photos?

After You Watch

Discuss these questions with a partner.

1. Do you want to explore a volcano?
2. Why or why not?
3. How can people travel to difficult places?

While You Watch

A • Tell students to watch the video the first time and match the sentence parts. Play the video.
• Check answers.

Answers: 1. b, 2. e, 3. f, 4. a, 5. d, 6. c

B • Tell students to watch the video again and answer the questions. Have the students read the questions. Explain any unknown words. Play the video.
• Check answers.

Answer: 1. the oldest lava lake, 2. from the earth, 3. 2,000 degrees, 4. tired

C • Match students with a partner and have them take turns saying things they learned from the reading.
• Have them look at the photos and say what they see.
• Compare answers with the class.

After You Watch

• Match students with a partner and have them talk about the questions.
• Compare answers with the class.

Teacher Tip: Roles in group work

It can be helpful to assign roles to students in each group. Some possibilities:
Leader—asks questions and keeps the discussion on topic
Secretary—takes notes on the group's ideas
Reporter—tells the group's answers to the class
Recorder—records the number of times each group member speaks, and tells each member how often they spoke when the activity ends
Be sure to rotate these roles often.

- Direct students' attention to the pictures. With the class, look at each picture in turn and talk about the activities in each one: relaxing, bungee jumping, playing tennis, eating together.
- Talk about other free-time activities and compile a list on the board. (Use the *-ing* form of the verb.) Ask students which activities they enjoy.
- Have students work with a partner to ask and answer the questions.
- Go over the Unit Goals with the class, explaining and/or translating as necessary.

FREE TIME

1. What are these people doing?

2. What activities do you do in your free time?

UNIT GOALS

Identify activities that are happening now
Talk about activities that are happening now
Talk about abilities
Talk about sports

74

Unit Goals	Grammar	Vocabulary	Listening	Speaking and Pronunciation	Reading and Writing
• Identify activities that are happening now • Talk about activities that are happening now • Talk about abilities • Talk about sports	Present continuous tense **I'm not watching** television. **I'm reading**. *Can* (for ability) He **can't** play the guitar. He **can** sing.	Pastimes Sports	Listening for specific information Telephone conversation	Describing personal activities happening now *sh* and *ch* sounds	"Sports—Then and Now" Writing about abilities

UNIT 7

75

Unit Theme Overview

- With working hours gradually becoming shorter in most countries, people around the world have an increasing amount of time available for their leisure activities. Some of the activities they pursue in their free time are the same as those enjoyed by previous generations: spending time with family and friends, relaxing at home, playing sports. Others are new and based on technological changes: sending and reading email, playing computer games, downloading music and movies from the Internet.

- This unit focuses on some of the most common leisure-time activities and on sports and things people have learned to do. Students begin by learning vocabulary for free-time pursuits and then learn to talk about their current activities. They acquire words for sports and practice talking about things they can and can't do. Finally, they learn about unusual sports and athletes around the world.

Identify Activities That Are Happening Now

Vocabulary

A • Have students look at the pictures. Elicit any words from the pictures that the students already know.

• Read the names of the people and have students repeat them with you.

• Tell students to listen to the recording and write the activities under the correct pictures. Read the activities in the box to them.

• Play the recording one or more times. **(CD2 T2)**

• Check answers.

Answers: 2. playing the guitar, 3. cooking, 4. reading, 5. listening to music, 6. drawing, 7. going to the movies, 8. going for a walk

B • Have students work individually to classify the activities in the chart.

• Call on students to tell you one thing they like or don't like.

Grammar

• Introduce the present continuous tense. Mime reading a newspaper and say, *I'm reading.* Write on the board, *I'm reading.* Repeat the process with several other verbs: *writing/eating/sitting.* Have students mime other actions and give/elicit the verbs.

• Introduce the negative: Mime and say, *I'm reading. I'm not writing.* Give/elicit more examples using mime.

• Introduce *yes/no* questions and short answers. Point to a student and ask, *Is he eating/reading/ writing?* Elicit *Yes, he is./No, he isn't.*

• Introduce *wh-* questions. Ask a student to mime eating/ reading and ask the class, *What is she eating?* Introduce *where* for location.

• Go over the information in the box.

Vocabulary

🎧 Track 2-2   **A.** Listen and write the words from the box under the correct picture.

| going to the movies | watching TV | playing the guitar | reading |
| drawing | going for a walk | listening to music | cooking |

Katie   Lok   Ben   Omar

1. _watching TV_   2. _____   3. _____   4. _____

Mariko   Crystal   Tom and Susan   Tony

5. _____   6. _____   7. _____   8. _____

B. Write the activities in exercise **A** in the correct column.

I like	I don't like

Grammar: Present continuous tense

Statement (negative)	*Yes/no* question	Short answer	*Wh-* question
I **am (not) reading**.	**Am** I **reading**?	Yes, I am. No, I'm not.	Where am I going?
You/we/they **are (not) reading**.	**Are** you/we/they **reading**?	Yes, you/we/they are. No, you/we/they aren't.	What are you/we/they doing?
He/she **is (not) reading**.	**Is** he/she **reading**?	Yes, he/she is. No, he/she isn't.	What is he/she doing?

*We use the present continuous tense to talk about things that are happening at the moment.

Word Bank: Activities

playing the piano   visiting friends

writing email   shopping

playing computer   studying
games

cleaning the house   exercising

Grammar: Present continuous tense

The present continuous is used to talk about things that are happening at the moment of speaking:
I'm watching TV right now.
It contrasts with the simple present tense, which is used to talk about habits and facts:
I always watch the news at nine o'clock.

A. Unscramble the words to write sentences.

1. the guitar / is playing / Charlie _____
2. Marian / watching TV / is not _____
3. is listening / Asha / to music _____
4. cooking lunch / is not / Bernardo _____
5. Ju / drawing / Is _____

B. Complete the conversation.

Dan: Is Miriam _____ TV?
Beth: No, she _____.
Dan: What is she _____?
Beth: _____ drawing.

 C. Take turns practicing the conversation in exercise **B** with a partner. Use the pictures on page 76.

Conversation

 A. Listen to the phone call. What is Dave doing?

Track 2-3

Dave: Hi, Mom.
Mom: Dave! Where are you? What are you doing?
Dave: Mom, don't worry! I'm at <u>Paul's</u>. We're <u>listening to music</u>.
Mom: Well, don't be home late.
Dave: Mom, I'm <u>17</u> years old. Chill!

B. Practice the conversation with a partner. Switch roles and practice it again.

C. Change the underlined words and make a new conversation.

Real Language

We can use these expressions to tell someone not to worry.

Formal ←——————→ Informal
Don't worry! Relax! Take it easy! Chill!

✓ **Goal 1** **Identify activities that are happening now**

What is he/she doing?

Work with a partner. Look at the pictures on page 76. Ask and answer questions.

Grammar Practice: Present continuous tense

Mime an action and tell the class to guess what you're doing using the present continuous: *You're watching TV. You're watching a scary movie.* Tell the class when they have guessed correctly. Divide the class into pairs and have them plan a similar mime for the class to guess. When all pairs are ready, have one student from each pair come to the front of the class and present their mime for the class to guess. At the end of the activity, talk about any funny/difficult/surprising mimes.

A • Have students work individually to write sentences.
  • Check answers.

Answers: 1. Charlie is playing the guitar. 2. Marian is not watching TV. 3. Asha is listening to music. 4. Bernardo is not cooking lunch. 5. Is Ju drawing?

B • Have students work individually to complete the conversation.
  • Check answers.

Answers: watching, isn't, doing, She's

C • Match students with a partner and have them make new conversations about all of the pictures on the previous page.
  • Call on student pairs to present a conversation to the class.

Conversation

A • Have students close their books. Write the question on the board: *What is Dave doing?*
  • Play the recording. **(CD2 T3)**
  • Check answers.

Answer: listening to music

B • Play or read the conversation again for the class to repeat.
  • Practice the conversation with the class in chorus.
  • Have students practice the conversation with a partner and then switch roles and practice it again.

C • Have students work with the same partner to make a new conversation.
  • Call on student pairs to present their conversation to the class.

✓ **Goal 1**
  • Have students work with a partner to talk about the pictures. Compare answers with the class.

Talk about Activities That Are Happening Now

Listening

A • Tell students they are going to listen to three phone conversations. They should number them in the order they hear them.

• Play the recording one or more times. **(CD2 T4)**

• Check answers.

Answers: 3, 2, 1

B • Tell students to listen to the conversations again and answer the questions. Go over the questions.

• Play the recording one or more times. **(CD2 T4)**

• Check answers.

Answers: 1. He's reading (a guitar magazine). 2. No, she isn't. 3. She's meeting some clients. 4. No, she isn't. 5. She's listening to music.

Listening

 A. Look at the pictures and listen to the telephone conversations. In what order do you hear the conversations? Write the number.
Track 2-4

 B. Answer the questions. Listen again to check your answers.
Track 2-4

1. What is Mike doing? _____
2. Is Dave's wife taking a walk? _____
3. What is she doing? _____
4. Is Salma playing the guitar? _____
5. What is she doing? _____

For Your Information: Cell phone etiquette

Because a call can interrupt important activities, when calling someone on a cell phone it's considered polite to ask, *Is this a good time to talk?* In some countries it is illegal to talk on a cell phone while driving.

Pronunciation: *sh* and *ch* sounds

Track 2-5

A. Listen and check the word you hear.

1. watch ✓   wash
2. cheap   sheep
3. chair   share
4. chip   ship
5. cash   catch
6. chop   shop
7. choose   shoes

B. Take turns reading the words. Your partner points to the words you say.

Communication

Work with a partner. Imagine that you are talking on the phone to each other. Have a conversation about what you are doing right now. Be creative.

✓ **Goal 2**   **Talk about activities that are happening now**

Work with a partner. Take turns talking about what a friend or family member is doing right now.

Lesson B   **79**

Pronunciation

- Point out the difference between the *sh* and *ch* sounds in English. Read the pairs of words to the class for students to repeat.

A • Tell students they will hear one word in each pair. They should check the word they hear in the recording. Play the recording one or more times. **(CD2 T5)**

- Check answers.

Answers: 2. sheep, 3. share, 4. chip, 5. cash, 6. shop, 7. shoes

B • Match students with a partner and have them take turns reading a word from each pair. Their partner should point to the word they hear.

Communication

- Match students with a partner and have them imagine a phone call like the ones in the Listening activity and role-play the conversation, using their imagination.

- Call on student pairs to present their phone calls to the class.

☑ **Goal 2**

- Match students with a partner and have them take turns talking about what a friend or a family member is doing right now.

- Call on student pairs to say the most interesting thing their partner said.

Expansion Activity

Have student pairs repeat the Communication activity, role-playing a conversation with a famous person about what he/she is doing now. Call on student pairs to present their role-plays to the class.

Lesson B   **79**

Talk about Abilities

Language Expansion

- Go over the words in the box, pronouncing them for students to repeat.

A • Have students work individually to label the pictures.
- Check answers.

Answers: 1. swim, 2. play soccer, 3. play football, 4. play volleyball, 5. ski, 6. ice skate, 7. play golf, 8. play tennis

B • Have students answer the questions about themselves and then talk to two other students and record their answers.
- Compare answers with the class. Which sports are the most popular?

Language Expansion: Sports

A. Match the words in the box to the pictures.

ice skate	ski	play soccer	play tennis
play volleyball	play golf	swim	play football

1. _____ 2. _____ 3. _____ 4. _____

5. _____ 6. _____ 7. _____ 8. _____

B. Answers the questions. Then interview two classmates.

Do you . . .	Me	Classmate 1	Classmate 2
play soccer?			
ski?			
ice skate?			
play golf?			
play tennis?			
swim?			
play volleyball?			
play football?			

Word Bank: Sports

basketball	martial arts
baseball	diving
ice hockey	waterskiing
wrestling	surfing
boxing	windsurfing
horse racing	rowing
car racing	

Grammar: *Can* for ability

English has several ways to express ability, including *can, know how to, be able to.*

Can is the most general expression of ability, including skills and physical ability. (*I can play the piano. I can run one mile in six minutes. I can meet you at ten o'clock.*)

Grammar: *Can* for ability

Statement	Negative	*Yes/no* question	Short answer
I/you/she/we/they **can** swim.	He **can't** play the guitar.	**Can** you ski?	Yes, I **can**. No, I **can't**.

A. Write about yourself. Complete the sentences with *can* or *can't*.

1. I _____ swim.
2. I _____ play soccer.
3. I _____ play golf.
4. I _____ ski.
5. I _____ play tennis.

B. Complete the conversations.

1. **A:** _____ play volleyball?
   B: No, I can't but I _____ play football.
2. **A:** _____ Damien swim?
   B: Yes, _____.

Conversation

Track 2-6

A. Listen to the conversation. What can Yumi's boyfriend do?

Julie: Hi, Yumi. I hear you have a new boyfriend.
Yumi: Yes, he's cute. He can <u>play the guitar</u>.
Julie: Wow!
Yumi: Yes, and he can <u>ski</u> and <u>ice skate</u>.
Julie: Hey! I can ski and ice skate.
Yumi: Sorry, Julie. He's taken!

B. Practice the conversation with a partner. Switch roles and practice it again.

C. Change the underlined words and make a new conversation.

✓ Goal 3 Talk about abilities

Ask a partner questions. Find out what he or she can do.

Can you ski?
No, I can't but I can ice skate.

Lesson C **81**

Grammar

- Introduce *can*. Tell the class, *I can swim. I can play tennis. What about you? Can you swim?* Elicit *Yes, I can./No, I can't*. Ask about other sports. Then have students make up new questions to ask you and their classmates.
- Go over the information in the box.

A • Have students work individually to complete the sentences.
- Compare answers with the class.

B • Have students work individually to complete the conversations.
- Check answers.

Answers: 1. Can you, can, 2. Can, he can

Conversation

A • Have students close their books. Write the question on the board: *What can Yumi's boyfriend do?*
- Play the recording. **(CD2 T6)**
- Check answers.

Answer: He can play the guitar, ski, and ice skate.

B • Play or read the conversation again for the class to repeat.
- Practice the conversation with the class in chorus.
- Have students practice the conversation with a partner and then switch roles and practice it again.

C • Have students work with the same partner to make a new conversation.
- Call on student pairs to present their conversation to the class.

✓ Goal 3

- Match students with a partner and have them ask questions about each other's abilities.
- Call on students to tell the class one interesting thing they learned about their partner.

Grammar Practice: *Can* for ability

Read this description to the class: *He can fly. He can jump over buildings. He can see through walls. Who is he?* (Answer: Superman.) If students can't guess, let them ask questions with *Can he*... until they find the answer. Give students time to write a similar description of what a person or animal can do. Then divide the class into groups of five or six students and have them take turns reading their descriptions for the group to guess. Have each group choose one description for the class to guess.

Lesson C **81**

Talk about Sports

Reading

A • Introduce the topic of the reading. Talk about the sports in the pictures and ask if students can do them.

B • Tell students to read the article and mark the sentences *true* or *false*. Tell them to circle any words they don't understand.

• Check answers.

Answers: 1. T, 2. T, 3. F, 4. F, 5. T

• Go over the article with the class and answer any questions from the students about vocabulary.

D   GOAL 4   TALK ABOUT SPORTS

▲ gymnastics

▲ ski jumping

Reading

A. Look at the pictures. Which of these sports can you do?

B. Read the article. Circle **T** for *true* and **F** for *false*.

1. Percy Hedge is a modern athlete.   T   F
2. Modern athletes don't carry trays of drinks.   T   F
3. Javier Sotomayor is a gymnast.   T   F
4. The high jump world record was 245 centimeters in 1912.   T   F
5. Many gymnasts are young.   T   F

Sports— Then and Now

Percy Hodges, a British athlete, is jumping a hurdle in this photo. He is also carrying a tray of drinks.

Modern athletes can run very quickly, but they don't carry trays of drinks.

For Your Information: World records

At every Olympic Games, old world records are broken and new world records are made, and at times, athletes do things that were previously considered impossible. For example, for many years, it was thought that no human being could run a mile in less than four minutes, but this was first done by Roger Bannister from the UK in 1954. Within three years, 16 other runners had broken the record. Since 1954, the record time has been lowered by almost 17 seconds.

In this photo from July 1936, Olympic champion Jesse Owens is jumping hurdles on board the ship *Manhattan*. He is traveling to the Olympic Games in Berlin.

The world record for the high jump in 1912 was 1 meter, 98 centimeters. Today Javier Sotomayor from Cuba is the world record holder. He can jump 2 meters, 45 centimeters.

This young Chinese boy is performing at a railway station in 1920.

Today many of the world's top gymnasts are very young, but it is not an easy life.

Writing

Write sentences about the things you can do and the things you can't do.

I can play basketball, but I can't swim.

_____

_____

_____

_____

_____

_____

_____

_____

Communication

Look at the pictures on these pages. Take turns asking and answering questions about the activities.

What's she/he doing?

Can you do this?

✓ Goal 4 | Talk about sports

Work with a partner. Talk about your favorite sports. Say what sports you like to watch. Say what sports you like to play.

Writing

- Have students write about things they can and can't do. Tell them to think about things like sports, languages, and hobbies.
- Have students exchange papers with a partner. Ask students to mark corrections and suggestions for improvements on their partner's paper.
- If desired, have students rewrite their papers, to be collected for marking.

Communication

- Have students work with a partner to talk about the pictures on the page.
- Compare answers with the class.

✓ Goal 4

- Match students with a partner and have them talk about sports they enjoy watching and playing.

After Reading

Talk about the greatest athletes from the students' country and what they can do.

Video Journal

Before You Watch

- With the class, go over the reasons why people play different sports.

A • Have students work individually to write the sports on the chart.

- Compare answers with the class.

B • Have students look at the picture of a Vanuatu land diver. Then have them discuss with a partner why people might do this.

E VIDEO JOURNAL *LAND DIVERS OF VANUATU*

Before You Watch

People play sports and games . . .

▲ for money   ▲ for exercise   ▲ for fun

A. Why do people play these sports? Write the name of the sport in the correct column. You can write the name in more than one column.

▲ skateboarding   ▲ golf   ▲ jogging   ▲ bungee jumping   ▲ ski jumping

For money	For exercise	For fun

B. Why do you think the people of Vanuatu dive from a tower?

For Your Information: Vanuatu

Vanuatu is an island nation in the Pacific, 1,090 miles/1,750 kilometers east of Australia. It became an independent country in 1980, after being ruled by Britain and France as "New Hebrides." It has a population of 215,000 people and a subtropical climate with nine warm, rainy months a year, and three cooler, drier months. Farming, cattle raising, and financial services are the main contributors to the economy. Traditional culture is still very important in Vanuatu, but the most popular sport is cricket.

While You Watch

A. Watch the video and check your answer to exercise **B** on page 84.

B. Watch the video again. Circle **T** for *true* and **F** for *false*.

1. Bungee jumping started in New Zealand.   T   F
2. The tower is 40 feet high.   T   F
3. The men dive from the tower for money.   T   F
4. Land diving is not dangerous.   T   F
5. Only people from Vanuatu can jump from the tower.   T   F

After You Watch

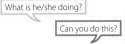
Look at the pictures on page 84. Take turns asking each other these questions.

What is he/she doing?

Can you do this?

Hiu
Tëgua
Torres Islands
Uréparapara
Mota Lava
Vanua Lava
Wasaka
BANKS ISLANDS
Avire
Santa Maria
Makéoné
Olpoi
Nokuku
Espiritu Santo
Malao
Kolé
Aoba (Omba)
Marino
Maéwo
Narovorovo
Lolowai
Wusi
Nduindui
Patteson Passage
Luganville
Aóre
Namaram
Nazareth
Malo
Pentecost (Île Pentecote)
Ranwas
Bougainville Strait
Norsup
Lakatoro
Mégham
Malakula
Ambrym
Paama
Lamap
Moriu
Epi
Votlo
Tongoa (Kuwaé)
Shepherd Islands
Émaé
Nguna
Moso
Éfaté (Île Vaté)
Mélé Bay
Port Vila

Potnarvin
Erromango

Tanna
Lowital
Waïsisi
Isangel

VANUATU

0 mi   80
0 km   80
NG MAPS

(Kéamu) Anatom
Aneighowhat

While You Watch

A • Tell students to watch the video the first time and find the reason why people dive from the towers. Play the video.

   • Check answers.

Answer: The people of Vanuatu believe this will make their crops grow.

B • Tell students to watch the video again and answer *true* or *false*. Have the students read the statements. Play the video.

   • Check answers.

Answers: 1. F, 2. T, 3. F, 4. F, 5. T

After You Watch

   • Match students with a partner and have them take turns asking and answering questions about the pictures.

   • Compare answers with the class.

Teacher Tip: Checking answers

There are many ways to check students' answers to activities, all with advantages and disadvantages.

Teacher reads the answers out loud, students check their work—the fastest way, but requires the least student involvement.

Teacher calls on students to give their answers—also fast, but may make students feel anxious.

Students correct each other's work—gives students more responsibility, but they may not correct all mistakes.

Volunteers each write the answer to one question on the board—gives the class an opportunity to work with common errors, but uses a lot of class time.

Teacher corrects outside of class—an opportunity for detailed feedback, but requires a lot of work from the teacher!

- Introduce the theme of the unit. Direct students' attention to the pictures. With the class, look at each picture in turn. Talk about the clothes the people are wearing in each one.

- Have students work with a partner to answer the questions.

- Compare answers with the class, compiling a list of colors on the board.

- Go over the Unit Goals with the class, explaining and/or translating as necessary.

CLOTHES

1. Which of these clothes do you wear?

2. What colors can you see?

UNIT GOALS

Identify and buy clothes
Say what people are wearing
Express likes and dislikes
Learn about clothes and colors

86

	Unit Goals	Grammar	Vocabulary	Listening	Speaking and Pronunciation	Reading and Writing
✓	• Identify and buy clothes • Say what people are wearing • Express likes and dislikes • Learn about clothes and colors	*Can/could* (polite requests) **Can** *I try on these shoes?* Likes and dislikes *I* **love** *your sweater!* *She* **can't stand** *pink.*	Clothes Colors	Listening for specific details	Describing people's clothes *Could you*	"Chameleon Clothes" Writing about what people are wearing

UNIT 8

87

Unit Theme Overview

- "Clothes make the man," according to an old English saying. What we wear expresses our personality, but also our cultural values and our position in society. Because of this, clothing is a topic that fascinates people of all ages.

- In this unit, students begin by learning basic vocabulary and phrases to use in shopping for clothing. They learn to describe different kinds of clothing and to talk about their own preferences. Finally, they look at clothing in a wider context—both in its function to protect the wearer and in its cultural context in the Video Journal.

Identify and Buy Clothes

Vocabulary

A • Pronounce the colors in the chart for students to repeat. Then pronounce the articles of clothing and have the students repeat them.

• Have students take turns naming the items in the pictures.

• Check answers with the class.

B • Go over the meanings of the words and phrases in blue.

• Have students work individually to complete the sentences.

• Check answers.

Answers: 1. black shoes, 2. coat, 3. sweaters

Vocabulary

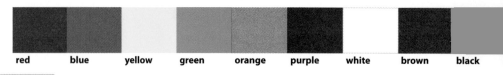

| red | blue | yellow | green | orange | purple | white | brown | black |

 This is a black hat.

👥 **A.** Look at the color chart. Take turns describing the photos to a partner.

▲ shirt

▲ pants

▲ dress

▲ skirt

▲ shoes

▲ sweater

▲ jacket

▲ coat

▲ tie

▲ hat

B. Complete the sentences. Notice the words in **blue**.

1. Ruben is **trying on** a pair of _____.
2. Lucy is **paying** for the _____ **by** credit card.
3. The sales assistant is **bringing** more _____.

Word Bank: More clothes

suit	raincoat
vest	sweatshirt
shorts	sweatpants
uniform	gloves
sandals	mittens
boots	baseball cap
sneakers	

Grammar: *Can/could* (polite requests)

Using *can/could* and *please* soften a request and make it more polite. English-speaking parents teach their young children that they must always say *please* when asking for something. (*Daddy, give me more milk. Say please! Daddy, give me more milk, please!*)

Grammar: *Can/could* (polite requests)

Can/could
Can I try it on, please?
Could you bring another pair, please?
Can and *could* are used to make polite requests.

Write the polite requests.

1. You want to try on a blue dress.   <u>Can I try on this blue dress, please?</u>
2. You want to see some red shoes. _____
3. You want to pay by credit card. _____
4. You want to try on a green sweater _____
5. You want the sales assistant to bring a size 7. _____

Conversation

Track 2-7

A. Listen to the conversation. What color shoes does the customer want?

Customer:	Do you have any white shoes?
Sales Assistant:	Yes, we do.
Customer:	Could I see them, please?
Sales Assistant:	Yes, of course.
Customer:	Ah, these look nice. Can I try them on, please?
Sales Assistant:	Sure.

 B. Practice the conversation with a partner. Switch roles and practice it again.

Real Language
We can show we agree by saying:
Formal ◄──────────────► Informal
Of course   Yes   Sure

Goal 1 **Identify and buy clothes**

Work with a partner. Take turns role-playing a sales assistant and a customer. Buy some clothes.

Grammar

- Go over the sentences with *can* and *could* in the box. Point out that these sentences are used in stores to talk to the sales assistant. Discuss other places where polite requests would be used (in a bank, post office, office, etc.). Point out the use of *please* to make requests more polite.
- Have students work individually to write the requests.
- Check answers.

Answers: 2. Could I see some red shoes, please? 3. Can I pay by credit card, please? 4. Can I try on the green sweater, please? 5. Could you bring a size 7, please?

Conversation

A
- Have students close their books. Write the question on the board: *What color shoes does the customer want?*
- Play the recording. **(CD2 T7)**
- Check answers.

Answer: white

B
- Play or read the conversation again for the class to repeat.
- Practice the conversation with the class in chorus.
- Have students practice the conversation with a partner and then switch roles and practice it again.

☑ Goal 1

- Have students work with the same partner to make new conversations about buying clothes.
- Call on student pairs to present their conversation to the class.

Grammar Practice: *Can/could* (polite requests)

Explain to students that they can use *can/could* to make polite requests in the classroom, too, such as when they need a piece of paper or don't understand something. (*Could you give me a piece of paper/say that again, please?*) Have students work with a partner to role-play a classroom situation with a polite request. Call on student pairs to present their role-play to the class.

Say What People Are Wearing

Listening

A • Tell students they are going to hear descriptions of four people's clothes. Pronounce the names in the box for the class.

• Play the recording one or more times. **(CD2 T8)**

• Check answers.

Answers: 1. Jenny, 2. Helen, 3. Dave, 4. Zahra

B • Match students with a partner and have them take turns talking about the pictures.

• Call on students to describe a picture to the class.

Listening

A. Listen to the descriptions. Match the names to the pictures.

Track 2-8

| Helen | Dave | Zahra | Jenny |

Jenny is wearing . . .

1. _____   2. _____

3. _____   4. _____

B. Take turns describing the picture to a partner.

For Your Information: Calling a taxi

The woman in the second photo is *calling a taxi*. In some large cities in English-speaking countries, such as New York, there are many taxis, and they drive around looking for customers. A customer who needs a taxi raises his/her hand and waves to the driver. In smaller cities, the taxis don't drive around, and customers must call them by phone or go to a *taxi stand* (a line of taxis waiting in front of a hotel or other important building).

Pronunciation: *Could you*

Track 2-9

A. Listen and check (✓) the box of the form you hear.

	Full form	Short form
1. Could you call a taxi, please?	✓	
2. Could you call a taxi, please?		✓
3. Could you help me, please?		
4. Could you help me, please?		
5. Could you repeat that, please?		
6. Could you repeat that, please?		

 B. Take turns reading the following sentences using the short form.

1. Could you open the window, please?
2. Could you pass the water, please?
3. Could you say that again, please?
4. Could you tell me the time, please?
5. Could you open the door, please?
6. Could you repeat that, please?

Communication

 Take turns describing another classmate's clothing and guess the name of the classmate.

She is wearing blue pants and a red sweater.

It's Andrea.

That's right.

 Goal 2   **Say what people are wearing**

Find photos you like in this book. Tell a partner what people in the photos are wearing.

Pronunciation

- Explain to students that in fast, casual speech, native English speakers often put words together and pronounce them in a short form. Emphasize that this is not incorrect English. Practicing short forms will help make students' English sound more natural.
- Introduce the full form and short form of *could you*.

A • Tell students to listen to the recording and mark the form they hear.
- Play the recording several times. **(CD2 T9)**
- Check answers.

Answers: 3. short, 4. full, 5. full, 6. short

B • Have students work with the same partner to practice saying the sentences using the short form. Walk around checking for good pronunciation.
- Call on students to read a sentence to the class.

Communication

- Match students with a partner and have them take turns describing clothing and guessing who is being described.
- Call on students to describe a classmate's clothes for the whole class to guess.

✓ Goal 2

- Match students with a partner. Tell them to look through the whole book (not just this unit) and describe interesting clothes they see.
- Call on students to tell the class about a photo they like, giving the page number.

Expansion Activity

For homework, have students find a magazine or Web site photograph of clothes they like and bring it to class. Divide the class into groups of four or five students and have them take turns describing the photos they brought. For more practice, have groups exchange photos and then describe or discuss the photos they received.

Express Likes and Dislikes

Language Expansion

- Pronounce the names of the colors for students to repeat.

A • Have students work individually to fill in the names of colors.

- Check answers.

Answers: 2. orange, 3. dark blue, 4. light green, 5. purple

B • Have students work individually or in pairs to list as many things as they can in the chart.

- Compare answers with the class, compiling lists on the board.

Grammar

- Explain that there are different ways of expressing degrees of *likes* and *dislikes*.
- Go over the sentences in the chart.

Language Expansion: More clothes and colors

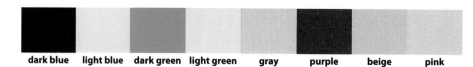

| dark blue | light blue | dark green | light green | gray | purple | beige | pink |

A. Write the colors of these clothes.

1. _light blue_ jeans   2. _____ socks   3. _____ blouse   4. _____ scarf   5. _____ t-shirt

B. Write all the clothes you know in the correct column.

Clothes men wear	Clothes women wear	Clothes men and women wear
		jeans

Grammar: Likes and dislikes

Likes and dislikes	
☺☺	I **love** jeans.
☺	I **like** pink t-shirts.
☹	I **don't like** hats.
☹☹	I **hate** white socks.
*We use these expressions to express likes and dislikes.	

Word Bank: More colors

navy blue	turquoise
sky blue	lemon yellow
olive green	gold
lavender	silver

Grammar: Likes and dislikes

All of these expressions can be used with all kinds of nouns and gerunds (for activities). A very common expression for strong dislikes is *I can't stand (pizza)*.

A. Complete the first column of the chart with other things that are not clothes. Then check (✓) the columns to show your likes and dislikes.

	😊😊 I love . . .	😊 I like . . .	☹ I don't like . . .	☹☹ I hate . . .
1. black jeans				
2. purple socks				
3. red clothes				
4.				
5.				
6.				
7.				
8.				

B. Take turns asking about a partner's chart.

Conversation

A. Chung and Brenda are buying a present for Brenda's boyfriend. Listen to the conversation. What present do they buy?

Track 2-10

Chung: What clothes does he like?
Brenda: He likes casual clothes. Jeans and t-shirts, you know.
Chung: What colors does he like?
Brenda: He loves dark colors. He hates colors like yellow or white.
Chung: OK, so buy him a black t-shirt.

B. Practice the conversation with a partner. Switch roles and practice it again.

C. Practice the conversation again, but buy a present for a person that you both know.

What things do you love?

I love traveling.

✓ **Goal 3** **Express likes and dislikes**

Tell a partner about things you love and things you hate.

A
- Tell students to write five other things in the first column of the chart. These can be things (for example, *dogs, hip-hop music, ice cream*) or verbs with *-ing* (for example, *cooking, skiing, studying*).
- Have students mark their opinions of the things listed.

B
- Match students with a partner and have them take turns asking and answering questions.
- Call on students to tell the class something interesting they learned about their partner.

Conversation

A
- Have students close their books. Write the question on the board: *What present do they buy?*
- Play the recording. **(CD2 T10)**
- Check answers.

Answer: a black t-shirt

B
- Play or read the conversation again for the class to repeat.
- Practice the conversation with the class in chorus.
- Have students practice the conversation with a partner and then switch roles and practice it again.

C
- Have students work with the same partner to make a new conversation.
- Call on student pairs to present their conversation to the class.

✓ Goal 3
- Match students with a partner and have them take turns talking about likes and dislikes.

Grammar Practice: Likes and dislikes

Have students work individually to make a new questionnaire like the one in exercise **A** using six of their own ideas. Then match them with a partner and have them take turns interviewing each other, asking, *What do you think about (dogs)?* and writing their partner's answers. As a class, discuss interesting answers they received.

Learn about Clothes and Colors

Reading

A • Match students with a partner and have them discuss their favorite color. Are they wearing that color today?

B • With the class, work through the exercise. Explain that they will see these words in the reading.

Answers: 1. b, 2. d, 3. e, 4. a, 5. c

C • Tell students to read the article and mark the sentences *true* or *false.*

• Point out the words in the Word Focus box.

• Tell students to circle any other words they don't understand as they read.

• Check answers.

Answers: 1. T, 2. F, 3. T, 4. F, 5. F

• Go over the article with the class and answer any questions from the students about vocabulary.

D **GOAL 4** **LEARN ABOUT CLOTHES AND COLORS**

Reading

A. Tell a partner your favorite clothes color.

B. Match the word and the definition.

1. chameleon ___   a. a person who fights in a war
2. invisible ___   b. an animal that changes color
3. to change ___   c. the part of the body you can see
4. soldier ___   d. something you can't see
5. skin ___   e. to make something different

C. Circle **T** for *true* and **F** for *false.*

1. Chameleons change color when they are angry.   T   F
2. Blue is a powerful color.   T   F
3. Pink is the color of love.   T   F
4. You can buy clothes that change color.   T   F
5. Soldiers are invisible.   T   F

> **Word Focus**
>
> **powerful** = strong
> **romantic** = loving
> **calm** = quiet

Chameleon Clothes

Chameleons can change the color of their skin. Sometimes they change color so they are difficult to see and become almost invisible. Sometimes they change color to show that they are angry or happy or looking for a partner.

Of course, humans can't change the color of their skin but we can change our clothes. Dark clothes make a person look more **powerful**. Pink is **romantic**; blue is **calm**. The color of your clothes says a lot about you.

Scientists are working on clothes that can change color when you press a button. They are not ready yet, but the idea is to make pants that can change from white to black or a shirt that can change from white to pink or red. Chameleon clothes!

94 Clothes

For Your Information: Chameleons

There are about 160 different species of chameleons, living in warm desert and tropical environments across Asia, Africa, and southern Europe. Some (but not all) chameleons can change their body color to fit in with their surroundings or to send a signal to other chameleons. The colors include blue, green, black, red, orange, brown, yellow, and turquoise. The color is produced by special cells in the lower layers of skin. When a person is described as "a chameleon," it means that he or she is able to fit into different social situations easily by making changes in personality and behavior.

But clothes that change color are also useful for soldiers. Like the chameleon, soldiers sometimes need to be invisible. Chameleon clothes make the soldiers difficult to see.

So, one day maybe you will be able to change your clothes from powerful to romantic to invisible, at the press of a button.

Writing

Write about what you or a classmate is wearing.

> Ibrahim is wearing a brown shirt with a green sweater. He is also wearing black trousers and black shoes. I like his clothes. He looks great.

Communication

👥 Take turns asking a partner about the clothes in the picture.

What is she wearing?
What color is it?
Do you like it?

✓ **Goal 4** | **Learn about clothes and colors**

Ask your partner these questions.
What is your favorite color?
What are your favorite clothes?

Writing
- Have students work individually to describe their own clothes or a classmate's clothes.
- Have students exchange papers with a partner. Ask students to mark corrections and suggestions for improvements on their partner's paper.
- If desired, have students rewrite their papers, to be collected for marking.

Communication
- Match students with a partner and have them talk about the people in the picture and what they're wearing.
- Call on students to describe one person's clothes to the class.

✓ **Goal 4**
- Have students work with the same partner to discuss the colors and clothes they like.

After Reading

Have students go online to a shopping Web site and find and print out a photo of clothes they like. If necessary, tell them which Web sites they should use. Divide the class into groups and have them take turns describing the pictures they found.

Video Journal

Before You Watch

- With the class, go over the reasons why people wear clothes.
- Have students work individually to write a sentence for each picture.
- Check answers.

Answers: 2. He is wearing fur pants to be warm and to be dry. 3. She is wearing a vest to carry things. 4. She is wearing an evening gown to look good. 5. He is wearing waterproof gear to be dry.

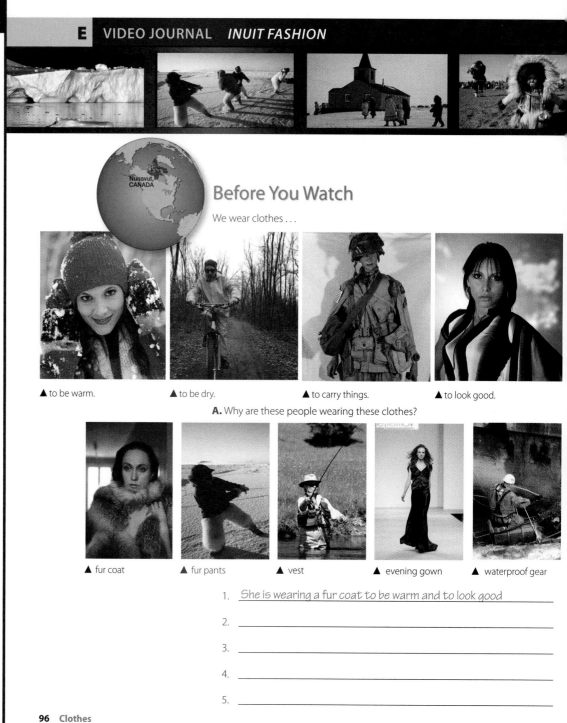

E VIDEO JOURNAL *INUIT FASHION*

Before You Watch

Nunavut, CANADA

We wear clothes . . .

▲ to be warm.　　▲ to be dry.　　▲ to carry things.　　▲ to look good.

A. Why are these people wearing these clothes?

▲ fur coat　　▲ fur pants　　▲ vest　　▲ evening gown　　▲ waterproof gear

1.　*She is wearing a fur coat to be warm and to look good*

2.　_____

3.　_____

4.　_____

5.　_____

96　Clothes

For Your Information: The Inuit

The Inuit are a group of native people who live in the far north of Alaska, Canada, and Greenland. Although most Inuit families today have at least one person working for money, hunting is still an honored and important occupation in their culture. People still eat traditional foods like seal and walrus meat, and they wear clothes made of polar bear, seal, and caribou skins. In many families, one woman works at a job to earn money to pay for electricity, guns, ammunition, and other needs, so that the men can continue to hunt full-time. The Inuit's Inuktitut language is still widely spoken, and traditional storytelling and dance are still practiced across the region.

While You Watch

 Watch the video. Circle the correct answers. There is more than one correct answer.

1. The models are wearing ___.
   a. hats
   b. jackets
   c. skirts
2. Aaju Peter is a ___.
   a. designer
   b. model
   c. photographer
3. Inuit women wear the Amouti to ___.
   a. be warm
   b. look good
   c. carry babies
4. Inuit kill seals for their ___.
   a. meat
   b. fur
   c. fat

After You Watch

The Inuit make clothes from seal fur. We also make clothes from other animals.

A. Match the animals and the material.

Word Focus

model = a person who shows new designs in clothes
fur = the hair that covers an animal's body

1. sheep _____   2. cow _____   3. rabbit _____

▲ fur   ▲ wool   ▲ leather

> We make shoes from leather.

B. Discuss with a partner what clothes we make from wool, leather, and fur.

Video Journal   97

While You Watch

- Tell students to watch the video and circle all of the correct answers. Play the video.
- Check answers.

Answers: 1. a, 2. a, 3. c, 4. a, b, c

After You Watch

A • Have students work individually to match the animals and the materials.
- Check answers.

Answers: 1. wool, 2. leather, 3. fur

B • Match students with a partner and have them talk about clothes made from animal products.
- Compare answers with the class.

Teacher Tip: Giving students more responsibility

Giving students responsibility for everyday classroom tasks not only lightens the teacher's workload, but gives students more of a feeling of involvement. Here are some tasks that your students may be able to perform:

- handing back homework
- distributing papers
- calling the class to order at the beginning
- setting up audio equipment
- erasing/washing the board at the end of class

- Direct students' attention to the pictures. With the class, look at each picture in turn and have students name as many foods as they can in each picture. Write lists on the board.

- Have students tell a partner about their favorite food.

- Compare answers with the class, compiling a list of favorite foods on the board.

- Go over the Unit Goals with the class, explaining and/or translating as necessary.

EAT WELL

1. What food do you see in the pictures?

2. What is your favorite food?

UNIT GOALS

Order a meal
Plan a party
Talk about a healthy diet
Talk about food for special occasions

98

Unit Goals	Grammar	Vocabulary	Listening	Speaking and Pronunciation	Reading and Writing
• Order a meal • Plan a party • Talk about a healthy diet • Talk about food for special occasions	*Some* and *any* *There's **some** ice cream in the freezer.* *How much* and *how many* **How many** *oranges do we need?* **How much** *chocolate do we have?*	Food Meals Countable and uncountable nouns	Listening for specific details Conversation to confirm a shopping list	Planning a dinner *And*	"Special Days, Special Foods" Writing about special foods

UNIT 9

Unit Theme Overview

- Food and food issues are in the news nearly every day. News reports talk about increases in food prices and changes in the way our food is grown. There is more and more debate about the healthiest way to eat and whether traditional or modern diets are better for us. Our choices in what to eat reflect many different factors: culture, economics, scientific information, and personal preference.

- In this unit, students approach the topic of food from a personal perspective (higher levels in *World English* look at the geographical and cultural aspects of food). Students learn the names of common foods and how to order in a restaurant. They practice the use of quantifiers such as *some* and *any* for food and learn to ask questions about amounts of countable and uncountable nouns. They consider whether their own diets are healthy and unhealthy. Finally they learn about foods connected with celebrations around the world.

Order a Meal

Vocabulary

- Pronounce the names of foods for the class to repeat.

A • Go over the terms on the menu. Have students work individually to list the items in the correct categories.

- Check answers.

Answers: Breakfast: cereal, eggs; Lunch and dinner: steak, fish, salad, pasta, chicken; Drinks: coffee, tea, fruit juice; Desserts: chocolate cake, ice cream

B • Match students with a partner and have them discuss what they like to eat at each meal.

- Compare answers with the class.

Vocabulary

▲ cereal   ▲ eggs   ▲ steak   ▲ fish

▲ salad   ▲ pasta   ▲ chicken   ▲ fruit juice

▲ coffee   ▲ tea   ▲ chocolate cake   ▲ ice cream

A. Write the food in the correct place on the menu.

Breakfast
(7:00 a.m. to 12:00 p.m.)

_____

Lunch & Dinner
(12:00 p.m. to 8:00 p.m.)
All served with salad

_____

Drinks

_____

Desserts

_____

B. Tell a partner what you like to eat for breakfast, lunch, and dinner.

Word Bank: More food

Breakfast: toast, oatmeal/porridge, pancakes, waffles
Lunch/dinner: ham, beef, pork, lamb, potatoes, beans, peas, soup
Drinks: iced tea, mineral water, lemonade, soda, beer, wine
Desserts: fruit salad, pie, pastry, cookies, brownie

Grammar: *Some/any*

Some is used in positive sentences, *any* is used in questions and negatives, and both are used in questions that make offers. This rule has been simplified somewhat, but will always produce grammatical sentences. (Native speakers generally use *some* in offers when they anticipate a positive answer: *Do you want some ice cream?* They use *any* when they anticipate a negative answer: *Do you want any more ice cream, or should I put it away?*)

Grammar: *Some* and *any*

Some and any

Statement	Negative	Question
There's **some** ice cream in the freezer.	We don't have **any** chicken.	Do you have **any** chocolate cake?

*We use *some* for questions with *can* and *could*.
Can I have **some** water, please?*

A. Complete the sentences with *some* or *any*.

1. There's _____ chocolate ice cream for dessert.
2. We don't have _____ coffee.
3. There's _____ chicken salad for your lunch.
4. Can I have _____ coffee, please?
5. Is there _____ fish?

B. Unscramble the words to write sentences.

1. some coffee/There's/on the table _____ .
2. some/I have/chocolate/Could/ice cream _____ ?
3. have/We/don't/fruit juice/any _____ .
4. fish/we have/any/Do _____ ?
5. eggs/next to/some/the milk/There are _____ .

Conversation

A. Listen to the conversation. What does the customer order?

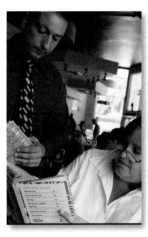

Waiter:	Good morning.
Customer:	Could I have some <u>coffee</u>, please?
Waiter:	Sure.
Customer:	Do you have any <u>strawberry ice cream</u>?
Waiter:	No, I'm sorry. We don't have <u>strawberry</u>. We only have <u>chocolate</u>.
Customer:	OK, I'll have some <u>chocolate ice cream</u>.

B. Practice the conversation with a partner. Switch roles and practice it again.

C. Change the underlined words and make a new conversation.

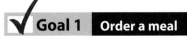 **Goal 1** | **Order a meal**

Change partners. Role-play ordering a meal.

Grammar

- Go over the information about *some* and *any* in the box.

- Point out that *any* is generally used in negative statements and questions. Point out that with polite requests we use *some*.

- Elicit examples of food from students. List them on the board. Elicit sample sentences and questions from students.

A • Have students work individually to complete the sentences.

- Check answers.

Answers: 1. some, 2. any, 3. some, 4. some, 5. any

B • Have students work individually to write the sentences.

- Check answers.

Answers: 1. There's some coffee on the table. 2. Could I have some chocolate ice cream? 3. We don't have any fruit juice. 4. Do we have any fish? 5. There are some eggs next to the milk.

Conversation

A • Have students close their books. Write the question on the board: *What does the customer order?*

- Play the recording. **(CD2 T11)**

- Check answers.

Answer: coffee and chocolate ice cream

B • Play or read the conversation again for the class to repeat.

- Practice the conversation with the class in chorus.

- Have students practice the conversation with a partner and then switch roles and practice it again.

C • Have students work with the same partner to make a new conversation.

- Call on student pairs to present their conversation to the class.

☑ Goal 1

- Match students with a new partner and have them role-play ordering some of their favorite foods in a restaurant.

- Call on student pairs to present their role-play to the class.

Grammar Practice: *Some/any*

Tell students to look at the restaurant menu in Vocabulary exercise **A** and cross out any five items. These are things that the restaurant has "run out of." Then match students with a partner and have them role-play a scene in the restaurant. One student is the customer and the other is the waiter. The customer should order, and the waiter will tell the customer what they don't have. Then have students change roles and practice again.

Plan a Party

- Tell students they are going to hear two people planning a party. With the class, look at the picture and talk about the items in it.

A • Tell students to listen to the conversation and complete the shopping list.

- Play the recording one or more times. **(CD2 T12)**

- Check answers.

Answers: 12 bottles of soda, 1 bag of ice, 20 hamburgers, 10 hot dogs

B • Match students with a partner and have them role-play a scene in a store where they must ask for the items on the list.

Listening

Miguel and Diana are planning a party. Miguel is writing a shopping list.

A. Listen and complete Miguel's shopping list.

Track 2-12

_____ bottles of soda
1 bag of _____
20 _____
10 _____

B. Role-play buying the food on Miguel's shopping list.

Could I have some soda, please?

How many bottles do you want?

102 Eat Well

Word Bank: Party food

potato chips and dip	cheese and crackers
corn chips	pretzels
peanuts	sandwiches
cake	cookies
coffee, tea	lemonade
punch	beer, wine

Pronunciation: *And*

Track 2-13

A. Listen and check the correct column. Listen and check (✓) the correct column of the form you hear.

	Full form	Short form
1. pasta and salad	✓	
2. pasta and salad		✓
3. fruit juice and cereal		
4. fruit juice and cereal		
5. chocolate cake and ice cream		
6. chocolate cake and ice cream		

B. Take turns reading the following sentences using the short form.

1. I like hot dogs and hamburgers.
2. Jill and David are good friends.
3. How many brothers and sisters do you have?
4. We have strawberry ice cream and chocolate ice cream.

Communication

Plan a dinner.

1. Decide who to invite.
2. Make a menu for the party.
3. Decide where the guests sit.

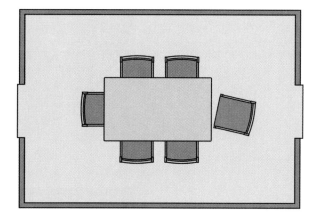

 **Goal 2** **Plan a party**

Join another group. Explain your menu and table seating.

Pronunciation

- Remind students that in fast, casual speech, native English speakers often pronounce words in a short form. Practicing short forms will help make students' English sound more natural.

- Introduce the full form and short form of *and*.

A • Tell students to listen to the recording and mark the form they hear. Play the recording several times. **(CD2 T13)**

- Check answers.

Answers: 3. short, 4. full, 5. full, 6. short

B • Have students work with the same partner to practice saying the sentences using the short form. Walk around checking for good pronunciation.

- Call on students to read a sentence to the class.

Communication

- Divide the class into groups of three and have them follow the directions to plan an imaginary party. If desired, you can allow them to invite famous people to their party (living and/or dead!).

☑ Goal 2

- Combine the groups to form groups of six and have them take turns describing their party plans.

- Call on each group to tell the class about their menu and guest list.

Expansion Activity

If appropriate, have the students plan an actual party for class time, with snacks, music in English, and games in English (give help as needed in finding and setting up the games).

Talk about a Healthy Diet

Language Expansion

- Talk about the meaning of diet—all the food you eat. Ask students, *Is your diet good or bad? Why?*

- Introduce the idea of countable nouns (like apples, oranges, hamburgers) and uncountable nouns (like coffee, tea, and water).

- Have students look at the plate and talk about the foods on the plate.

A • Have students write the foods in the correct part of the chart.

- Check answers.

Answers: Countable nouns: oranges, apples, carrots, potatoes, eggs, cookies
Uncountable nouns: salad, rice, bread, meat, fish, beans, cheese, butter, milk, candy

B • With the class, make a list of other foods that could go in the chart.

Language Expansion: Countable and uncountable nouns

The Eatwell Plate
The Eatwell Plate helps you to eat a good diet. It shows the types of food to eat and also how much of each type of food to eat.

A. Write the food in the correct column.

Countable nouns (plural ending -s)	Uncountable nouns
oranges	rice

B. Add the names of other food to the Eatwell Plate. Then list each as a countable or uncountable noun.

Word Bank: Fruit and vegetables

bananas	grapes	peaches
cherries	melon	strawberries
blueberries	mangoes	papayas
pineapples	lettuce	tomatoes
squash	zucchini	onions
peas	celery	spinach

Grammar: Countable and uncountable nouns

Countable nouns are things that are viewed as separate units:
one potato, two potatoes
Uncountable nouns are things that are viewed as substances:
water, bread
For many uncountable nouns, there are units that make them countable:
one <u>cup</u> of water, two <u>slices</u> of bread

Grammar: *How much* and *how many*

How much and *how many*	
Countable nouns	**Uncountable nouns**
How many oranges do you need?	**How much** milk do we have?

How much and *how many* are used to ask about quantities.

A. Complete the sentences. Use *how much* or *how many*.

1. _____ oranges do you eat every week?
2. _____ candy do you eat?
3. _____ milk do you drink every day?
4. _____ cookies do you eat every day?
5. _____ bread do you eat every day?

B. Take turns asking and answering the questions in exercise **A** with a partner.

Conversation

A. Listen to the conversation. Does the patient eat well?

Track 2-14

Doctor: Tell me about the food you eat. How much <u>fruit</u> do you eat?
Patient: I eat <u>an apple</u> every day. Sometimes I have <u>an orange</u> as well.
Doctor: Very good! Do you eat <u>meat</u>?
Patient: Yes, I love <u>meat</u>. I eat a big <u>steak</u> every day.
Doctor: And <u>vegetables</u>. Do you eat <u>vegetables</u>?
Patient: No, I don't like <u>vegetables</u>.

B. Practice the conversation with a partner. Switch roles and practice it again.

C. Change the underlined words and make a new conversation.

✓ **Goal 3**   **Talk about a healthy diet**

Ask a partner about his/her diet. Is it a healthy diet?

Grammar

- Review the idea of countable and uncountable nouns. Go over the information in the box. Have the class practice asking questions. Say, for example, *I eat hamburgers. (How many hamburgers do you eat?) I drink tea. (How much tea do you drink?)*

A • Have students work individually to complete the questions.
  - Check answers.

Answers: 1. How many, 2. How much, 3. How much, 4. How many, 5. How much

B • Match students with a partner and have them practice asking and answering the questions. Remind them that they can also say (for example), *I don't eat candy.*

Conversation

A • Have students close their books. Write the question on the board: *Does the patient eat well?*
  - Play the recording. **(CD2 T14)**
  - Check answers.

Answer: no

B • Play or read the conversation again for the class to repeat.
  - Practice the conversation with the class in chorus.
  - Have students practice the conversation with a partner and then switch roles and practice it again.

C • Have students work with the same partner to make a new conversation.
  - Call on student pairs to present their conversation to the class.

✓ Goal 3

- Review the idea of a diet. Then match students with a partner and have them talk about their diets.
- Compare answers with the class. Discuss what kinds of food are in a healthy diet.

Grammar Practice: Countable and uncountable nouns

Match students with a partner. Have them close their books. Tell them to work together to list 10 count nouns and 10 non-count nouns as fast as they can. They should raise their hands when finished. Note the names of the first three pairs to finish. When all students have finished, call on the first three pairs to write their lists on the board. With the class, go over each list and correct any mistakes. The pairs with the most correct answers are the winners.

Talk about Food for Special Occasions

Reading

A • Introduce the topic of the reading. Go over the ideas of *ordinary* (usual) and *special* (not usual).

• Match students with a partner and have them talk about the foods in the pictures, saying which ones are special. Compare answers with the class.

B • Have students read the article to answer the questions. Tell them to circle any words they don't understand.

• Check answers.

Answers: 1. on New Year's Day; 2. three days; 3. they don't like to do any work during the holiday; 4. Mexico; 5. make a wish

• Go over the article with the class, answering any questions from the students about vocabulary.

Reading

 A. Look at the pictures. Take turns saying which food is ordinary and which food is special.

▲ wedding cake ▲ fried rice ▲ turkey

▲ corn flakes ▲ sandwich ▲ banana flambé

A wedding cake is special food.

 B. Answer the questions.

1. When do the Greeks eat *vasilopita*?
   _____

2. How long is the Japanese New Year holiday? _____

3. Why do the Japanese make *Osechi* boxes?
   _____

4. In what country do people eat *Rosca de Reyes*? _____

5. What do people do when they blow out the candles on a birthday cake?
   _____

Word Focus

coin = metal money
doll = a small toy figure like a child

Special Days, Special Food

All over the world, people eat special food on special days. At the New Year in Greece, people eat a special cake called *vasilopita*. Inside the cake, there is a **coin**. They cut the cake, and the person who gets the coin gets good luck.

The Japanese have a three-day holiday at the New Year. They don't like to do any work during the holiday, so they cook the food before it begins. They put the food in boxes called *Osechi* boxes. The food is very beautiful. It is also delicious.

For Your Information: More birthday customs

In India, Hindu people celebrate their birthdays only until they are 16 years old. It's a religious celebration and they bring flowers to the temple.

In Brazil, people pull on the birthday person's ear once for each year of their age. The person gives the first piece of birthday cake to his or her favorite relative.

In Hungary, a birthday child brings candy to school for everyone in the class.

In France, people celebrate their "name day"—the religious feast day of the saint they were named for.

n January 6 in Mexico, people eat a special cake called *sca de Reyes*. Inside the cake is a small plastic **doll**. The rson who gets the doll has to have a party on February 2 d invite the other people.

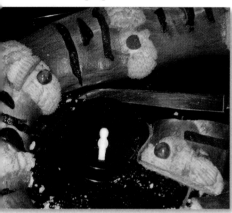

t the best known all special foods the birthday cake. l over the world, ople celebrate eir birthdays with ake with candles. ople blow out the ndles and make vish.

Communication

👥 Answer the questions in the first column. Then ask two classmates the questions.

	Me	Classmate 1	Classmate 2
What do you eat for breakfast?			
How much fruit do you eat each day?			
What do you eat at the New Year?			

Writing

Write about what you eat each day and what you eat on special days.

I usually have eggs for breakfast and a sandwich for lunch. I have dinner at six o'clock. We usually have rice, meat, and vegetables.

At the New Year we eat special noodles, and of course for my birthday I have a birthday cake.

✓ **Goal 4** **Talk about food for special occasions**

Work with a partner. Make a list of all the special food in your country.

Communication

- Have students work individually to complete the first column.
- Have students talk with two classmates to complete the other two columns.
- Compare answers with the class.

Writing

- Go over the model writing passage with the class.
- Then have students write about their own food habits, both for ordinary days and for special days.
- Have students exchange papers with a partner. Ask students to mark corrections and suggestions for improvements on their partner's paper.
- If desired, have students rewrite their papers, to be collected for marking.

✓ Goal 4

- Match students with a partner and have them work together to list food for special occasions.
- With the class, compile a list on the board and talk about any differences in what students eat to mark special days.

After Reading

Ask students to find information about a special food from another country and tell the class about it in English. Where is the food from? What is in it? When do people eat it?

Video Journal

Before You Watch

A • With the class, go over the names of the foods in the pictures. Introduce the idea of *fast food* and ask students for examples of restaurants that serve it.

   • Have students work individually to list the foods in the chart.

   • Check answers.

Answers: Fast food: hamburger, pizza, hot dogs, french fries; Slow food: fish, mushrooms, fruit, cheese

B • Match students with a partner and have them discuss foods they like and dislike (both foods from the chart and other foods).

E VIDEO JOURNAL *SLOW FOOD*

Before You Watch

A. Write the food in the correct column.

| hamburger | cheese | fish | mushrooms |
| pizza | hot dogs | french fries | fruit |

▲ cheese ▲ mushrooms ▲ french fries

▲ fruit ▲ pizza

Fast food	Slow food
hamburger	cheese

B. Tell a partner what foods you like and what foods you don't like.

For Your Information: Slow Food

The Slow Food movement was started in Italy in the 1980s, to fight the rise of fast food and industrialized living. It was begun by Carlo Petrini. Now there are more than 83,000 members in 122 chapters in Italy, and 450 regional chapters of the organization around the world. The goals of the Slow Food movement are to promote traditional foods, to start seed banks to save the seeds of traditional crops, and to organize celebrations of local cuisine in different regions of the world. It also tries to educate people about the problems and dangers of industrial agriculture.

While You Watch

Answer the questions.

1. Is Greve a big city? _____
2. What three things do the people of Chianti produce? _____
3. Does the mayor want to change Greve? _____
4. What is the goal of the Slow Food Movement? _____
5. What do the farmers of Pistoia produce? _____

After You Watch

A. How can you slow down your life? Label the pictures with the phrases in the box.

| spend time with friends and family | take a nap in the afternoon |
| get more exercise | eat healthy food |

_____   _____

B. Discuss with a partner: In what other ways can you slow down your life?

While You Watch

- Tell students to watch the video and answer the questions. Go over the questions with the class.
- Play the video one or more times.
- Check answers.

Answers: 1. no; 2. wine, cheese, mushrooms; 3. no; 4. keep good living, good food, family, and friends; 5. a special cheese

After You Watch

A • Talk about the idea of slow food and why people like to do things more slowly.
- Have students work individually to label the pictures.
- Check answers.

Answers: eat good food, take a nap in the afternoon, get more exercise, spend time with friends and family

B • Match students with a partner and have them talk about more ideas for slowing down their lives.
- With the class, compile a list on the board. Ask students which ideas they would like to try.

Teacher Tip: Sharing students' work

There are a number of ways that students can share their work with their classmates:
- give oral presentations in front of the class
- make large posters to display in front of the class (brown wrapping paper for packages is cheap and works well for this)
- tape students' papers around the classroom walls and allow time for students to walk around and read their classmates' work
- have students write or draw on a transparency and show these to the class on an overhead projector
- photocopy students' papers into a class magazine/newspaper and make a copy for each student

- Direct students' attention to the pictures. With the class, look at each picture in turn and have students talk about what they see in each one.

- Introduce the theme of the unit. Answer the questions together with the class. If students tell you about health problems, give them the English names of the problems.

- Go over the Unit Goals with the class, explaining and/or translating as necessary.

HEALTH

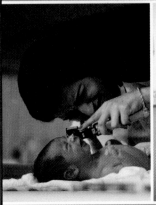

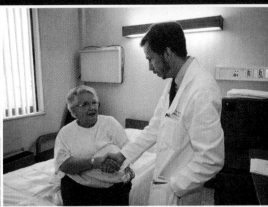

1. Are the people in the pictures healthy?

2. What do you do to stay healthy?

UNIT GOALS

Identify parts of the body to say how you feel
Ask about and describe symptoms
Identify remedies and give advice
Learn and talk about prevention

110

Unit Goals	Grammar	Vocabulary	Listening	Speaking and Pronunciation	Reading and Writing
• Identify parts of the body to say how you feel • Ask about and describe symptoms • Identify remedies and give advice • Learn and talk about prevention	Feel/look + adjective John **looks** terrible. I **feel** sick. My back **hurts**. Should (for advice) You **should** take an aspirin.	Parts of the body Common illnesses Remedies	Listening for general understanding and specific details Telephone conversations to make a doctor's appointment	Describing symptoms and illnesses; giving advice Word stress	"Preventing Disease" Writing rules for kitchen workers

UNIT 10

Unit Theme Overview

- The human body is the same all over the world, but people's experiences with health and illness vary widely, both among individuals and among cultures. For even a simple problem such as a cold, there are widely different reactions and remedies in different places. Some people will go to a doctor when they have a cold; others will use commercial medicines; others will employ old household remedies, ranging from onions on the chest to strong drink; and some will just wait for the cold to pass.

- In this unit, students approach the topic of health by beginning with the universal. They learn to describe how they feel, and they learn the names of body parts to talk about problems. They talk about common conditions and learn to give advice about remedies. In the reading, they learn about preventing some of the most serious illnesses around the world.

111

Identify Parts of the Body to Say How You Feel

Vocabulary

A • Have students look at the illustration of the body parts. Tell them to listen to the recording and repeat the words. Play the recording one or more times. **(CD2 T15)**

B • Direct students' attention to the pictures. Talk about the problems shown in each one and pronounce the names of health problems for students to repeat.

• Go over the words in the box for how people feel. Point out that they go from *terrible* (very, very bad) to *great* (very, very good).

• Have students complete the sentences, individually or with a partner.

• Check answers.

Answers: 1. sick, 2. well, 3. OK, 4. great, 5. terrible

Grammar

• Go over the information in the box. Point out the difference between feel (inside yourself) and look (outside to other people). Explain that sometimes people feel sick, but they don't look sick.

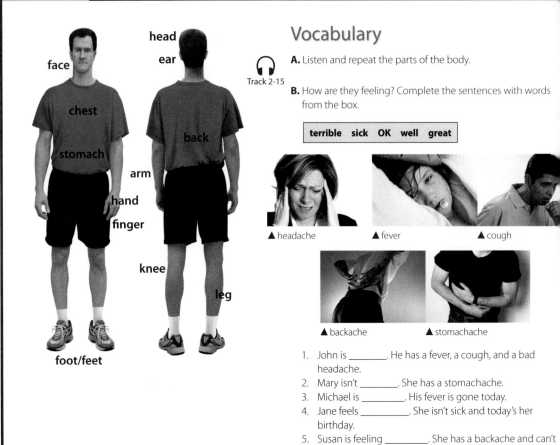

Vocabulary

A. Listen and repeat the parts of the body.

Track 2-15

B. How are they feeling? Complete the sentences with words from the box.

| terrible   sick   OK   well   great |

▲ headache   ▲ fever   ▲ cough

▲ backache   ▲ stomachache

1. John is _____. He has a fever, a cough, and a bad headache.
2. Mary isn't _____. She has a stomachache.
3. Michael is _____. His fever is gone today.
4. Jane feels _____. She isn't sick and today's her birthday.
5. Susan is feeling _____. She has a backache and can't move.

Grammar: *Feel, look*

Statement	Negative	*Yes/no* questions	Information questions
I **feel** sick. He/she **looks** sick.	Hilary **doesn't feel** great. You **don't look** well.	**Do** you **feel** OK? **Does** he/she **look** tired?	How do you feel?
*The verbs *look* and *feel* are followed by an adjective.			

112   Health

Word Bank: Internal body parts

lungs
heart
brain
liver
stomach
intestines
kidneys

nerves
muscles
veins
arteries
bones
joints

Grammar: *Feel, look*

Feel and *look* are copular verbs—verbs that describe states. They link the subject to additional information about the subject (= the complement) and are not usually used in continuous tenses.

A. Match the sentences with the responses.

1. How do you feel? ___
2. Do you feel OK? ___
3. Does Alan look well? ___
4. How do they feel? ___
5. Sarah doesn't look well. ___

a. No, she isn't feeling well.
b. I feel fine.
c. No, he doesn't. He looks sick.
d. No, I feel terrible.
e. They feel OK.

B. Complete the sentences.

1. **A:** Do you feel OK?
   B: Yes, I _____
2. **A:** How is Melanie?
   B: She doesn't _____ well.
3. **A:** How _____?
   B: I feel terrible.
4. **A:** You don't look very well.
   B: No, I _____.
5. **A:** Does Gerardo look OK?
   B: No, _____ sick.

> **Real Language**
>
> We can ask about someone's health by using the following questions.
>
> Formal ◄─────────────► Informal
> *What's the matter?   What's wrong?   What's up?*
>
> *How are you?* is a greeting. We do not normally use it to ask about someone's health.

Conversation

Track 2-16

A. Listen to the conversation. What's wrong with Kim?

Stephanie: What's the matter, Kim? You don't look well.
Kim: I don't feel well. My <u>head</u> hurts.
Stephanie: Oh, dear!
Kim: And I feel <u>sick</u>.
Stephanie: Maybe you have the flu.

 B. Practice the conversation with a partner. Switch roles and practice it again.

 C. Change the underlined words and make a new conversation.

 Goal 1 **Identify parts of the body to say how you feel**

Take turns asking a partner how he or she feels today. Be creative with your aches and pains.

A • Have students work individually to match the columns.
• Check answers.

Answers: 1. b, 2. d, 3. c, 4. e, 5. a

B • Have students work individually to fill in the blanks.
• Check answers.

Answers: 1. do, 2. feel, 3. are you, 4. don't feel well, 5. he looks

Real Language

• Point out that we use these questions when we see a problem.

Conversation

A • Have students close their books. Write the question on the board: *What's wrong with Kim?*
• Play the recording. **(CD2 T16)**
• Check answers.

Answer: her head hurts

B • Play or read the conversation again for the class to repeat.
• Practice the conversation with the class in chorus.
• Have students practice the conversation with a partner and then switch roles and practice it again.

C • Have students work with the same partner to make a new conversation.
• Call on student pairs to present their conversation to the class.

✓ Goal 1

• Match students with a partner and have them take turns talking about their health. Tell them to make up interesting health problems!
• Call on students to tell the class about their partner's problems.

Grammar Practice: *Feel, look*

Have students work with a partner to look through their books (both this unit and earlier units) to find pictures of people and talk about how they feel and how they look. Have them choose three photos and for each one write down the page number and two sentences (*He feels cold. He looks happy.*). Call on each pair of students to tell the class about one picture.

Ask about and Describe Symptoms

Listening

A • Introduce the topic. Ask students about when they go to the doctor. *What does the patient do? What does the doctor do?* Talk about the idea of symptoms—signs that you are sick.

• Tell students they are going to hear two conversations in doctors' offices. They should listen and write the patients' symptoms.

• Play the recording one or more times. **(CD2 T17)**

• Check answers.

Answers: Patient 1: headache, backache, fever; Patient 2: cough, stomachache, fever

B • Go over the pictures and read the sentences for students to repeat. If necessary, explain that measles is a health problem common in children, but adults sometimes get it too. It's a big problem if adults get measles.

• Match students with a partner and have them ask and answer questions about the people in the pictures.

• Call on student pairs to present a conversation to the class.

B GOAL 2 ASK ABOUT AND DESCRIBE SYMPTOMS

Listening

🎧 **A.** Listen to the conversations. List the patients' symptoms.
Track 2-17

Patient 1	Patient 2

B. Look at the pictures. Take turns asking about these people and describing their symptoms.

▲ She has a cold.

▲ He has an earache.

▲ He has a toothache.

▲ She has a sore throat.

▲ They have measles.

What's the matter with her?

Her throat hurts.

She has a fever.

For Your Information: Measles

Measles is a contagious disease that is more common in children. It is caused by a virus that spreads very easily. Up to 90 percent of people will catch measles if someone else in their household has the disease. The symptoms are fever, cough, runny nose, red eyes, and a rash all over the body. When children have measles, it is often not severe, but in adults, measles can cause brain infections and permanent damage to the eyes. Measles can cause death if the person has other serious health problems. For this reason, children in developed countries are usually given a vaccination against the disease before they are 18 months old.

Pronunciation: Word Stress

Track 2-18

A. Listen and notice the stressed syllables.

Doctor:	How can I <u>help</u> you?
Patient:	I don't feel very <u>well</u>. I have a <u>head</u>ache.
Doctor:	Anything <u>else</u>?
Patient:	Yes, I have a <u>fe</u>ver.
Doctor:	OK. I think I need to ex<u>a</u>mine you.

Track 2-19

B. Listen to the conversation. Underline the stressed syllables.

Dentist:	How are you today?
Patient:	I have a terrible toothache.
Dentist:	Where does it hurt?
Patient:	Right here.
Dentist:	I see the problem.

Communication

 Role-play the following situations.

Situation 1

Student A
You are a doctor. Ask your patient how she/he feels.

Student B
You are the patient. You have a cough, a headache, and a fever.

Situation 2

Student B
You are a dentist. Ask your patient how she/he is.

Student A
You are the patient. You have a toothache.

> Where does it hurt?

> Does it hurt a lot?

✓ **Goal 2**   **Ask about and describe symptoms**

Work with a partner. Make a list of ailments. Then take turns describing the symptoms of each one.

Pronunciation

- Introduce the idea of stress— words and parts of words that sound "stronger" when we're speaking. Tell students that every language has its special pattern for stress. If desired, give examples from the students' language.

A • Tell students that an English word has stress on one or more of its syllables. In English, the most important word in a sentence gets a strong stress on the syllable.

- Tell them to listen to the recording and read the sentences, paying attention to the underlined syllables. Play the recording one or more times. **(CD2 T18)**

B • Tell students to listen to the recording and mark the stressed syllables. **(CD2 T19)**

- Check answers.

Answers: How are <u>you</u> today? I have a terrible <u>tooth</u>ache. Where does it <u>hurt</u>? Right <u>here.</u> I see the <u>prob</u>lem.

- Have students read the conversation with a partner, paying attention to the stressed syllables.

Communication

- Match students with a partner and have them work together to role-play the situations, switching roles for situation 2.

✓ Goal 2

- Explain that *ailments* are health problems. Match students with a partner and have them list as many ailments and symptoms as they can.

- With the class, compile a list on the board.

Expansion Activity

Have students discuss with a partner or a group which ailments are serious and which are not serious. Which ones should you go to the doctor for? Compare answers with the class.

Identify Remedies and Give Advice

Language Expansion

- Introduce the idea of remedies—things you can do at home when you have a simple ailment.

- Read the remedies for students to repeat.

- Have students work individually to answer the questions. Tell them that more than one remedy may be correct for an ailment. Compare answers with the class.

Suggested answers: 1. take some aspirin; 2. take some aspirin, lie down, go to bed, see a doctor; 3. take some cough medicine, see a doctor ; 4. take some aspirin, see a dentist; 5. take some aspirin, lie down, go to bed, see a doctor

Grammar

- Tell students, *I feel terrible. I have a cold. What should I do?* Model advice with *should: You should take some cold medicine.* Elicit ideas and write them on the board.

- Go over the information in the box. Give/elicit more examples.

Language Expansion: Remedies

▲ go to bed

▲ see a doctor

▲ lie down

▲ see a dentist

▲ take some cough medicine

▲ take some aspirin

Answer the questions. Use the phrases above.

1. What do you do when you have a headache? _____
2. What do you do when you have a backache? _____
3. What do you do when you have a cough? _____
4. What do you do when you have a toothache? _____
5. What do you do when you have a fever? _____

Grammar: *Should* (for advice)

Statement	Negative	*Yes/no* question	*Wh-* question	Short answers
You **should** go to bed. He **should** take some cough medicine.	He **shouldn't** go to work today.	**Should** I see a doctor?	What **should** I do?	Yes, you **should**. No, you **shouldn't**.

*We use *should* to ask for and give advice.

Word Bank: Remedies

drink tea/hot water/orange juice
eat spicy food/chicken soup
take vitamin C/garlic tablets
put a cold cloth on your forehead
take a bath in warm/cool water
go to bed early

Grammar: *Should* (for advice)

The modal *should* is used for various functions in English, including predictions, intentions, and advice. Native speakers often use the word *maybe* to soften the advice and make it more polite: *Maybe you should go home.*

A. Match the questions and the answers.

1. Should I see a doctor? ___
2. I have a headache. What should I do? ___
3. Paul has a toothache. What should he do? ___
4. Should Helen see a doctor? ___
5. Hilary has a cough. What should she do? ___

a. You should take some aspirin.
b. He should see a dentist.
c. She should take some cough medicine.
d. Yes, you should.
e. No, she shouldn't.

 B. Complete the conversations and then practice them with a partner.

1. **A:** I have a headache. What should I do?
   B: _____

2. **A:** I think I have the flu. What should I do?
   B: _____

3. **A:** I have a stomachache. What should I do?
   B: _____

4. **A:** I think my computer has a virus. What should I do?
   B: _____

Conversation

 A. Listen to the conversation. What does Casey think Brenda
Track 2-20   should do?

Casey: Hi. What's up, Brenda?
Brenda: I don't feel well. I <u>think I have the flu</u>. What should I do?
Casey: I think you should <u>go home and go to bed</u>.
Brenda: Do you think I should see a doctor?
Casey: No, I don't think so.

 B. Practice the conversation with a partner. Switch roles and practice it again.

 C. Change the underlined words and make a new conversation.

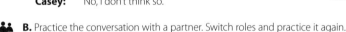 **Goal 3** **Identify remedies and give advice**

Work with a partner. Take turns naming an ailment and suggest a
remedy or give advice.

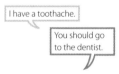

I have a toothache.

You should go
to the dentist.

Lesson C   **117**

A • Have students work individually to match the columns.
   • Check answers.

Answers: 1. d, 2. a, 3. b, 4. e, 5. c

B • Have students work individually to complete the conversations. If necessary, explain that flu is a short word for influenza, and a computer virus is like an "ailment" that computers get from other computers. Compare answers with the class.

Suggested answers: 1. You should take some aspirin. 2. You should go to the doctor. 3. You should drink some tea. 4. You should go to the computer store and ask for help.

   • Have students practice the conversations with a partner.
   • Call on student pairs to present a conversation to the class. Discuss any interesting remedies that students think of.

Conversation

A • Have students close their books. Write the question on the board: *What does Casey think Brenda should do?*
   • Play the recording. (**CD2 T20**)
   • Check answers.

Answer: She should go home and go to bed.

B • Play or read the conversation again for the class to repeat.
   • Practice the conversation with the class in chorus.
   • Have students practice the conversation with a partner and then switch roles and practice it again.

C • Have students work with the same partner to make a new conversation.
   • Call on student pairs to present their conversation to the class.

✓ Goal 3
   • Have students work with a different partner to talk about problems (health or other kinds of problems) and give advice.
   • Call on student pairs to present a conversation to the class.

Grammar: *Should* (for advice)

Talk about the idea of home remedies—easy things that people can do at home when they are sick to feel better. Point out that some remedies are very old. Choose a common health problem such as a cold or the hiccups (demonstrate this word) and ask students to tell you as many remedies as they can think of using *should*:
You should drink hot tea with lemon.
Write them on the board. Ask, *Which ones are very old? Which ones really work?*

Lesson C   **117**

Learn and Talk about Prevention

- Introduce the topic of the reading. Talk about preventing something—stopping something bad from happening.

A • Have students work individually to mark the things that people can prevent.

- Match students with a partner and have them compare answers and talk about ways to prevent flu and toothaches.

B • Tell students to read the article and answer *true* or *false*. Read through the statements with the class. Tell them to circle any words in the reading that they don't understand.

- Check answers.

Answers: 1. T, 2. F, 3. F, 4. F, 5. F

- Go over the article with the class and answer any questions from the students about vocabulary.

Reading

A. Check the things we can prevent. Compare your answer with a partner's answers. How can we prevent them?

☐ flu
☐ rain
☐ toothache
☐ headache

Word Focus

prevent = avoid a problem before it happens
infectious disease = a disease you can get from another person
vaccine = medicine to prevent a disease

B. Read the article. Circle **T** for *true* and **F** for *false*.

1. There is a vaccine for measles.   T   F
2. About 40,000 children die from malaria every day in Africa.   T   F
3. There is a vaccine for malaria.   T   F
4. Mosquito nets are expensive.   T   F
5. Influenza is a problem in hot countries.   T   F

Preventing Disease

Many people, especially children, die from **infectious diseases** every year. We can **prevent** many infectious diseases. Let's look at the most dangerous ones.

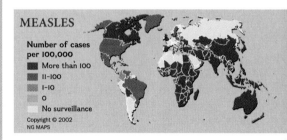

MEASLES
Number of cases per 100,000
■ More than 100
■ 11–100
■ 1–10
□ 0
□ No surveillance
Copyright © 2002
NG MAPS

Measles is mainly a children's disease. There is a very good, cheap **vaccine** for measles. All children should get the vaccine but unfortunately not all do. About 900,000 children die every year from measles.

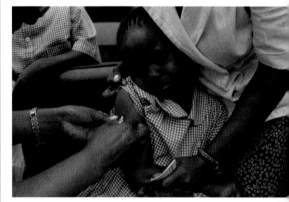

▲ All children should get a measles shot.

For Your Information: Infectious diseases

Malaria: This disease is caused by microorganisms that are carried by mosquitoes. Every year, there are about 350–500 million cases of malaria in the world, which kill 1–3 million people. Most of these deaths are in Africa.

Influenza/"flu": This disease is caused by a number of types of viruses and is spread through the air when people cough. New kinds of flu virus can develop and spread quickly around the world. In this unit in the Student Workbook, a reading gives students more information about the flu.

Measles: Please see For Your Information on page 114.

MALARIA

Risk

- Significant
- Low
- None

Copyright © 2002
NG MAPS

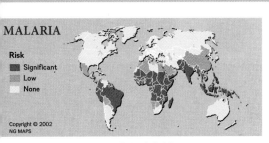

Imagine seven Jumbo jets full of children. Now, imagine that all the Jumbos crash and all the children are killed. That's how many children die from malaria in Africa *every day*. There is no vaccine for malaria, but it is not difficult to prevent. All you need is a $5 mosquito net.

▲ Children should sleep under a mosquito net.

INFLUENZA (FLU)

Outbreaks

- Widespread
- Regional
- Local
- Sporadic
- Negligible or no surveillance

Copyright © 2002
NG MAPS

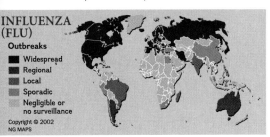

Influenza (or flu) is caused by a virus. The virus changes every year so scientists have to make a new vaccine every year. People at risk—for example, older people—should have a flu shot every year. There are good years and bad years. In a bad year, influenza can kill millions of people.

Writing

👥 Complete this notice. Use the words and expressions in the box.

cover	gloves	switch off	wash your hands	clean

You should always:

_____ before entering the kitchen.

_____ your hair.

Use oven _____.

Keep the kitchen _____.

_____ electrical equipment.

Communication

👥 Discuss how you can prevent these problems.

toothache	car accidents
heart attacks	computer viruses

You should brush your teeth.

You shouldn't eat a lot of candy.

You should see a dentist every six months.

✓ **Goal 4** **Learn and talk about prevention**

Share your best ideas from the communication activity with the class.

Writing

- Review the idea of preventing illness. Talk about how dirty food causes some illness, and talk about preventing problems in the kitchen.
- Tell students to look at the words and pictures and complete the notice.
- Check answers.

Answers: wash your hands, cover, gloves, clean, switch off

Communication

- With the class, go over the problems listed.
- Match students with a partner and have them discuss and list ideas for preventing each problem.

✓ **Goal 4**

- Call on student pairs to tell the class about some of their ideas.

After Reading

With the class, talk about a serious health problem in the students' country, such as malaria, HIV/AIDS, or tuberculosis. What are the best ways to prevent this problem? Make a list on the board.

Video Journal

Before You Watch

A • Go over the names of the animals in the photos. Ask students to work with a partner to rank them in order of their danger.
  • Compare answers with the class.

B • Introduce the vocabulary in the box, and go over the meanings of the words.
  • With the class or individually, have students complete the sentences.
  • Check answers.

Answers: 1. flowers, 2. repellant, 3. sun-dried, 4. dry climate, 5. insecticide

---

Before You Watch

A. Look at the pictures. How dangerous do you think these animals are? Rate them 1 to 4.

▲ lion   ▲ mosquito   ▲ tarantula   ▲ leopard

B. Complete the sentences. Use the words in the box.

insecticide   repellent   flowers   sun-dried   dry climate

1. Today's my mother's birthday. I always give her _____.
2. We need mosquito _____ when we go fishing at the lake.
3. This tomato sauce is very good. Does it have _____ tomatoes?
4. It never rains here. We have a very _____.
5. Please buy some _____. There are insects in the house.

For Your Information: Malaria

Malaria is a disease caused by parasites that are carried by mosquitoes. It is found in tropical and subtropical areas of the Americas, Asia, and Africa. There are between 350 and 500 million cases of malaria every year, killing up to a million people, mostly children. It is one of the world's most common infectious diseases. Currently, there is no vaccination against malaria, but research is being done. Attempts to control the disease involve destroying the habitat of the mosquitoes who carry it and preventing the insects from reproducing. An effective way of protecting the most vulnerable people such as children and elderly people is by providing them with insecticide-treated mosquito nets to cover their beds.

While You Watch

A • Tell students to watch the video and answer *true* or *false*. Play the video one or more times.

• Check answers.

Answers: 1. T, 2. T, 3. F, 4. T, 5. T

B • Tell students to work with a partner and talk about countries where malaria is common.

• With the class, list countries where malaria occurs.

• If it occurs in the students' country, talk about ways to prevent malaria.

After You Watch

• Divide the class into groups of three or four students and have them talk about other useful plants that are good for our health.

• Call on groups to present their ideas to the class.

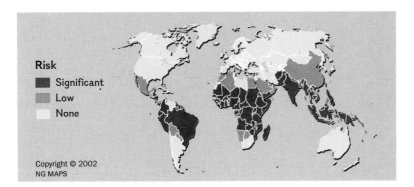

Risk

Significant

Low

None

Copyright © 2002
NG MAPS

While You Watch

A. Circle **T** for *true* and **F** for *false*. Watch the video again to check your answers.

1.	Pyrethrum flowers attract malaria mosquitoes.	T	F
2.	Mosquitoes are resistant to many insecticides.	T	F
3.	Doctors make medicine from pyrethrum flowers.	T	F
4.	Many children die each year from malaria.	T	F
5.	Pyrethrum flowers grow well in dry climates.	T	F

B. Study the map. With a partner locate the countries around the world where malaria is a serious disease.

After You Watch

Discuss other plants and flowers that prevent or cure illnesses. Report to the class.

_____

_____

_____

_____

_____

Video Journal   121

Teacher Tip: "Fillers"

Here are some activities to "fill in" a few extra minutes at the end of a lesson:

• The Blackboard Game (if you have filled the board with vocabulary and other notes): Have a volunteer sit with his/her back to the board. Students take turns giving definitions of words on the board. When the volunteer says the correct word, you step up and erase it. The game ends when all the words are erased.

• Error Quiz: On the board, write 10 incorrect sentences that you have heard or seen in the students' recent work. Have students work with a partner to correct as many as they can in five minutes. When the time is up, ask the class for corrections and rewrite the sentences on the board.

• Spelling Practice: Dictate 10 to 15 words that students find difficult. Let them compare answers with a partner before giving the correct answers.

- Direct students' attention to the pictures. With the class, look at each picture in turn and talk about what is happening in each picture.

- Introduce the theme of the unit. With the class, talk about future plans—for the weekend and for their life. (Students will learn *be going to* and *would like to* in this unit. At this point, they can answer with phrases: *go shopping/watch videos/get a job/study abroad*.)

- Go over the Unit Goals with the class, explaining and/or translating as necessary.

MAKING PLANS

1. What are your plans for the weekend?

2. What are your plans for your life?

UNIT GOALS

Plan special days
Plan holidays
Make life plans
Express wishes and plans

122

	Unit Goals	Grammar	Vocabulary	Listening	Speaking and Pronunciation	Reading and Writing
	• Plan special days • Plan holidays • Make life plans • Express wishes and plans	*Be going to* What **are** you **going to** do? We **are going to** have a party. *Would like* for wishes I **would like** to be a doctor.	Celebrating special days American holidays Professions	Listening for general understanding and specific details Conversations to discuss special dates or events	Talking about holiday celebrations *Be going to* (short form)	"Life's Milestones" Writing about wishes and plans

UNIT 11

Unit Theme Overview

- Many students are learning English with an eye to the future. They hope to use their new language to get a job, to interact with foreign colleagues, to study abroad, or to travel internationally. They may need English skills to qualify for higher levels of education, or they may just want to use their new language to gain access to a broader range of information or entertainment. For any of these goals, learning English is intimately linked with goals and plans—and this unit teaches students to explore and express theirs in English.

- They begin by learning to use *going to* and talking about short-term plans for special days, whether it's next weekend or an upcoming birthday or anniversary. They move on to learn the use of *would like to* to talk about future desires. They talk about their own life plans and finally read and watch a video about the life plans of several people in countries around the world.

123

Plan Special Days

Vocabulary

A • Direct students' attention to the pictures and introduce the vocabulary.

• Have students look at the Year Planner page. Introduce/ review the names of the months presented and the remaining months—August, September, October, November and December—pronouncing them for students to repeat.

• Have students work individually to write their ideas about how to celebrate each occasion.

• Compare answers with the class. Answers will vary.

B • Match students with a partner and have them talk about how they usually celebrate their birthdays.

• Call on students to tell the class about their birthday activities.

Vocabulary

▲ go out for dinner   ▲ have a party   ▲ have a barbeque

▲ go to a club   ▲ go to the movies   ▲ have a family meal

January 7th, Dad's birthday

February 17th, John's birthday

March

April   1st, Mom and Dad's anniversary

May   14th, My birthday

June   3rd, Mom's birthday

July   24th, Grandpa and Grandma's anniversary

A. Look at the Year Planner and pictures. Decide the best way to celebrate. Complete the sentences.

1. On Dad's birthday, we usually __have a party__.
2. On Mom's and Dad's anniversary, they usually _____
3. On John's birthday, we usually _____
4. On Mom's birthday, she usually _____
5. On my birthday, _____
6. On Grandpa and Grandma's anniversary, we _____

> What do you usually do on your birthday?

B. Tell a partner what you usually do on your birthday.

124   **Making Plans**

Word Bank: More plans

have a picnic	have a
have a graduation party	housewarming party
get together with friends	have a wedding/
clean my house/apartment	baby shower
go shopping	stay home
	go to bed early

Grammar: *Be going to*

English uses a variety of different structures to talk about future time. One of them is *be going to*, which is used to talk about plans and intentions. It is also used informally for making predictions. One common error to watch out for is omitting the *be* verb—*We going to watch videos*.

Grammar: *Be going to*

Be going to

Statement	Negative	*Yes/no* question	*Wh-* question
I **am going to** have a party.	**We are not going to** have a big meal.	**Are you going to** go to the movies?	What **are you going to** do? When **are we going to** go?

*We use *be going to* for making plans.
*We also use these time expressions: *tomorrow, next Saturday/week/year.*

A. Complete the sentences. Use the words in parentheses and *be going to*.

1. **A:** What _____ (you do) for your birthday?
   B: I _____ have a BIG party!
2. **A:** _____ (you have) a barbeque on the weekend?
   B: No, we _____ (go) to the movies.
3. **A:** Where _____ (Brenda and Alan go) on New Year's?
   B: They _____ go to Times Square.

 B. Practice the conversations with a partner.

Conversation

 A. Listen to the conversation. When is Susan's birthday?

Track 2-21

Sally:	When is your birthday?
Susan:	It's on <u>May 21</u>.
Sally:	Hey, that's next week. Are you going to <u>have a party</u>?
Susan:	No, I'm going to <u>go out for dinner with my parents</u>.

B. Practice the conversation with a partner. Switch roles and practice it again.

C. Change the underlined words and make a new conversation.

✓ **Goal 1**   **Plan special days**

Take turns asking a partner how he or she celebrates birthdays.

Grammar Practice: *Be going to*

Have students take a piece of paper and make seven columns with the days of the week at the top. This is their "calendar" for next week. Then have them write an activity (real or imaginary) for five of the seven days (such as see a movie, study English, etc.). Have students work with a partner to plan an activity (such as have a cup of coffee) they want to do together. They should not look at their partner's calendar. Model sentences like, *I'm going to do the laundry on Monday night* and *What are you going to do on Tuesday night?* When all student pairs have finished, call on students to talk about their plans.

Grammar

- Introduce the structure. Tell students, *I have a lot of plans this weekend. I'm going to read your homework papers. I'm going to see my friends. And I'm going to watch TV.* Write the sentences on the board.
- Ask, *What about you? What are you going to do?* Elicit answers with *going to* and write them on the board.
- Go over the information in the box, and give/elicit more examples.

A • Have students work individually to complete the sentences.
- Check answers.

Answers: 1. are you going to do, am going to; 2. Are you going to have, are going to go; 3. are Alan and Brenda going to go, are going to

B • Match students with a partner and have them practice the conversations.
- If time permits, have students make new conversations with their own ideas.

Conversation

A • Have students close their books. Write the question on the board: *When is Susan's birthday?*
- Play the recording. **(CD2 T21)**
- Check answers.

Answer: May 21

B • Play or read the conversation again for the class to repeat.
- Practice the conversation with the class in chorus.
- Have students practice the conversation with a partner and then switch roles and practice it again.

C • Have students work with the same partner to make a new conversation.
- Call on student pairs to present their conversation to the class.

✓ **Goal 1**
- Match students with a partner and have them take turns telling about their birthday celebrations.

Plan Holidays

Listening

A • Tell students they are going to hear people talking about their plans for holidays.

• Have students read about American holidays. Go over the photos and information about the holidays.

B • Tell students to listen to the conversations and write the name of each holiday. Tell them they will NOT hear the name of the holiday—they must think about the information in the conversation. Play the recording one or more times. **(CD2 T22)**

• Check answers.

Answers: New Year's Day, Independence Day

C • Tell students to listen again to answer the questions. Have them read the questions.

• Play the recording one or more times. **(CD2 T22)**

• Check answers.

Answers: 1. There are too many people. 2. stay home with her family, 3. to a party with his girlfriend, 4. go downtown and watch the fireworks, 5. six o'clock

Listening

A. Read about American holidays.

American Holidays

▲ On Thanksgiving Day, people have a family meal.

▲ All over the United States, people celebrate Independence Day with fireworks.

▲ On New Year's in New York, people go to Times Square to celebrate.

▲ At Christmas, people decorate their houses and give presents.

B. Listen and write which holidays the people are talking about.

Track 2-22

Linda and Kenichi are talking about _____

Tom and Maria are talking about _____

C. Listen again and answer the questions.

Track 2-22

1. Why isn't Linda going to go to Times Square? _____
2. What is she going to do? _____
3. Where is Kenichi going to go? _____
4. What are Tom and Maria going to do? _____
5. What time is Tom leaving? _____

126 **Making Plans**

For Your Information: American holidays

The activity talks about four of the most important holidays in the United States.

Thanksgiving is the fourth Thursday in November. People travel long distances to eat a traditional dinner with their family, including turkey and pumpkin pie. They talk and think about all the good things in their life that they're thankful for.

Independence Day is July 4. It is celebrated with parades (floats, marching bands, and patriotic displays) and each city has fireworks in the city parks at night.

On *New Year's Eve*, people usually have big parties with drinks and dancing. At midnight, they kiss for good luck.

Christmas is December 25. People attend religious services, give presents to family and friends, and cook and eat special foods, especially cookies.

Pronunciation: *Be going to* (short form)

Track 2-23

A. Listen and check the correct column of the form you hear.

	Full form	Short form
1. We're going to have a party	✓	
2. We're going to have a party		✓
3. I'm going to go to Paris.		
4. I'm going to go to Paris.		
5. They're not going to come.		
6. They're not going to come.		

B. Practice the dialogs with a partner. Use the short form of *be going to.*

A: What are you going to do on the weekend?
B: I'm going to go to the beach.

A: Are you going to go to Kim's party?
B: No, I'm going to stay home this weekend.

Communication

Write a list of holidays in your country. Discuss what you are going to do on *those* days.

✓ **Goal 2** **Plan holidays**

Join another pair of students and tell them about two holidays on your list.

Lesson B **127**

Pronunciation

A
- Explain to the class that in casual speech, *be going to* is pronounced with the short form *gonna*. This is very common, and practicing it will help make students' speech more natural. Emphasize that this form is used only in speaking, NOT in writing. (Learners sometimes write *gonna* in the mistaken belief that this makes their English more native-like.)
- Tell students to listen and mark the form they hear. Play the recording one or more times. **(CD2 T23)**
- Check answers.

Answers: 3. short, 4. full, 5. full, 6. short

- Play the recording again, one or more times, for students to repeat.

B
- Match students with a partner and have them practice the conversations, using the short form each time.
- Call on student pairs to present a conversation to the class.

Communication
- Have students work with their partner to list holidays in their country. Help with vocabulary as needed. Then have them talk about their plans for each holiday using *going to.*

✓ **Goal 2**
- Combine student pairs into groups of four and have them take turns talking about their plans for two holidays.

Expansion Activity

As a follow-up to Goal 2, assign each group two different holidays and have them write descriptions similar to those of the American holidays on the previous page. Then have them share their descriptions with the class.

Make Life Plans

Language Expansion

- Introduce the idea of life plans. Ask, *Why do people usually choose a profession? Do people sometimes change their professions? Why?*

- Have students look at the pictures. Read the professions and have students repeat them.

- Clarify the difference between the person's job and the profession/field. Explain, *I'm a teacher. That's my job. I work in education. That's my profession.*

- Have students work individually to match the columns.

- Check answers.

Answers: 1. b, 2. e, 3. a, 4. f, 5. d, 6. c

Grammar

- Introduce the idea of *would like to* for wishes in the future. Go over the information in the box. Point out that *would like to* is used with a verb in the base form.

Language Expansion: Professions

▲ law

▲ nursing

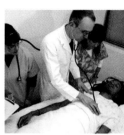
▲ medicine

▲ music

▲ acting

▲ psychology

Match the person to the profession.

1. doctor _____   a. music
2. lawyer _____   b. medicine
3. musician _____   c. psychology
4. nurse _____   d. acting
5. actor _____   e. law
6. psychologist _____   f. nursing

Grammar: *Would like to* for wishes

Statement	Yes/no question	Short answer	*Wh-* question
I **would like to** be a doctor. Danny **would like to** study law.	**Would** you **like to** study engineering? **Would** you **like to** be a nurse?	Yes, I **would**. No, I **wouldn't**.	What **would** you **like to** be?

Word Bank: Professions

education	engineering
science	business
government	the military
technology	the ministry (religion)
agriculture	

Grammar: *Would like to*

Would like to is slightly more polite and "softer" than *want to* in expressing a desire. It is used with the base form of the verb.

A. Unscramble the words to write sentences.

1. to be a would like I musician. _____
2. Eleanor like What would to be? _____
3. to be Would you a doctor? like _____
4. Deng nursing. would to study like _____
5. What like to be? would you _____

B. Write the wishes or plans.

Wish	Plan
1. *I would like to be an actor.*	I am going to be an actor.
2. Danny would like to study medicine.	_____
3. _____	I am going to be a doctor.
4. We would like to leave at seven o'clock.	_____
5. _____	They are going to study nursing.

Conversation

Track 2-24

A. Listen to the conversation. What would Wendy like to be?

Father: So, Wendy, you're 18 years old today. What are you going to do with your life?

Wendy: Well, I'd like to get married and have children.

Father: Whoa! Not so quick!

Wendy: Only joking! I'd like to be a <u>lawyer</u>. I'd like to study <u>law</u> and become a <u>lawyer</u>.

 B. Practice the conversation with a partner. Switch roles and practice it again.

 C. Change the underlined words and make a new conversation.

Real Language

We can say *Only joking* to show we are not serious.

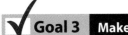 **Goal 3** **Make life plans**

Talk to a partner. What would you like to do with your life?

Lesson C **129**

A • Have students work individually to write the sentences.
 • Check answers.

Answers: 1. I would like to be a musician. 2. What would Eleanor like to be? 3. Would you like to be a doctor? 4. Deng would like to study nursing. 5. What would you like to be?

B • Have students work individually to write the wishes/plans.
 • Check answers.

Answers: 2. He is going to be a doctor. 3. I would like to study medicine. 4. We are going to (see the fireworks). 5. They would like to be nurses.

Conversation

A • Have students close their books. Write the question on the board: *What would Wendy like to be?*
 • Play the recording. **(CD2 T24)**
 • Check answers.

Answer: a lawyer

B • Play or read the conversation again for the class to repeat.
 • Practice the conversation with the class in chorus.
 • Have students practice the conversation with a partner and then switch roles and practice it again.

C • Have students work with the same partner to make a new conversation.
 • Call on student pairs to present their conversation to the class.

☑ Goal 3

 • Match students with a partner and have them talk about their life plans. Tell them that this can be a job or profession, or some other important plan.

Grammar Practice: *Would like to* and *be going to*

Prepare a list of 8 to 10 sentences with *am going to* and *would like to* about yourself. (For example, *I am going to take a vacation next week. I would like to go skiing.*) Some should be true, others not true. Dictate the sentences one at a time to the class. Tell them to think about the sentence and to write it down only if they think it's true. After you've dictated all the sentences, ask which sentences the students wrote down and give them the correct answers. You can repeat the activity by having students write their own list of true and false statements and dictate the statements to a partner. This activity can be done to practice many different structures.

Express Wishes and Plans

Reading

A • Introduce the topic of the reading. Ask students, *Do you think wishes and plans are the same in every country?* Ask them to explain their answers.

• Have students look at the pictures and guess where the people are from.

• Have students read the article to check their guesses. Tell them to circle any words they don't understand.

• Check answers.

Answers: Cuba, South Africa, Ukraine

• Go over the article with the class, answering any questions from the students about vocabulary.

B • Have students read the article again to answer the questions.

• Check answers.

Answers: 1. 15, 2. an actress, 3. Havana, 4. she is going to get married, 5. no, 6. their anniversary, 7. have a meal and dance all night

C • Have students read the sentences and mark the answers.

• Check answers.

Answers: 1. wish, 2. plan, 3. wish, 4. plan

Reading

A. Look at the pictures. Where do you think these people come from? Read and check your guesses.

B. Read and answer the questions.

1. How old is Annalien? _____
2. What would she like to be? _____
3. Where would she like to study? _____
4. Why is today Zanelle's big day? _____
5. Does Zanelle have children? _____
6. What are Vasili and Olga celebrating? _____
7. What are they going to do? _____

C. Check (✓) the correct box.

	Wish	Plan
1. Annalien: I would like to study acting.	☐	☐
2. Zanelle is going to get married.	☐	☐
3. Zanelle would like to have a lot of children.	☐	☐
4. Vasili and Olga are going to dance all night.	☐	☐

Life's Milestones

In some Central American and Caribbean countries, a girl's 15th birthday is very important.

Here, Elsa Mendoza prepares her niece, Annalien, for her 15th-birthday photographs.

Annalien would like to study acting in Havana. Her aunt told her that she has to finish school first. "She's not ready to go to the big city yet."

Zanelle is an Ndebele from South Africa. Today is her big day. She is going to get married. However, she is not truly married until she has her first child. She says, "I would like to have a lot of children. But most of all, I would like to be happy."

For Your Information: *Quince Años*

Girls in Mexico and other countries in Latin America celebrate their fifteenth birthday to mark the transition from girl to young woman in a special celebration called Quince Años. The girl wears a beautiful and very expensive dress that looks a little bit like a wedding dress. On the morning of her birthday, the girl goes to church with her family and all of her friends. In the evening, there is a huge party in a restaurant, with a cake and decorations in the same colors as the girl's dress. People enjoy music and dancing until very late at night.

This is Vasili and Olga Karezin. They are from the Ukraine. Today is their golden wedding anniversary. They got married 50 years ago. What are they going to do on this special day? They are going to have a meal with their family and friends. And then they are going to dance—all night.

Writing

Write a wish and a plan.

I would like to visit Europe. So, I am

going to learn English and I am going

to save some money.

✓ **Goal 4** | **Express wishes and plans**

Share your wishes and plans with a partner.

What would you like to do with your life?

How are you going to do it?

Writing

- Have students write about one wish they have for the future and their plan for getting this wish.

- Have students exchange papers with a partner. Ask students to mark corrections and suggestions for improvements on their partner's paper.

- If desired, have students rewrite their papers, to be collected for marking.

✓ **Goal 4**

- Call on students to read their papers to a partner or have them read them to a small group.

After Reading

With the class, talk about the wishes and plans of the people in the reading. Are they the same as in the students' country? What is similar? What is different?

Video Journal

Before You Watch

A • Match students with a partner and have them discuss the meanings of the items in bold. (Point out that the pictures can give them more information.)

• Go over the vocabulary with the class.

B • With the class, list other kinds of martial arts, such as karate, judo, kung fu, tae kwon do, aikido, and so forth.

Before You Watch

A. Read about the video. With a partner try to guess the meanings of the words in bold.

> ### Video Summary
>
> Thai **boxing,** or Muay Thai, is a traditional **martial art** from Thailand. Thai boxers use their hands, heads, and legs. Manat is a 12-year-old boy from a poor family who is living at a Thai boxing **training camp**. He trains seven hours a day, seven days a week. He wishes to become a boxing champion. He works very hard.

B. What martial arts do you know? Make a list.

_____

_____

_____

_____

_____

_____

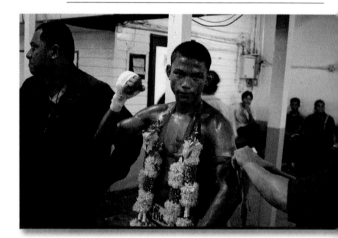

For Your Information: Thai boxing

Thai boxing is called Muai Thai in the Thai language and is a martial art and the national sport of Thailand. In contrast to western boxing, the hands, shins, elbows, and knees are all used against the opponent. It is performed in a ring and gloves are used. Training for a Thai boxer involves running, rope jumping, and intense daily practice of punches and kicks. Because of the difficulty of the sport, most Thai boxers retire from fighting after only a short career and work as trainers instead. Thai boxers are usually from poor families and become professional boxers to support their families. Wealthier people do take up the sport, but only as amateurs.

While You Watch

 A. Watch the video. Order the things that you see.

___ Manat doesn't win.
___ Manat goes into the ring for a ceremony.
___ The fight begins.
___ Manat trains very hard.
___ Manat will become a champion.

 B. Watch the video again. Complete the sentences with words from the box.

| family   champion   poor   trains   win |

1. Manat comes from a _____ family.
2. Manat's coaches believe he will be a _____.
3. When Manat wins, he wants to send the money to his _____.
4. Manat doesn't _____.
5. Manat _____ very hard.

After You Watch

 Answer these questions with a partner.

1. Do you think Manat will get his wish to become a Thai boxing champion?
2. What do you think about the training camp? Name positive and negative things.

While You Watch

A • Tell students to watch the video the first time and write numbers to put the events in order. Play the video.

 • Check answers.

Answers: 5, 2, 4, 1, 3

B • Tell students to watch the video again and complete the sentences. Have the students read the statements. Play the video.

 • Check answers.

Answers: 1. poor, 2. champion, 3. family, 4. win, 5. trains

After You Watch

 • Match students with a partner and have them discuss the questions.

 • Compare answers with the class.

Teacher Tip: Fun with English outside of class

Encourage students to find language activities that they enjoy to get more practice outside of class. Some ideas:

• sing along with English songs on cassette or CD (lyrics can be found on the album liner or on Web sites)
• speak in English with a friend or classmate outside of class time
• read an English comic book or a magazine on a topic that is well-known in the native language (for example, soccer or fashion)
• watch English-language movies with native-language subtitles
• talk to yourself in English!

- Introduce the theme of the unit. Talk about the meaning of move— to change your home to another place. Point out that sometimes one person or family moves; other times large groups of people move.

- Direct students' attention to the pictures. With the class, look at each picture in turn, and talk about where the picture was taken and what is happening in it.

- Discuss the questions with the class.

- Go over the Unit Goals with the class, explaining and/or translating as necessary.

MIGRATIONS

1. Why do people move from one country to another?

2. Why do animals move from one place to another?

UNIT GOALS

Talk about moving in the past
Talk about moving dates
Talk about preparations for moving
Discuss migrations

134

	Unit Goals	Grammar	Vocabulary	Listening	Speaking and Pronunciation	Reading and Writing
✓	• Talk about moving in the past • Talk about moving dates • Talk about preparations for moving • Discuss migrations	Simple past tense *He moved to California.* *When did they leave Germany?*	Moving Dates Preparations for a move	Listening for general understanding and specific details Biographies of famous American immigrants	Talking about people moving from place to place *-ed* sounds	"Human Migration" Writing a travel postcard

UNIT 12

135

Unit Theme Overview

- We live in an increasingly mobile world. Every day, countless people around the world move to a new city or even a new country to pursue better opportunities for work or education. And, tragically, large groups of people are forced to leave their homes because of war, hunger, or ethnic persecution.

- In this unit, students talk and think about why people moved to a new home, both individually and in large groups, and learn to talk about past events. They begin by talking about individual changes in the past. They learn to talk about the dates when things happened. They consider how people prepared to move to a new home. Finally, they learn about larger patterns of human migration in the past and compare animals' migration across vast distances.

Talk about Moving in the Past

Vocabulary

- Introduce the vocabulary in the pictures. Explain that these words are verbs—words for actions—and that they are used together with the prepositions to show direction. Read the verb/preposition combinations for students to repeat.

- Have students work individually to choose the correct verbs.

- Check answers.

Answers: 1. leave, 2. arrive, 3. stay, 4. staying, 5. go

Grammar

- Tell the class, *I usually leave school at four thirty. But yesterday, I left at six o'clock. What about you? When did you leave?* From different students elicit, *I left at (three thirty).* Write on the board, *I usually leave at four thirty. Yesterday, I left at six o'clock.* Tell students that this is the simple past tense. We use it to talk about things in the past, like yesterday, last year, and so forth.

- Go over the information in the chart. Point out that there are two kinds of verbs. Regular verbs use a rule to make the simple past tense: add *-ed*. Most verbs are regular. Some verbs are irregular. They don't use *-ed* to form the simple past tense. They are all different. Students have to memorize them. Go over the irregular verbs in the chart.

- Explain/review how the verb changes in the *yes/no* question and the information question.

Vocabulary

▲ leave   ▲ arrive in/at   ▲ return to/from   ▲ go to

▲ come from/to   ▲ move from/to   ▲ stay in/at

Circle the correct verb in parentheses.

1. People (move/leave) their homes when they go to work.
2. They are going to (arrive/come) from Paris tomorrow.
3. I am going to (come/stay) at Jim's house tonight.
4. At the moment, John is (staying/returning) in Toronto.
5. Children (go/stay) to school at eight o'clock.

Grammar: Simple past tense

Simple past tense		
Statement	Negative	*Wh-* questions
He **moved** from New York to San Francisco.	I **didn't stay** in California.	When **did they leave** Germany? How long **did you stay** in France?

*We use the simple past tense to talk about completed actions or conditions.

*Some verbs are regular in the simple past. They have an *-ed* ending.		*Some verbs are irregular in the simple past. They have many different forms.	
return	returned	go	went
stay	stayed	come	came
arrive	arrived	leave	left
move	moved		
live	lived		

Word Bank: Useful irregular verbs

see	saw	have	had	make	made
sit	sat	think	thought	take	took
say	said	write	wrote	know	knew
read	read	tell	told	meet	met
do	did	give	gave	eat	ate
drink	drank				

Grammar: Simple past tense (statements, negative, and information questions)

The simple past is used to talk about actions that were completed in the past. Irregular verbs are those that don't follow the rule in forming the past tense and so must be learned individually (practice with flash cards is a good way to do this). Tell students that if they are unsure about a verb, dictionaries usually have a list of irregular verbs in the back.

A. Match the questions and the answers.

1. When did you move to Oman? _____   a. He lived there for eight years.
2. How long did you stay in Taipei? _____   b. She came in 2008.
3. When did Michelle come to Chile? _____   c. They left in 2002.
4. When did Al and Lorena leave Argentina? _____   d. I moved there in 2007.
5. How long did George live in Texas? _____   e. I stayed there for two years.

B. Complete the questions and answers.

1. **A:** When did you leave Canada?
   B: I _____ in 2000.
2. **A:** How long _____ in Saudi Arabia?
   B: I stayed there for three years.
3. **A:** Where did you live in Brazil?
   B: We _____ in São Paulo.
4. **A:** When did you arrive in the United States?
   B: I _____ three years ago.

 C. Practice the questions and answers in exercise **B** with a partner.

Conversation

 A. Listen to the conversation. When did Fatima arrive in Canada?

Track 2-25

Ed: <u>Fatima</u>, you're not <u>Canadian</u>. Do you mind if I ask where you're from?
Fatima: Well, I was born in <u>Syria</u>, but later my parents moved to <u>France</u>.
Ed: How long did you stay in <u>France</u>?
Fatima: Twelve years. But then I left <u>France</u> when I was 18 to study in the <u>United States</u>.
Ed: And when did you come to <u>Canada</u>?
Fatima: I came here five years ago.

B. Practice the conversation. Switch roles and practice it again.

C. Change the underlined words and make a new conversation.

✔ **Goal 1**   **Talk about moving in the past**

With a partner trace two or three moves that you made (or wanted to make). Make notes of the names of the places. Take turns asking each other about your moves.

A • Have students work individually to match the columns.
   • Check answers.

Answers: 1. d, 2. e, 3. b, 4. c, 5. a

B • Have students work individually to complete the sentences.
   • Check answers.

Answers: 1. left, 2. did you stay, 3. lived, 4. arrived

C • Match students with a partner and have them practice the conversations in exercise **B** together.
   • Call on student pairs to present their conversation to the class.

Conversation

A • Have students close their books. Write the question on the board: *When did Fatima arrive in Canada?*
   • Play the recording. **(CD2 T25)**
   • Check answers.

Answer: five years ago

B • Play or read the conversation again for the class to repeat.
   • Practice the conversation with the class in chorus.
   • Have students practice the conversation with a partner and then switch roles and practice it again.

C • Have students work with the same partner to make a new conversation.
   • Call on student pairs to present their conversation to the class.

☑ **Goal 1**
   • Have students take turns asking and answering questions about where they lived in the past.

Grammar Practice: Simple past tense

Have students work individually to write three sentences about themselves using the past tense verbs they have learned. Collect the papers, read each student's sentences to the class, and have them guess who wrote the sentences. Ask follow-up questions about any interesting statements.

Talk about Moving Dates

Listening

- Go over the information in the Word Focus box. Tell students that in English, we say years as pairs of digits: *1850 is eighteen fifty.* The exception is 2000 to 2009, when we say (for example), *two thousand six.* Write more years on the board and have students practice saying them.

A • Introduce the idea of an immigrant—a person who comes from another country to live in a new place.

- Tell students they are going to hear information about four immigrants in the United States. They should write the name with the correct photo. Have them read the names.
- Play the recording one or more times. **(CD2 T26)**
- Check answers.

Answers: 1. Albert Einstein, 2. Salma Hayek, 3. Jerry Yang, 4. Anna Kournikova

B • Tell students to listen again for the dates and circle *true* or *false.* Have them read the sentences.

- Play the recording one or more times. **(CD2 T26)**
- Check answers.

Answers: 1. T, 2. F, 3. T, 4. F

C • Tell students to listen again and find the information. Have them read the questions.

- Play the recording one or more times. **(CD2 T26)**
- Check answers.

Answers: 1. in Switzerland, 2. her aunt, 3. California, 4. when she was five years old

---

Listening

Track 2-26

A. Do you know these people? Write the name under the photos. Listen and check.

| Albert Einstein   Jerry Yang   Salma Hayek   Anna Kournikova |

Famous immigrants to the United States

Word Focus

We say years like this:

1980 = nineteen eighty
2000 = two thousand
2009 = two thousand nine

1. _____

2. _____

3. _____

4. _____

Track 2-26

B. Listen carefully for the dates. Circle **T** for *true* and **F** for *false.*

1. Albert Einstein moved to the United States in 1933.   T   F
2. Salma Hayek was born in 1976.   T   F
3. Jerry Yang moved to San Jose in 1976.   T   F
4. Anna Kournikova moved to the United States in 1990.   T   F

Track 2-26

C. Listen again and answer the questions.

1. Where did Albert Einstein go to school? _____
2. Who did Salma Hayek live with in the United States? _____
3. Where did Jerry Yang move to in the United States? _____
4. When did Anna Kournikova start to play tennis? _____

138 Migrations

For Your Information: Immigrants

Albert Einstein, a physicist, is best known for his theory of relativity. He received the Nobel Prize for physics in 1921.

Salma Hayek is an actress, director, and TV and film producer. She is also active in groups to stop violence against women.

Jerry Yang created a Web site in 1994 called "Jerry's Guide to the World Wide Web." This became yahoo.com

Anna Kournikova is famous as a tennis player but also as a fashion model for swimsuits and sports clothes.

Pronunciation: -ed endings

A. Listen and check the correct column.

Track 2-27

B. Practice these sentences with a partner.

1. He moved to Peru in 1989.
2. They wanted to go to Egypt.
3. My mother cooked a delicious meal.
4. We walked to the beach.
5. I traveled from Buenos Aires by plane.
6. Kris wanted to buy a new coat.

	/d/ ending	/t/ ending	/ld/ ending
1. returned			
2. moved			
3. wanted			
4. traveled			
5. cooked			
6. stayed			
7. lived			
8. walked			

Communication

Look at the arrows on the map. Take turns asking where and when Alonso and Trudy went. The map shows where. You add the dates.

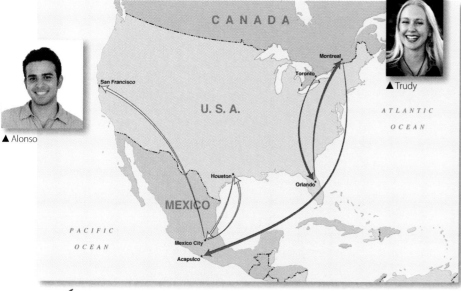

▲ Trudy

▲ Alonso

Goal 2 **Talk about moving dates**

Think of a friend or family member that has moved a lot in the past. Tell a partner where and when he or she moved.

> When did Alonso leave Mexico City?

> Where did he go?

Pronunciation

A • Remind the class that regular verbs in the simple present tense add *-ed* at the end. Point out that the *-ed* has different pronunciations (/d/ after a voiced sound, /t/ after a voiceless sound, and /id/ after *t* or *d* sounds). Tell them to listen to the pronunciations. Play the recording. **(CD2 T27)**

• Point out the differences in pronunciation. Play the recording again and have students mark the sound they hear.

• Check answers.

Answers: 1. /d/, 2 /d/, 3. /id/, 4. /d/, 5. /t/, 6. /d/, 7. /d/, 8. /t/

• Tell students to listen again and repeat the words. Play the recording.

B • Match students with a partner and have them take turns reading the sentences. Walk around listening for good pronunciation.

• Call on students to read a sentence to the class.

Communication

• Match students with a partner. Assign each partner to think of and write in dates for one of the people (Alonso or Trudy).

• Then have them ask and answer questions to get the dates that their partner wrote in.

✓ Goal 2

• Have students tell their partners about a person they know who has moved a lot.

• Compare stories with the class.

Expansion Activity

With the class, talk about what kinds of people move frequently to other countries (businesspeople, diplomats, soldiers, etc.). Would students like to have this kind of a life? Why, or why not?

Talk about Preparations for Moving

Language Expansion

- Go over the expressions for pre-moving activities. Point out the irregular past forms of the verbs in the Word Focus box.

A • Look at the checklist with the class. Then have students work individually to write sentences.
- Check answers.

Answers: 2. we didn't sell the house, 3. we sold the car, 4. we didn't get the visas, 5. we closed the bank account

Grammar

- Review the simple past tense. Go over the information in the box. Ask students a series of questions about their activities the day before: *Did you buy something new/go to a movie/get food at the supermarket?* and so on to elicit, *Yes, I did./No, I didn't.* Have students ask you questions.

Language Expansion: Preparing to move

Word Focus

Note the following irregular past tenses:

sell—sold	buy—bought
get—got	have—had

▲ sell the house   ▲ buy the tickets   ▲ pack   ▲ get a passport

▲ sell the car   ▲ close the bank account   ▲ have a farewell party

Write sentences from the checklist.

- ☑ buy the tickets
- ☐ sell the house
- ☑ sell the car
- ☐ get the passports
- ☑ close the bank account

1. _We bought the tickets._ _____
2. _____
3. _____
4. _____
5. _____

Grammar: Simple past tense

Simple past tense	
Yes/no questions	Short answers
Did they **return** to New York?	Yes, they **did**. No, they **didn't**.

Word Bank: Moving activities

rent an apartment
buy a house
find a new school for the children
notify the post office
get a new driver's license
get the water/electricity/gas turned on

For Your Information: Study in Australia

To study in Australia, international students need to get a student visa. They must submit a document stating the institution they want to apply to and the type of course they want to study; records of their previous educational qualifications; and scores on an international English test. They must pass a medical examination and show proof that they have purchased medical insurance for their time in Australia.

A. Unscramble the words to write questions.

1. farewell / party / have a / Did / they _____ ?
2. you / the / sell / house / Did _____ ?
3. Did / the / tickets / Ian / buy _____ ?
4. close / the / Did / we / windows _____ ?
5. pack / they / their / Did / things _____ ?

B. Complete the sentences. Practice them with a partner.

1. **A:** _____ buy the tickets?
   B: Yes, I _____.
2. **A:** Did you _____?
   B: No, I _____.
3. **A:** Did they _____ the house?
   B: No, _____.

Conversation

Track 2-28

A. Where are David and Liana moving? Listen to the conversation.

David: Did you <u>get the tickets</u>?
Liana: Yes, I did. Here they are.
David: Great!
Liana: And did you <u>sell the car</u>?
David: Yes, I did. I got <u>$3,000</u> for it.
Liana: Wow! Now I can buy some nice warm clothes for Canada.

B. Practice the conversation. Switch roles and practice it again.

C. Change the underlined words and make a new conversation.

✓ **Goal 3** | **Talk about preparations for moving**

You are going to Australia to study English for the summer. Make plans with a partner. Write a checklist.

Answers: 1. Did they have a farewell party? 2. Did you sell the house? 3. Did Ian buy the tickets? 4. Did we close the windows? 5. Did they pack their things?

B • Have students work individually to complete the sentences.
• Check answers.

Answers: 1. Did you, did; 2. close the windows, didn't; 3. sell, they didn't

• Match students with a partner and practice the conversations.

Conversation

A • Have students close their books. Tell them to listen to the conversation.
• Play the recording. **(CD2 T28)**

B • Play or read the conversation again for the class to repeat.
• Practice the conversation with the class in chorus.
• Have students practice the conversation with a partner and then switch roles and practice it again.

C • Have students work with the same partner to make a new conversation.
• Call on student pairs to present their conversation to the class.

✓ **Goal 3**

• Have students work with a partner to list all the things they will need to do before going to Australia.
• Compare lists with the class.

Grammar Practice: Simple past

Have students choose a trip they took in the past and think about their preparations. Then match students with a partner and have them ask and answer questions to write a list of things their partner did before the trip. Whose list is longer? Did they have a good trip?

Discuss Migrations

Reading

A • Introduce the topic of the reading. Talk about the idea of ancestors—your relatives a long time ago. With the class, look at the map and talk about where people's ancestors came from.

B • Have students read the article and find all the regular and irregular verbs. Tell them to mark any words they don't understand.
• Check answers.

Answers: regular: appeared, arrived, migrated, moved, stayed; irregular: left

• Go over the article with the class, answering any questions from the students about vocabulary.

C • Have students read the article again to answer the questions.
• Check answers.

Answers: 1. in Africa, 2. to the Middle East, 3. from the East to the West, 4. People move to find work/a good life. 5. People move because of wars.

Reading

A. At some time in the past, your ancestors moved to your country. Maybe it was 100 years ago; maybe it was 100,000 years ago. Look at the map. Where did they come from?

B. Read and underline the regular verbs and circle the irregular verbs in the simple past tense.

C. Answer the questions.

1. Where did humans first appear?
   _____

2. Where did they migrate to first?
   _____

3. How did people move across the United States? _____

4. Give an example of economic migration.
   _____

5. Give an example of forced migration.
   _____

Word Focus

migrate = to move from one place to another
economic = about money
forced = when something is not what you want
war = a fight

Human Migration

We think that modern humans appeared in Africa about 200,000 years ago. But they didn't stay in Africa. They migrated out of Africa to the Middle East and then to the rest of the world. Throughout history, people have **migrated** from one place to another. People, it seems, like to move.

▲ People moved from the East Coast of the United States to the West Coast in wagon trains.

Since the 17th century, many European people have moved from Europe to the Americas. They left Spain and Portugal and moved to South America. Many Northern Europeans migrated to North America. In the United States, most people arrived in New York. Some stayed on the East Coast, but many people migrated to the West Coast.

142 Migrations

For Your Information: Early human migration

The first humans (Homo sapiens) began to move out from Africa about 70,000 years ago and had spread all across Australia, Asia, and Europe in the following millennia. Humans reached the Americas around 15,000 years ago. The Pacific Islands were the last place to be populated, around 2000 years ago. There have been many other migrations of civilizations, such as the movement of the Turks east across Asia between the 6th and 11th centuries AD. The Vikings, Germans, and Roma ("gypsy") people all migrated across Europe during medieval times.

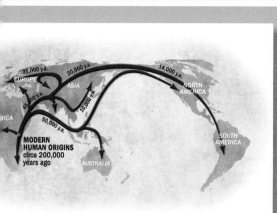

Modern Human Origins
circa 200,000 years ago

So, why do people move? First, there is **economic** migration. People move to find work and a good life. Second, there is **forced migration**. People move because of **wars**; it is not safe to stay in their homes.

These people are from the Congo, in Africa. They left their homes during the war, but now they are returning.

Of course, many people don't migrate. They stay in the same place all their lives. But people like to visit different countries on their vacations. People, it seems, just like to move.

Writing

Read the brochure and write a holiday postcard.

European Three Capital Tour

June 15th	Leave home.
June 16th	Arrive in London. The Tower of London
June 18th	London to Paris. Eiffel Tower, The Louvre
June 20th	Paris to Rome. The Coliseum
June 22nd	Rome to London.
June 23rd	London to home.

We left home on the 15th and arrived in London on the 16th. We visited

_____

_____

_____

_____

_____

Communication

 Where would you like to migrate to? Why would you like to live there? Explain to a partner and then to the class.

✓ **Goal 4** **Discuss migrations**

Animals also migrate. What animals migrate? Where do they migrate to and from? Why do they migrate?

Writing

- Ask students if they have ever gone on a tour. Where did they go? Did they write postcards about their trip?
- Go over the tour brochure and talk briefly about the places mentioned.
- Have students complete the postcard using information from the brochure.
- Have students exchange papers with a partner. Ask students to mark corrections and suggestions for improvements on their partner's paper.
- If desired, have students rewrite their papers, to be collected for marking.

Communication

- Match students with a partner and have them explain where they would like to move to and why they want to move there.
- Call on students to say interesting things they heard.

✓ **Goal 4**

- Have students tell a partner what they know about animal migrations. If necessary, introduce/review names of animals and countries.
- Then call on students to tell the class about these migrations.

After Reading

With the class, talk about groups of people who have migrated to the students' country. Where did they come from? Why did they migrate? How is their life different now?

Video Journal

Before You Watch

A • Have students complete the sentences, referring to their dictionaries as needed.

• Check answers.

Answers: 1. fragile, 2. spectacle, 3. forest, 4. Logging, destroy, 5. preserve, 6. environment, disaster

B • Have students work individually to categorize the words.

• Check answers.

Answers: positive: spectacle, preserve; negative: fragile, disaster, destroy; neutral: forest, logging, environment

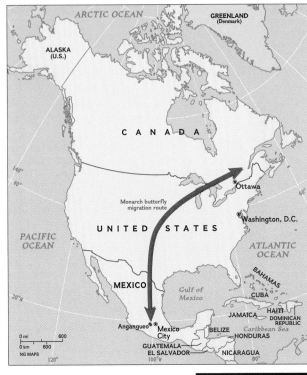

Before You Watch

A. Complete the sentences with words from the box. Use your dictionary.

spectacle	forest	fragile	environment
disaster	logging	destroy	preserve

1. Monarch butterflies are very _____. Cold temperatures can kill them.
2. The monarch migration is very beautiful. It is a _____.
3. Monarch butterflies migrate to a _____ in Mexico.
4. _____, cutting down trees, is going to _____ the forest.
5. Governments and organizations want to _____ the forest.
6. Millions of monarchs will die without their natural _____. It will be a _____.

B. Write each of the words in the box in the correct column.

Positive meaning (+)	Negative meaning (−)	Neutral meaning

144   Migrations

For Your Information: Monarch butterflies

The monarch butterfly lives mainly in North America but is also found in Australia, New Zealand, and occasionally in Western Europe. Its wingspan is about 3½ to 4 inches (9 to 10 centimeters). It was named monarch because of its large size and also its large range. To defend against predators, it produces a poisonous chemical with a bad taste, and its brilliant color pattern warns other animals not to eat it.

While You Watch

A. Watch the video. Match to complete the sentences.

1. Monarch butterflies ____
2. Monarch Watch ____
3. Loggers ____
4. The Mexican government ____

    a. pays the landowners $18 per cubic meter of wood they do not cut down.

    b. work at the University of Kansas and observe the butterfly migration.

    c. travel more than 2,000 miles every year.

    d. cut down the trees and destroy the forest.

B. Watch the video again. Write the numbers you hear.

1. More than _____ million monarch butterflies migrate each year.
2. The butterflies travel _____ miles from northern America and Canada to a Mexican forest.
3. In January 2002, a rainstorm and freezing temperatures killed _____ million butterflies.
4. Almost _____ percent of the population in the *El Rosario* butterfly sanctuary died from the cold.
5. There are _____ butterfly sanctuaries in Mexico.
6. In the last _____ years, logging destroyed nearly half the forests the monarchs need.

After you Watch

Discuss the problems of the Monarch migration in your group. Write a list of things that people can do to save these butterflies.

Communication

With a partner think of an animal or plant that has a similar problem in your country or region. Answer these questions:

1. What is the animal or plant?
2. What problem does it have?
3. How can this animal or plant be saved?

While You Watch

A • Tell students to watch the video the first time and match the sentence parts. Play the video.

    • Check answers.

Answers: 1. c, 2. b, 3. d, 4. a

B • Tell students to watch the video again and find the numbers. Have the students read the statements. Play the video.

    • Check answers.

Answers: 1. 300, 2. 2,000, 3. 250, 4. 80, 5. six, 6. 20

After You Watch

• Divide the class into groups of three or four students and have each group make a list of ways that people can help the butterflies.

• Compare lists with the class.

Communication

• Match students with a partner and have them list animals or plants that have a similar problem in their region.

• Have them answer the questions.

• Have student pairs present the problems of plants and animals in their region.

Teacher Tip: Self-evaluation

At the end of the course, it's useful to have students spend some time reflecting on the progress they've made and their goals for future learning. One way to do this is by having them fill in a questionnaire in English or their own language and then (if time permits) having a brief meeting with each student to discuss his/her answers.

Here are some possible questions you could use:

How much have you improved in these areas? Write "A lot," "Some," or "A little": Speaking/Listening/Writing/Reading/Vocabulary/Grammar

Which activities in class helped you the most?

Which activities didn't help you?

What will you do differently in your next class?

HOW TO USE THIS SECTION?

These pair and group work activities are intended to take about 5 minutes. They can be used when a lesson finishes early or for a quick break from a lesson.

Students will probably need some help with vocabulary. If a pair asks you for a word and you think it is useful for the other students, write it on the board.

Don't worry if the students make mistakes, the idea is to get them to make the best use of their limited English.

After the class has finished you may want to share information about the photo or photos they used.

Activity 1

- Review/introduce the names of countries where it snows. Review/introduce vocabulary for jobs as well as adjectives to describe people.

- Match students with a partner and have them take turns asking and answering the questions.

Activity 2

- Review vocabulary for parts of a house/apartment as well as vocabulary for electronic products. Ask questions about students' living space and electronic products they own.

- Review prepositions of place.

- Match students with a partner and have them take turns asking and answering the questions.

Activity 1
Units 1 & 2

 Take turns asking and answering the questions.

   a. Where is the Brown family from?

   b. Is it hot or cold in their country?

   c. What is Mr. Brown's job?

   d. Are they young or old?

   e. Is Mr. Brown handsome?

   f. Are the children pretty?

▲ the Brown family

Real Language

We use *I think . . .* or *Maybe . . .* when we are not sure about an answer.

I think they are from Canada.

Maybe they are from Canada.

Activity 2
Units 3 & 4

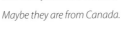 Take turns answering the questions.

   a. What furniture can you see in the house?

   b. Where is the furniture?

   c. What electronic products can you see?

   d. Where are they?

   e. What personal possessions can you see?

   f. Where are they?

Activity 3
Units 5 & 6

 Imagine a person who lives in this city. Think about these questions, then tell a partner about that person.

a. What is the person's name?
b. Where does the person live?
c. Where does the person work?
d. How does he/she get to work?
e. What route does he/she take?
f. What does he/she do at work?
g. What does the person do when he/she gets home from work?

Activity 4
Units 7 & 8

 Take turns asking and answering the questions.

a. What are these people doing?
b. What are they wearing?
c. What color are their clothes?

World English **147**

Activity 3

- Have students look at the photo. Elicit vocabulary related to the picture that they know.

- Elicit from students information about where they live, work, and leisure activities. Elicit the route for how they get to work/school. Review vocabulary for giving directions.

- Explain that individually each student will invent a fictional character. Refer students to the activity and the questions they will need to answer and have them generate a profile for their character.

- Match students with a partner and have them take turns asking and answering the questions.

Activity 4

- Have students look at the photos. Elicit vocabulary related to the picture that they know.

- Review vocabulary for clothing and colors.

- Elicit from students descriptions of the clothes they are wearing and colors. Encourage them to use the present continuous in their answers.

- Match students with a partner and have them take turns asking and answering the questions.

Activity 5

- Have students look at the first picture. Match students with a partner and have them generate a list of the fruits and vegetables they see in the picture.

- Do a class check. Provide the vocabulary any fruits and vegetables they don't know.

- Have students look at the second photo. Match students with a partner and have them generate a list of the foods they see in the picture.

- Have students focus on the questions. Model the questions and elicit answers from students.

- Match students with a partner and have them take turns asking and answering the questions about all the foods in the pictures.

Activity 5
Units 9 & 10

 What is a healthy diet? Take turns asking and answering questions like these:

    a. Should you eat _____?

    b. How much _____ should you eat every day?

148   Communication Activities

Activity 6
Units 11 & 12

Deluxe World Tour
The Tour of a Lifetime

▲ Eiffel Tower
June 20 Paris, France

▲ The Pyramids
June 22 Egypt

▲ Wildbeest migration
June 25 Kenya

▲ the Taj Mahal
June 28 India

▲ the Great Wall
July 1 China

▲ Disneyland
July 3 Los Angeles,
California, USA

STUDENT A

You are going to go on this tour. Student B took this tour last year. Ask questions like:

a. Where did you go?

b. When did you arrive in _____ ?

c. How long did you stay in _____ ?

d. What did you do in _____ ?

STUDENT B

You went on the tour last year. Student A is taking the tour this year. Ask questions like:

a. Where are you going to go?

b. How long are you staying in _____ ?

c. What are you going to do in _____ ?

Activity 6

- Elicit information of recent vacations that students have taken. Ask, *Where did you go? How long did you stay? What did you do there?*

- Elicit information of vacation trips that students are planning. If they do not have a firm plan, have them imagine one. Ask, *Where are you going to go? How long are you staying? What are you going to do there?*

- Have students look at the photos. Elicit vocabulary related to the picture that they know.

- Match students with a partner. Assign roles. Have them role-play the situation.

- When they finish, have them exchange roles and practice again.

Grammar

adjectives, 8
    + *be,* 8–9
    demonstrative, 41
    possessive, 5
    some and *any,* 101
indefinite articles, 17
how much and *how many,* 105
nouns
    countable and uncountable, 104
    plural endings, 28
prepositions of place, 32–33, 65
there is/there are, 28–29
verbs, 8
    be + adjective, 8–9
    be + adjective + noun, 20–21
    be + *not,* 16
    be going to, 125
    can for ability, 81
    can/could (polite requests), 89
    contractions with *be,* 5, 16, 19
    feel, look, 112
    have, 45
    have to, 69
    imperatives, 65
    likes and dislikes, 92–93
    present continuous tense, 76–77
    present tense *be,* 5
    questions with *be* and short answers, 9
    should for advice, 116
    simple past tense, 136–137, 140
    simple present tense–questions and answers, 56–57
    simple present tense–statements and negatives, 52–53
    would like to for wishes, 128–129

Listening

biographical information, 138
conversations, 5, 6, 9, 17, 21, 29, 33, 41, 42, 45, 53, 57, 65, 69, 77, 78, 81, 89, 93, 114, 117, 125, 137, 141
descriptions, 30–31, 81, 90, 114
discussions, 126
interviews, 18, 54, 57
introductions, 5, 6
party planning, 102
telephone conversations, 77, 78
walking tours, 66

Pronunciation

and, 103
be going to (short form), 127
contractions with *be,* 19
could you, 91
-ed endings, 139
falling intonations on statements and information questions, 55
final-*s,* 31
/r/ sound, 7
sh and *ch* sounds, 79
short *i* and long *e* sound, 43
word stress, 115
yes/no questions, 67

Reading skills, 10, 18, 22, 34, 46, 58, 64, 70, 82, 94, 106, 118, 130, 142

Readings

Chameleon Clothes, 94–95
Different Farmers, 22–23
Families around the World, 10–11
Human Migration, 142–143
Jewelry, 46–47
Life's Milestones, 130–131
Preventing Disease, 118–119
Robots at Work, 58–59
Shackleton's Epic Journey–a Diary, 70–71
Special Days, Special Food, 106–107
Sports–Then and Now, 82–83
Unusual Houses, 34–35

Speaking

asking for/giving directions, 67
asking/answering questions, 19, 21, 29, 41, 42, 43, 47, 54, 55, 57, 61, 65, 67, 68, 69, 95, 105, 107, 133, 139, 141, 145
comparing, 35
conversations, 5, 9, 17, 21, 29, 33, 41, 45, 53, 57, 65, 69, 77, 79, 81, 93, 105, 113, 115, 117, 119, 125, 129, 137, 139, 141
describing, 7, 11, 23, 25, 31, 91, 115
discussing, 23, 115, 127, 143
giving advice, 117, 119
greetings and introductions, 4
interviewing, 19, 57, 80, 105
making plans, 102, 103, 129, 131
ordering food, 101

party planning, 102, 103
role playing, 115
telephone conversations, 77, 79

Test-taking skills

checking off answers, 31, 43, 48, 61, 79, 91, 93, 103, 118, 130, 139
circling answers, 10, 97, 136
fill in the blanks, 7, 8, 17, 25, 28, 35, 44, 49, 64, 65, 133, 145
labeling answers, 12, 24, 40, 44, 72, 76, 109
matching, 9, 30, 37, 41, 49, 57, 73, 90, 94, 97, 113, 117, 128, 137
multiple choice, 70, 97, 145
ranking answers, 133
sentence completion, 10, 13, 22, 25, 29, 33, 44, 45, 49, 52, 53, 57, 61, 64, 65, 69, 72, 77, 81, 88, 101, 105, 113, 119, 120, 124, 137, 141, 144
true or false, 6, 12, 17, 25, 31, 37, 42, 46, 58, 82, 85, 94, 118, 121, 138
underlining answers, 7, 9, 142
unscrambling sentences, 5, 21, 29, 53, 77, 101, 129, 141

Topics

Clothes, 86–97
Daily Activities, 50–61
Eating Well, 98–109
Free Time, 74–85
Friends and Family, 2–13
Getting There, 62–73
Health, 110–121
Houses and Apartments, 26–37
Jobs around the World, 14–25
Making Plans, 122–133
Migrations, 134–145
Possessions, 38–49

Video Journals

Animal Families, 12–13
Inuit Fashion, 96–97
A Job for Children, 24–25
Land Divers of Vanuatu, 84–85
Making a Thai Boxing Champion, 132–133
Monarch Butterflies, 144–145
Pyrethrum, 120–121
Slow Food, 108–109
Uncovering the Past, 48–49
A Very Special Village, 36–37
Volcano Trek, 72–73
Zoo Dentists, 60–61

Vocabulary

body parts, 112
clothing, 92
colors, 92
countable/uncountable nouns, 104
countries and cities, 20
directions, 64
electronic products, 44
foods, 100
furniture and household objects, 32
greetings and introductions, 4
ground transportation, 68
health and illness, 112, 116
jobs, 16
leisure activities, 76, 80, 124
moving, 136, 140
personal descriptions, 8
personal possessions, 40
planning activities, 124
professions, 128
remedies, 116
rooms in a house, 28
sports, 76, 80
time expressions, 52, 53
work activities, 56

Writing

activities, 83
descriptions, 11, 35, 47, 95
diaries, 71
interviews, 47
job descriptions, 59
meals, 107
notices, 119
paragraphs, 23, 35
personal descriptions, 47, 83
postcards, 143
sentences, 83
wishes and plans, 131

ILLUSTRATION

iv-v: National Geographic Maps; **6:** Ted Hammond/IllustrationOnline.com; **7:** Nesbitt Graphics, Inc.; **8:** Ted Hammond/IllustrationOnline.com; **11, 12, 20, 22, 23:** National Geographic Maps; **24, 25:** (all) Bob Kayganich/IllustrationOnline.com; **28:** (both) Patrick Gnan/IllustrationOnline.com; **29:** Nesbitt Graphics, Inc.; **32, 33, 35:** (all) Patrick Gnan/IllustrationOnline.com; **36:** (t) Mapping Specialists, Ltd. Madison, WI, USA, (br) Bob Kayganich/IllustrationOnline.com; **40:** Bob Kayganich/IllustrationOnline.com; **44, 52, 54:** Nesbitt Graphics, Inc.; **60:** National Geographic Maps; **64, 65:** Bob Kayganich/IllustrationOnline.com; **66:** National Geographic Maps; **68:** Nesbitt Graphics, Inc.; **70:** National Geographic Maps; **72:** (l) Mapping Specialists, Ltd. Madison, WI, USA, (r) Bob Kayganich/IllustrationOnLine.com; **78:** Keith Neely/IllustrationOnline.com; **85:** National Geographic Maps; **88:** (t) Nesbitt Graphics, Inc., (b) Keith Neely/IllustrationOnline.com; **92:** Nesbitt Graphics, Inc; **96:** National Geographic Maps; **102, 103, 104:** Bob Kayganich/IllustrationOnline.com; **112, 114:** Ralph Voltz/IllustrationOnLine.com; **118, 119, 121:** National Geographic Maps; **124:** Nesbitt Graphics, Inc.; **132:** National Geographic Maps; **136:** Ted Hammond/IllustrationOnline.com; **139:** Patrick Gnan/IllustrationOnline.com; **143, 144:** National Geographic Maps.

T194: Ted Hammond/IllustrationOnLine.com; **T196:** Patrick Gnan /IllustrationOnLine.com; **T197, T199:** Nesbitt Graphics, Inc.; **T201:** Ted Hammond/IllustrationOnLine.com.

PHOTO

Cover photo: Remi Benali/Corbis.

iv: (tl) PhotostoGo.com, (mr) Gail Johnson/Shutterstock, (b) Charles Shapiro/ Shutterstock; **v:** (tl) Kheng Guan Toh/Shutterstock, (tr) Upperhall/JupiterImages, (m) Steve Silver/AGE Fotostock, (b) David Reed/AGE Fotostock; **2–3:** (l to r) Annie Griffiths Belt/National Geographic Image Collection, Winfield Parks/National Geographic Image Collection, Ira Block/National Geographic Image Collection, Steve Winter/National Geographic Image Collection; **4:** (tl) photos.com, (tr) Sharon Dominick /iStockphoto, (tr, background) Rade Kovac/Shutterstock, (bl) Jacob Wackerhausen / iStockphoto, (br) BananaStock/JupiterImages; **6:** (l) Aldo Murillo/iStockphoto, (m) Blend Images/JupiterImages, (r) Jennifer Zolzer/iStockphoto; **8:** (top, l to r) iStockphoto (2), Stephanie phillips/iStockphoto, PhotostoGo.com, (middle, t to b) iStockphoto, Shelly Perry/iStockphoto, iStockphoto, Pete Collins/iStockphoto; **9:** (t) AVAVA/Shutterstock, (b) Kevin Russ/iStockphoto; **10:** (t) Joey Nelson/iStockphoto, (b) Michael S. Yamashita/National Geographic Image Collection; **11:** (l) Kris Leboutillier/National Geographic Image Collection, (right, clockwise from tl) Jacob Wackerhausen/iStockphoto, Kevin Russ/iStockphoto, Oleg Dubas/Shutterstock, Carmen Martínez Banús/iStockphoto; **12–13:** (l to r) Dan Westergren/National Geographic Image Collection, Joel Sartore/National Geographic Image Collection, Maria Stenzel/National Geographic Image Collection, Clickit/Shutterstock, George F. Mobley/National Geographic Image Collection, Frans Lanting/National Geographic Image Collection, Clickit/Shutterstock, Dan Westergren/National Geographic Image Collection; **12:** (1) Michael Nichols/National Geographic Image Collection, (2) Nico Smit/iStockphoto, (3) Joel Sartore/National Geographic Image Collection, (4) photos.com, (5) Chris Johns/National Geographic Image Collection, (6) Nico Smit/iStockphoto; **13:** (bottom, l to r) Chris Johns/National Geographic Image Collection, Tubuceo/Shutterstock, iStockphoto, Joel Sartore/National Geographic Image Collection, John Pitcher/iStockphoto; **14–15:** (l to r) Charles O'Rear/National Geographic Image Collection, Tino Soriano/National Geographic Image Collection, Xinhua /Landov, George F. Mobley/National Geographic Image Collection; **16:** (1) PhotostoGo.com, (2) H. Edward Kim/National Geographic Image Collection, (3) Carrie Bottomley/iStockphoto, (4) Theo Westenberger/National Geographic Image Collection, (5) Comstock Images/JupiterImages, (6) Jose Manuel Gelpi Diaz/iStockphoto, (7) Andrew Lever/Shutterstock, (8) iStockphoto; **17:** PhotostoGo.com; **18:** (l) Bonnie Jacobs/iStockphoto, (m) Wilson Valentin/iStockphoto, (r) Diego Cervo/Shutterstock; **19:** Andrea Gingerich/iStockphoto; **20:** (l to r) Lars Christensen/iStockphoto, Giorgio Fochesato/iStockphoto, Vladimirs Koskins/Shutterstock, Surkov Vladimir/Shutterstock; **21:** Digital Vision/Getty Images; **22:** James L. Amos/National Geographic Image Collection; **23:** (top, l to r) Tish1/Shutterstock, Yali Shi/iStockphoto, John Scofield/National Geographic Image Collection, Jupiterimages/Getty Images, (b) W. Robert Moore/National Geographic Image Collection; **24–25:** (l to r) Franziska Lang/Shutterstock, Rita Januskeviciute/Shutterstock, Josep Pique Alecha/iStockphoto, Gail Johnson/Shutterstock, Sophie Demange/iStockphoto, Chris Pole/Shutterstock, Gail Johnson/Shutterstock, Sophie Demange/iStockphoto; **24:** (b) Sophie Demange/iStockphoto; **25:** (b) Robert S. Patton/National Geographic Image Collection; **26–27:** (l to r) Justin Guariglia/National Geographic Image Collection, Michael Shake/Shutterstock, PhotostoGo.com, Ed Kashi/National Geographic Image Collection; **29:** Justin Horrocks/iStockphoto; **30:** (tl) Keisuke Iwamoto/Sebun Photo/Getty Images, (tr) Steve Lovegrove/iStockphoto, (ml) RCPPHOTO/Shutterstock, (mr) David Hughes/Shutterstock, (b) Rohit Seth/Shutterstock; **31:** (l) Thierry Maffeis/Shutterstock, (r) Mike J Roberts/Shutterstock; **32:** (top, l to r) Stephanie Phillips/iStockphoto, Maksym Bondarchuk/iStockphoto, James Phelps/iStockphoto, Geoffrey Holman/iStockphoto, (middle, l to r) Lars Christensen/iStockphoto, Simon Krži/iStockphoto, Bonita Hein/iStockphoto, trailexplorers/Shutterstock, (bottom, l to r) Dmitry Kutlayev/iStockphoto, Arthur Fatykhov/iStockphoto, Margo Harrison/Shutterstock, White Smoke/Shutterstock; **33:** (top, l to r) Joy Brown/Shutterstock, Juriah Mosin/Shutterstock, photos.com, Harry Hu/Shutterstock, Ryan McVay/AGE Fotostock, (bl) Chris Rodenberg Photography/Shutterstock, (br) PhotostoGo.com; **34:** (l) George Steinmetz Photography, (tr) George Steinmetz/National Geographic Image Collection, (br) Norbert Rosing/National Geographic Image Collection; **35:** (t) Photodisc/Getty Images, (b) Tomasz Broszkiewicz; **36–37:** (l to r) PhotostoGo.com, Seet/Shutterstock, Massimo Bassano/National Geographic Image Collection, Antonio S./Shutterstock, PhotostoGo.com, Lucio Pompeo/iStockphoto, Antonio S./Shutterstock, Massimo Bassano/National Geographic Image Collection;

36: (ml) Antonio S./Shutterstock, (mr) Dan Clausen/Shutterstock, (bl) Knud Nielsen/Shutterstock; 37: (m) Bruno Morandi/AGE Fotostock, (b) Lucio Pompeo/iStockphoto; 38–39: (l to r) Bill Curtsinger/National Geographic Image Collection, Medford Taylor/National Geographic Image Collection, Saxpix.com/AGE Fotostock, Peter Cook/AGE Fotostock; 40: (1) Jon Helgason/iStockphoto, (2) José Luis Gutiérrez/iStockphoto, (3) Thomas Perkins/iStockphoto, (4) Wendell Franks/iStockphoto, (5) iStockphoto, (6) Igor Grochev/Shutterstock, (7) iStockphoto, (8) Alexphoto/Shutterstock, (9) BrunoSINNAH/Shutterstock, (10) iStockphoto, (11) Jocicalek/Shutterstock, (12) John Rawsterne/iStockphoto; 41: (t to b) Nicolaas Weber/iStockphoto, iStockphoto, Sebastien Cote/iStockphoto, iStockphoto, Dave White/iStockphoto; 42: (tl) Mario Tama/Getty Images, (tr) Jupiterimages/Getty Images, (b) Nikola Hristovski/iStockphoto; 43: (t) Iain Sarjeant/iStockphoto, (m) Catharina van den Dikkenberg/iStockphoto, (b) Damir Karan/Shutterstock; 44: (clockwise from tl) Dragan Trifunovic/iStockphoto, Aleksandr Doodko/Shutterstock, Gadom88/Shutterstock, Mark Blinch/Reuters/Landov, Lee Pettet/iStockphoto, Matjaz Boncina/iStockphoto, Michael Ransburg/Shutterstock, Jossnat/Shutterstock, Arvind Balaraman/Shutterstock; 45: photos.com; 46: (tl) Jodi Cobb/National Geographic Image Collection, (tm) Nathan Holland/Shutterstock, (tr) Carol Beckwith and Angela Fisher/Getty Images, (b) Sisse Brimberg/National Geographic Image Collection; 47: (t) Jonathan Blair/National Geographic Image Collection, (b) Sisse Brimberg/National Geographic Image Collection; 48–49: (l to r) iStockphoto (2), Maria Stenzel/National Geographic Image Collection, Stephen Alvarez/National Geographic Image Collection, photobank.ch/Shutterstock, Alf Ertsland/iStockphoto, iStockphoto, Maria Stenzel/National Geographic Image Collection; 48: (middle, clockwise from tr) Samantha Grandy/iStockphoto, Richard Barnes/National Geographic Image Collection, Kenneth Garrett/National Geographic Image Collection, Stephen Alvarez/National Geographic Image Collection (2), iStockphoto, (b) iStockphoto; 49: (bottom, l to r) Alf Ertsland/iStockphoto, Zoran Kolundzija/iStockphoto, Dave Willman/iStockphoto, iStockphoto; 50–51: (l to r) Yuri Arcurs/Shutterstock, Marcus Clackson/iStockphoto, Michael S. Yamashita/National Geographic Image Collection, Ira Block/National Geographic Image Collection; 52: (top, l to r) Rich Legg/iStockphoto, CW Images/Alamy, Stockbyte/Getty Images, Stephen Coburn/Shutterstock,

(bottom, l to r) Robyn Roper/iStockphoto, Александр Васильев/iStockphoto, photos.com, Catherine Yeulet/iStockphoto; 53: Zhang Bo/iStockphoto; 54: (all) Joel Sartore/National Geographic Image Collection; 55: iStockphoto; 56: (top, l to r) PhotostoGo.com, Michael DeLeon/iStockphoto, PhotostoGo.com, Dallas Events Inc/Shutterstock, (bottom, l to r) Junial Enterprises/Shutterstock, Sean Locke/iStockphoto, Creatas Images/JupiterImages, Rob Friedman/iStockphoto; 57: iStockphoto; 58: (t) Ljupco Smokovski/Shutterstock, (m) NASA, (b) George Steinmetz/National Geographic Image Collection; 59: (t) David Doubilet/National Geographic Image Collection, (m) Mike Segar/Reuters/Landov, (b) NASA; 60–61: (l to r) Andy Z./Shutterstock, Vadim Kozlovsky/Shutterstock, Alexey Arkhipov/Shutterstock, Henk Bentlage/Shutterstock, Ewan Chesser/Shutterstock, Leslie Banks/iStockphoto, Andy Z./Shutterstock, Henk Bentlage/Shutterstock; 60: (ml) Vadim Kozlovsky/Shutterstock, (mr) Karen Kuehn/National Geographic Image Collection, (1) Fritzkocher/Shutterstock, (2) David T Gomez/iStockphoto, (3) Auke Holwerda/iStockphoto, (4) Cen/Shutterstock, (5 & 6) Roberto A Sanchez/iStockphoto, (7) iStockphoto; 61: Alexey Arkhipov/Shutterstock; 62–63: (l to r) Richard Nowitz/National Geographic Image Collection, AGE Fotostock/SuperStock, Thomas Nord/Shutterstock, Kike Calvo/V&W/The Image Works; 65: Trista Weibell/iStockphoto; 66: Mark Bassett/Alamy; 67: Yegorius/Shutterstock; 68: (tl) PhotostoGo.com, (tr) Robert Pernell/Shutterstock, (ml) Charlie Hutton/Shutterstock, (mr) PhotostoGo.com, (bl) Michal Napartowicz/Shutterstock, (br) Corbis RF/JupiterImages; 69: Blend Images/JupiterImages; 70, 71: (all) Royal Geographical Society; 72–73: (l to r) Carsten Peter/National Geographic Image Collection, Valery Shanin/Shutterstock, Dengmh3602/Shutterstock, Steve Raymer/National Geographic Image Collection, James L. Amos/National Geographic Image Collection, Danny Warren/Shutterstock, Dengmh3602/Shutterstock, Steve Raymer/National Geographic Image Collection; 72: (m) iStockphoto, (bottom, l to r) Erick N/Shutterstock, Steve Raymer/National Geographic Image Collection, James L. Amos/National Geographic Image Collection, Danny Warren/Shutterstock, Borge Ousland/National Geographic Image Collection; 73: (ml) Sergio B./Shutterstock, (mr) Chad Truemper/iStockphoto, (b) Carsten Peter/National Geographic Image Collection; 74–75: (l to r) Jim Richardson/National Geographic Image

Collection, Michael Krinke/iStockphoto, Stefan Ataman/Shutterstock, Michael S. Yamashita/National Geographic Image Collection; 76: (1) iStockphoto, (2) Supri Suharjoto/Shutterstock, (3) iStockphoto, (4) Monkey Business Images/Shutterstock, (5) Orpheus/Shutterstock, (6) Stuart Cohen/The Image Works, (7) Andrew Rich/iStockphoto, (8) Ivonne Wierink-vanWetten/iStockphoto; 77: BananaStock/JupiterImages; 79: (l) Paul Kline/iStockphoto, (m) Edward Bock/iStockphoto, (r) Jason Stitt/Shutterstock; 80: (1) Schmid Christophe/Shutterstock, (2) Alberto L. Pomares G./iStockphoto, (3) Richard Paul Kane/Shutterstock, (4) Alan C. Heison/Shutterstock, (5) Wolfgang Amri/Shutterstock, (6) Wouter van Caspel/iStockphoto, (7) Ina Peters/iStockphoto, (8) Galina Barskaya/Shutterstock; 81: Daniel Deitschel/iStockphoto; 82: (t) Daniel Deitschel/iStockphoto, (ml) iStockphoto, (mr) Bettmann/Corbis, (b) Pete Niesen/Shutterstock; 83: (t) Jan and Terry Todd Collection/AP Images, (m) Dimitri Iundt, Franck Seguin/TempSport/Corbis, (bl) Guy Magee Jr./National Geographic Image Collection, (br) photos.com; 84–85: (l to r) Eldad Yitzhak/Shutterstock, Upperhall/JupiterImages, Danita Delimont/Alamy, Andreas Fischer/iStockphoto, Xavier Marchant/Shutterstock, Holger Mette/iStockphoto, Upperhall/JupiterImages, Danita Delimont/Alamy; 84: (ml) Studio DL/Corbis, (mc) Sean Locke/iStockphoto, (mr) Mandy Godbehear/Shutterstock, (bottom, l to r) Daniel Brunner/iStockphoto, Elena Talberg/Shutterstock, Bociek666/Shutterstock, Jan Kranendonk/Shutterstock, Ilja Mašík/Shutterstock; 85: (b) Upperhall/JupiterImages; 86–87: (l to r) Robert B. Goodman/National Geographic Image Collection, John Scofield/National Geographic Image Collection, DEX Image/JupiterImages, Radius Images/JupiterImages; 88: (top, l to r) iStockphoto, Elnur/Shutterstock, Terekhov Igor/Shutterstock, Karkas/Shutterstock, iStockphoto, (bottom, l to r) Alexander Kalina/Shutterstock, iStockphoto, Dario Sabljak/Shutterstock, Francesco Ridolfi/iStockphoto, iStockphoto; 89: Josef Philipp/iStockphoto; 90: (tl) iStockphoto, (tr) Justin Guariglia/National Geographic Image Collection, (bl) Joel Sartore/National Geographic Image Collection, (br) Reza/National Geographic Image Collection; 92: (l to r) Camilla Wisbauer/iStockphoto, photos.com (2), Kati Molin/iStockphoto, Jani Bryson/iStockphoto; 93: Brand X Pictures/JupiterImages; 94: (t) Gerry Ellis/Minden Pictures/National Geographic Image Collection, (b) Jason Edwards/National Geographic Image Collection; 95: (t both) Botanica/JupiterImages,

UNIT 1

LESSON B, LISTENING

Track 1-6

Carlos: My name is Carlos and this is my family. This is my mother. Her name is Elena. This is my father. His name is Jose Manuel. This is my sister. Her name is Karina.

Now, these are my grandparents. This is my grandfather. His name is Pedro and this is my grandmother. She's Susana. Here's another photo. These are our dogs. Their names are Lucy and Lulu. I love my family.

UNIT 2

LESSON A, VOCABULARY

Track 1-9

1. Oscar is a teacher.

2. Eun is an artist.

3. Jane is an engineer.

4. Dae-Jung is a chef.

5. Jim is a taxi driver.

6. Hannah is a doctor.

7. Harvey is a banker.

8. Fernanda is an architect.

LESSON B, LISTENING

Track 1-11

Michelle: Hello, my name is Michelle. I'm 35 years old and I'm an artist. I love my job. It's very interesting.

Carlos: Hi! My name is Carlos. I'm 43 years old and I'm a taxi driver. My job is not very interesting.

Salim: Hello. My name is Salim and I'm an architect. I'm 34. I like my job. It's interesting.

UNIT 3

LESSON B, LISTENING

Betty: Hello, my name is Betty and this is my house. It is a small house, but it has a big yard. There is just one bedroom in my house.

Joe: My name is Joe and this is my house. It is a big house with a very big garden. On the first floor there is the kitchen, dining room, and living room. On the second floor, there are five bedrooms and three bathrooms. My favorite place though is the garden.

Katsuro: My name is Katsuro and I am from Hokkaido in Japan. This is my house in winter. It is cold in Hokkaido and so there is a fireplace in my living room. Can you see the chimney outside?

Ramon: My name is Ramon Garcia and this is my house in Mexico City. I have a big family so I need a big house. There is a big living room and a dining room with a beautiful view. There are six bedrooms and seven bathrooms. But best of all, there is also an indoor swimming pool. We are lucky, we have a beautiful house.

Liling: Hello! My name is Liling and I am from Hong Kong. This is my apartment. It is *very* small. This is my bedroom. It is also my living room and my dining room! There's a kitchen and a bathroom, but they are also very small.

UNIT 4

LESSON B, LISTENING

Conversation 1

Security: Excuse me, madam. Is this your bag?

Gill: Yes, it is.

Security: What do you have in it?

Gill: There are my books: a notebook, a dictionary, and my *World English* book.

Security: Is that all?

Gill: Oh, yes, and my wallet.

Security: OK, thank you.

Conversation 2

Security: Excuse me, sir. Is that your bag?

Lee: Yes, it is.

Security: What do you have in it, sir?

Lee: My cell phone and my wallet.

Security: Is that all?

Lee: Yes, that's all.

Security: OK, thank you.

UNIT 5

🎧 LESSON B, LISTENING

Track 1-23

Interviewer: This morning we have Joel Sartore, the photographer, with us. Good morning, Joel.

Joel: Good morning, Jane.

Interviewer: First, can I say I love your photos.

Joel: Thank you.

Interviewer: So, what is your secret? How do you take such beautiful photos?

Joel: It's easy. I get up early, like at six o'clock, and take some photos. Then I take a nap at twelve o'clock.

Interviewer: You take a nap!

Joel: Yes, I take a nap. And then in the evening, like about eight o'clock, I take some more photos. The secret is the light. The light is good early in the morning and late in the evening.

Interviewer: I see. Thanks for the tip.

UNIT 6

LESSON B, LISTENING

Track 1-27

Tour guide:
Welcome to New York's Store Window Walking Tour. The tour starts at Bloomingdale's. From Bloomingdale's, walk two blocks along East 60th Street. Turn right on Madison Avenue and you will see Barneys. From Barneys, walk one block along East 61st Street and turn left on 5th Avenue. Walk for two blocks, and FAO Schwarz is across from Grand Army Plaza. Then cross 5th Avenue and there is Bergdorf Goodman on the corner of 5th Avenue and East 58th Street. And finally, on the corner of East 57th Street and 5th Avenue is Tiffany & Co.

UNIT 7

LESSON A, VOCABULARY

Track 2-2

1. Katie is watching TV.

2. Lok is playing the guitar.

3. Ben is cooking.

4. Omar is reading

5. Mariko is listening to music.

6. Crystal is drawing.

7. Tom and Susan are going to the movies.

8. Tony is going for a walk.

LESSON B, LISTENING

Track 2-4

Conversation 1

Angela: Hi, Mike! What are you doing?

Mike: Hi, Angela! Well, I'm reading.

Angela: Reading! You don't usually read. What are you reading?

Mike: I'm reading a guitar magazine.

Angela: OK, that's more like you!

Conversation 2

Husband: Hi, honey!

Wife: Hi, Dave. Look, can I call you back?

Husband: Why? What are you doing?

Wife: I'm meeting some clients. It's important.

Husband: OK, but don't forget. *I'm* important, too!

Conversation 3

Paul: Hi, Salma. What's happening?

Salma: Sorry, can you speak up. I can't hear you.

Paul: Sorry. What are you doing?

Salma: Oh, I'm listening to music.

Paul: Well, turn it down!

🎧 LESSON B, PRONUNCIATION
Track 2-5

1. watch

2. sheep

3. share

4. chip

5. cash

6. shop

7. shoes

UNIT 8

LESSON B, LISTENING

Track 2-8

Zahra is wearing black. All of her clothes are black.

This is Helen. She is calling a taxi. She is wearing a white coat and brown pants.

Dave is leaving for work. He is wearing a black jacket and a purple tie.

Jenny is walking in the park. She is wearing a coat, scarf, and hat.

LESSON B, PRONUNCIATION

Track 2-9

1. Could you call a taxi, please?

2. /kudjə/ call a taxi, please?

3. /kudjə/ help me, please?

4. Could you help me, please?

5. Could you repeat that, please?

6. /kudjə/ repeat that, please?

UNIT 9

LESSON B, LISTENING

Track 2-12

Miguel:　　OK, what do we need to buy for the party?

Diana:　　Well, we need some drinks. Get 12 bottles of soda.

Miguel:　　OK. And food?

Diana:　　Wait a minute. We need some ice. One bag, I think.

Miguel:　　OK, one bag of ice.

Diana:　　Now food. Do we have any hamburgers?

Miguel:　　No, we don't. So, we need, say, 20 hamburgers.

Diana:　　OK. Let me see. Anything else?

Miguel: Hot dogs?

Diana: Good idea. OK, 10 hot dogs.

 LESSON B, PRONUNCIATION

Track 2-13

1. pasta and salad

2. pasta 'n' salad

3. fruit juice 'n' cereal

4. fruit juice and cereal

5. chocolate cake and ice cream

6. chocolate cake 'n' ice cream

UNIT 10

 LESSON B, LISTENING

Track 2-17

Conversation A

Doctor: So, how can I help you?

Patient: I have a headache, doctor.

Doctor: Mmm. Anything else?

Patient: Yes, I have a backache as well.

Doctor: Do you have a fever?

Patient: Yes, doctor. I do.

Doctor: OK, I think you have malaria.

Conversation B

Doctor: Good morning, what can I do for you?

Patient: Good morning doctor. I have a cough and I don't feel well.

Doctor:	You don't feel well? Can you explain?
Patient:	Well, I have a stomachache and I have a fever as well.
Doctor:	Mmm, oh dear! OK, I think I need to examine you.

UNIT 11

 LESSON B, LISTENING

Track 2-22

Conversation 1

Kenichi:	So Linda, what are you going to do for the holiday?
Linda:	Well, I'm not going to go to Times Square this year.
Kenichi:	Why?
Linda:	Because there are too many people.
Kenichi:	So what are you going to do?
Linda:	I'm going to stay home with my family. What are you going to do, Kenichi?
Kenichi:	I'm going to go to a party with my girlfriend.
Linda:	Great. Hope you have a good time!
Kenichi:	And you!

Conversation 2

Tom:	What are you going to do for the holiday, Maria?
Maria:	I don't know. What are you going to do?
Tom:	Well, I'm going to go downtown and watch the fireworks. Do you want to come?
Maria:	Sure! What time?
Tom:	We're going to leave at about six o'clock. OK?
Maria:	Great!

LESSON B, PRONUNCIATION

Track 2-23

1. We're going to have a party.

2. We're /gʌnə/ have a party.

3. I'm /gʌnə/ go to Paris.

4. I'm going to go to Paris.

5. They're not going to come.

6. They're not /gʌnə/ to come.

UNIT 12

LESSON B, LISTENING

Track 2-26

1. Albert Einstein

Albert Einstein was born in Germany in 1879. His family moved to Milan, but Albert went to school in Switzerland in 1895. He graduated from college in Switzerland. He lived in Switzerland for 28 years and then moved to the United States in 1933.

2. Salma Hayek

Salma Hayek was born in Mexico in 1966. In 1978, at the age of 12, she moved to the United States to go to school, but soon returned to Mexico. Later, she again went to the United States to live with her aunt and did not return to Mexico until 1983. She moved to the United States again in 1991 and became an American citizen.

3. Jerry Yang

Jerry Yang was born on November 6, 1968, in Taipei, Taiwan. At the age of eight, in 1976 he moved to San Jose, California, with his mother and brother. When he arrived in America, he only knew one word of English—*shoe*. However, he learned quickly and, in 1994, with a partner started the company Yahoo! Inc.

4. Anna Kournikova

Anna Kournikova was born in Moscow in 1981. She started playing tennis when she was five years old. She moved to the United States in 1991 to study tennis.

UNIT 1

VIDEO JOURNAL *ANIMAL FAMILIES*

NARRATOR: People live in families. Some families are big. Other families are small.

Some animals live alone.

But many animals live in family groups as well.

These are lions. They live in family groups. There are usually 5 to 7 females in the group.

In the group, there is usually only one male. He has long hair on his neck. He is very handsome. He is the father of all the young lions. These are his sons and daughters.

This is a family of meerkats. It is a big family. There are 20 to 30 meerkats in the family.

This is the alpha pair. They are the leaders. They are the mother and father of all the young meerkats. Aren't they pretty!

This is a family of gorillas. This is the leader of the family. He has silver hair on his back. He is the father of all the young gorillas in the group. There are seven females. They are the mothers of all the young gorillas.

Families are important for animals and for people.

UNIT 2

VIDEO JOURNAL *A JOB FOR CHILDREN*

NARRATOR: Einar and his sister Andrea are from Heimaey, in Iceland, a small country in Europe. They have a very interesting job. They have a box. In their box they have two young puffins, or pufflings. Einar and Andrea help these birds. They want to rescue them.

EINAR, Age 14, Heimaey Resident: They don't survive if they stay in the town. Cats and dogs eat them, or they just die. It's really good to rescue them.

NARRATOR: The children of Heimaey rescue young puffins, or 'pufflings'. Every summer, they help pufflings get to the sea. It is their job.

AGNES, Heimaey Parent: The children rescue the birds. If they don't do it, the puffins die. The children's job is exciting.

NARRATOR: They take the lost pufflings to the beach. Then they throw the pufflings into the sky. How do the pufflings get lost?

The pufflings leave their nests in the cliffs. They fly out to sea. They see the lights of Heimaey and they fly into the town! People find the puffins on the streets. The children of Heimaey help them.

Each night in summer, mothers and fathers go with their children to look for lost pufflings. They use flashlights. The pier is a good place to look for pufflings. They rescue the pufflings from the streets. It's hard work. Olaf Holm and his six-year-old son Andrew are looking for pufflings. They look carefully. They have a bird!

OLAF AND ANDREW, Puffling Patrollers: We found this puffling in the parking lot.

NARRATOR: The next day, the children take the birds to the beach. The children point the birds to the sea. They throw the young puffin to the sea. The little puffins swim or fly to safety. The children like their job. They are happy.

There are eight to ten million puffins in Iceland. Every year, the children work to look for puffins. Here, children of Heimaey rescue lost pufflings.

UNIT 3

VIDEO JOURNAL *A VERY SPECIAL VILLAGE*

NARRATOR: Camogli is a town on the Italian coast. The sun shines on the houses next to the sea. But, this town is different.

In the town of Camogli, things look real…but they're not.

This fishing village near Genoa is full of *trompe l'oeil*— a special art. In *trompe l'oeil* things are not real.

In this village, windows open — in solid walls. Beautiful stonework is paint! And the flowers are not real. They are painted on the buildings!

In the past, Camogli's fishermen painted their houses in bright colors and unusual designs. The fishermen wanted to see their homes from the water.

Then, in the 1700s, this art made small, simple buildings look special and expensive.

There are thousands of *trompe l'oeil* houses in this area. But only a few artists paint them.

Raffaella Stracca is an artist. Raffaella uses old and new methods in her work.

"You find a lot of these painted facades in the area of Liguria a lot.

NARRATOR: It is difficult to be a good *trompe l'oeil* painter. Rafaella has worked for 20 years to paint stone so it looks real.

Carlo Pere is an artist. He paints *trompe l'oeil* for people who live in small houses or city apartments. They want Pere's *trompe l'oeil* terraces and balconies.

Carlo feels that *trompe l'oeil* Is special.

"*Trompe l'oeil* means bringing the central city of Milan to the sea, or the sea to the mountains…or even the mountains to the sea."

NARRATOR: Carlos uses an art book from the 1300s to study *trompe l'oeil*. He uses traditional-style paints.

He wants to protect the *trompe l'oeil* traditions.

In this part of Italy, you can still see the local culture everywhere. It's in the street, in the bay and in the cafés of the town. But in Camogli what you see is not always real.

UNIT 4

VIDEO JOURNAL *UNCOVERING THE PAST*

NARRATOR: These people are archeologists. They are looking for old things. Here, they find plates and bones.

Archaeology is the study of ancient things. They look at old buildings and houses. They look for things like jewelry, pots and plates.

Archeologists also study paintings in caves. They also study fossils—the bones of old animals. And they study human remains, like these skulls.

To find things archaeologists get dirty. Teams work with shovels and spades. It is slow work. The work can be exciting.

This is a Mayan city. The beautiful carvings made by the Maya tell their history. The archaeologists who found these writings are discovering Maya civilization.

Archeologists work in many places – in South America, in cities, in Asian jungles.-Sometimes the work is dangerous. But it is always interesting.

UNIT 5

VIDEO JOURNAL *ZOO DENTISTS*

NARRATOR: When an animal has a toothache, it doesn't go to the dentist's office. Dr. Sarah de Sanz is a 'people dentist'. She treats human patients in her office in San Francisco. However, she sometimes treats patients who don't come to her office, or sit in her chair.

What kind of patients are these? Animals! Dr. de Sanz is a part-time zoo dentist. She and her father, Dr. Paul Brown, work in the San Francisco area. They do checkups, fillings, and other dental work on anyone—or anything—that needs them.

DR. BROWN: Yes, I'm happy. I think it's a wonderful job.

NARRATOR: Going to the dentist is frightening for a lot of people. But when a dentist treats a zoo animal, it's the patient that can be scary. Some of these patients can bite off a dentist's hand. Dr. de Sanz and Dr. Brown work in the most dangerous animal jaws. They're happy to do it. These animals need them.

NARRATOR: These dentists do checkups on zoo animals. Today, they start with Artie the sea lion, one of the dentists' best patients.

ZOO EMPLOYEE: He's an excellent dental patient; he's better than most people. Aren't you, Artie? Aren't you?

DR. DE SANZ: He is an old animal. He's 30 years old, . . . and he's happy about it . . . so we're going to just look at his teeth and see if he has any particular dental problems.

NARRATOR: They take an X-ray. They get a clear picture. Artie's checkup goes well. Artie's teeth are fine: not bad for a 30-year-old who's never brushed his teeth!

ZOO EMPLOYEE: Want to hear him say 'ah'?

DR. DE SANZ: Yeah! Could you say 'ah' please? You are an excellent patient!

NARRATOR: The next visit is Dr. Brown's favorite animal—the elephant. He likes elephants because they have interesting teeth.

DR. BROWN: This is an elephant molar.

NARRATOR: Elephants get six sets of teeth in a lifetime. When the last set is gone, they can no longer eat and will die.

ZOO EMPLOYEE: This is Sue. She's a ten-year-old little female African elephant.

NARRATOR: An elephant's tusks are really teeth. The dentists check the teeth in Sue's mouth, and her tusks.

DR. BROWN: Perfect! She's in great shape. Her teeth look wonderful!

NARRATOR: Sue is the perfect patient and gets an excellent report. But not all animals do so well . . .

The next patient is the San Francisco Zoo's rare black jaguar. Sandy has a terrible toothache and needs surgery.

DR. DUNKER: We can't walk up to her and say 'Can I look in your mouth?' You may lose a few fingers maybe your head! This animal has to be anesthetized in order for us to look at it.

NARRATOR: Making an animal sleep is difficult. Sandy is 21 years old, takes her to the operating room. Everybody is worried. They start the surgery. Suddenly there's a problem . . .

DR. DUNKER: Hey Ron, why don't you come over here?

NARRATOR: Sandy stops breathing! First the doctors give her oxygen. Sandy takes one breath per minute! The team acts quickly.

Sandy's teeth are very bad. She needs two root canals—and a filling! Dr. de Sanz and Dr. Brown must now work carefully and quickly to take out the nerve of each bad tooth and then put fillings in the holes that are left. After a lot of hard work—the surgery is over.

NARRATOR: The jaguar's visit with the dentists is finished. Sandy will feel well again. She won't have a toothache!

NARRATOR: As the zoo dentists finish another day. It's all in a day's work for these zoo dentists!

UNIT 6

VIDEO JOURNAL *VOLCANO TREK*

NARRATOR: In a region of Ethiopia, hot lava erupts from the Erta Ale volcano. The temperature of this lava is more than 2,000 degrees Fahrenheit.

Now, a team of explorers wants to see Erta Ale. They want to learn about the volcano. It's a difficult trek, and the team has to use camels.

They reach the crater. Franck Tessier and Irene Margaritis are geologists and professors at the University of Nice. They travel very far to see Erta Ale!

In the crater, they see the black lava lake.

"It is quite exciting. I want to see it now."

NARRATOR: Erta Ale is in the Afar area of Ethiopia. The Afar triangle is in an area where three continental plates meet. These plates move every year.

The Erta Ale volcano has the oldest lava lake in the world. The lake is one of the lowest points on Earth. At Erta Ale, geologists study how the world started millions of years ago.

Red hot lava comes out from the earth. This lava forms Erta Ale's lava lake. When the lava cools, it is hard and black. Hot magma breaks through when the volcano erupts.

The geologists stand at the top of the active volcano and wait next to the crater. It's difficult to be there; there is a strong smell of sulfur. It's very, very hot.

Then, the group goes down into the crater. Professor Tessier wants to collect pieces of the red-hot lava. It's 2:00 in the morning when they return. They're very tired and, as Professor Margaritis says; "very hot," "I think this is fresh lava,"

NARRATOR: The pieces don't come directly from the lava lake. However, the team decides they're fresh.

The team goes back to analyze the pieces of lava. They want to learn new information to teach to others. They want to know what the lava of Erta Ale can teach them about how the world started millions of years ago.

UNIT 7

VIDEO JOURNAL *LAND DIVERS OF VANUATU*

NARRATOR: Most people think Bungee jumping —as we know it —started in New Zealand.

However a type of bungee jumping started in the small South Pacific island nation of Vanuatu.

At first, it looks like a traditional bungee jumping but it is very different.

Compared to this, bungee jumping is a walk in the park.

This is the Naghol, which means "land diving". The diver tries to touch the soil with his head. The people of Vanuatu believe this will make their crops grow.

They jump from this 70-foot wooden tower. High on the tower, one man, Rene, has some advice.

RENE, Land Diver: Whenever you are on the tower ready to jump, if you have second thoughts that means you must not jump.

NARRATOR: The first diver greets the crowd like a rock star. His dive goes well. He hits the ground hard, but he's okay. His friends run to him and free his ankles.

The second dive is not so good. The young boys think the vines are not good, but the older, more experienced divers say they are okay.

They aren't.

On the way down, one of the vines breaks and the young boy hits the ground. Everyone helps. But he's unconscious.

Jumping is sometimes dangerous. Sometimes people are seriously injured. But usually they are okay.

At last, the boy is better. He walks away with his friends and brothers.

One of the older men jumps next. He is standing on the tower. The crowd is excited. Eventually he jumps. It's a very good dive.

Westerners aren't allowed to jump, but we can tie a small camera to a diver's leg. We think this is the first time. The crowd loves it.

CAMERAMAN: Good job. Good job. Is the lens clean? Yes! Good job, good job. Are you all right? Good job. Amazing!

NARRATOR: The young man with the camera tells about his jumps in the local language, Raga.

LAND DIVER: The first dive was great. The second dive I broke a vine. But as long as I'm not hurt, everything is going well. I'm a lucky man.

NARRATOR: The last jump is by one of the most experienced divers in Pentecost. He jumps from the tower and everyone is happy.

When it's over, the children climb the tower. One day they might jump.

UNIT 8

VIDEO JOURNAL *INUIT FASHION*

NARRATOR: We usually think Inuit people don't wear clothes to look good. It is more important to be warm.

In the Canadian province of Nunavut, in the capital city of Iqaluit, we can see that this is not true.

It's high fashion in the high Arctic . . .

Beautiful jackets . . . coats . . . sweaters . . . coats . . . dresses

NAT SOT (English): So this is the seals I work with . . . beautiful.

From her home in Iqaluit, Aaju Peter designs clothes.

A lot of people like her clothes.

AAJU PETER, Designer: So when I take this I can turn it into anything.

NARRATOR: Anything from a coat to a skirt.

AAJU PETER, Designer: This one is taken from a southern made vest that my sister had given to me. This is just so beautiful this is the signature of the North.

NARRATOR: The Inuit still use seal skins but they also use modern materials like wool, cotton and synthetic materials. However, they still use traditional designs.

One of the most important is the Amouti … a jacket with a pouch for carrying a baby.

Women slip the baby over their head . . .

AAJU PETER, Designer: There it is inside the pouch and you're free to do whatever.

AAJU PETER, Designer: I think since the Inuit are the ones who designed this outfit, Inuit should be the ones showing the rest of the world how these Amouti's are made and how they are worn.

NARRATOR: Because they are worried about the killing of baby seals, the U.S. and Europe banned the sale of seal fur.

MADELEINE ALLAKARIALLAK, CBC Radio Canada: We weren't doing that of course, and to this day we don't do that, I mean we use every part of the seal. We eat the meat, we use the seal fat, but we need to use the skin to make money and it's not affecting the population, the seals are reproducing fine.

NARRATOR: But the Inuit say that the seals are not in danger. There are lots of them. They want to lift the ban.

Inuit clothes have changed but they still use ideas from the past.

UNIT 9

VIDEO JOURNAL *SLOW FOOD*

NARRATOR: This is Chianti, in Italy. It is famous for its wines.

Greve, is a small town in Chianti.

The people produce wine, cheese and mushrooms.

Life is slow in Chianti. Things do not change very quickly. The people like it that way.

"Our goal is to protect what makes Greve special. We want Chianti to remain a special place where things don't move too fast."

Greve's mayor helped start the Slow Food Movement.

The goal of the Slow Food Movement is to keep the pleasures of good living, good food, family and friends.

Now the Slow Food Movement is international. It has more than 66,000 members worldwide.

"It's very nice to live here because we have a nice atmosphere, we have nice landscapes. And so, when you have nice things to see, a nice place to live in, it's very easy."

NARRATOR: Salvatore Tescano had an American style hamburger restaurant in Florence. Now he has a restaurant in Greve.

"You have to take your time. Slow down. What you eat is important."

NARRATOR: In the mountains of Pistoia, in northern Tuscany, the farmers make a special cheese.

It is made from the milk of black sheep.

Many farmers stopped making the cheese. But the Slow Food Movement is helping. Now more farmers are making the cheese. It is very popular.

"Our cheese is famous now."

"From Singapore to Macao, in New York, in Rome, you always find the same pizza, the same hamburgers. Slow food doesn't want this. The Slow Food Movement wants people to eat special food."

NARRATOR: Greve wants the best of both the modern world and the traditional life of Italy.

UNIT 10

VIDEO JOURNAL *PYRETHRUM*

NARRATOR: One of the world's biggest killers is malaria.

It's spread by mosquitoes. These insects carry the disease.

With all the special and complex products for sale today, the best mosquito repellent comes from a flower.

Here on Kenya's Lake Nakuru we are looking for the world's most dangerous animal.

It is not the lion or the leopard. The most dangerous animal is much smaller.

This is it—the tiny but very deadly Anopheles mosquito, responsible for spreading Malaria.

All of these insects on this man's arm are OK because they are from The International Centre for Insect Physiology and Ecology outside Nairobi, Kenya. Here research into malaria is happening now.

MARY WAMBUI-NDUNGA, ICIPE: Malaria is still the most important parasitic disease in the wild and according to W.H.O estimates (World Health Organization) 1983, forty percent of the wild population would suffer a case of Malaria in one year. That accounts to about three to four hundred millions cases. In Africa we lose between one to two million children in one year.

NARRATOR: The most important, insecticide in the control of mosquitoes is not a synthetic chemical but a natural one produced by the flower Pyrethrum.

The plant is a type of Chrysanthemum which grows today all over the world.

Seventy percent of the world's production comes from here in Kenya.

This is ideal Pyrethrum country, because the plant grows best at a high altitude in a dry climate.

The flowers are picked and sun-dried.

The Pyrethrum insecticide has a fast knockdown effect on mosquitoes.

It kills them almost instantaneously.

The benefits of Pyrethrum over a synthetic insecticide are that it's an environmentally friendly insecticide and that insects have no time to build up any resistance to it.

This is a small farm in the Molo district of Kenya's Rift Valley.

Pyrethrum grows here.

This farmer is able to harvest four hundred kilograms of dried flowers from this area a year.

He makes eight hundred dollars of urgently needed cash.

The flowers go to large processing plants.

The Pyrethrum extract makes many insecticides. Its importance is growing around the world.

JOSHUA KIPTOON, Pyrethrum Board of Kenya: Pyrethrum is one of the most important plants in the world because it's used to kill insects that carry diseases that harm man. It fights his enemies.

NARRATOR: Most people never know that their insect repellent is made from a flower growing in Africa. Pyrethrum is one of the plants that is changing the world.

UNIT 11

VIDEO JOURNAL *MAKING A THAI BOXING CHAMPION*

NARRATOR: Thai boxing, or muay thai, is Thailand's oldest martial art. It looks like Western boxing, but it's very different. In Thai boxing you can use every part of your body: your hands, head, feet, knees—even elbows are okay.

The s port has a long history. Two thousand years ago, warriors trained in Thai boxing to protect their country from invaders. Now it's one of Thailand's most popular sports—everyone loves it. It's part of many festivals. You can see it on television around the country every day.

Many boxers in Thailand started boxing at the Lanna Muay Thai Training Camp in Chiang Mai. Right now, the camp is home for a 12-year-old boy named Manat. He and 15 other boys are here to become fighters.

Most of the boys are young and they come from very poor families. The camp pays for their training. While they are here, they only box. The boys train for seven hours a day, seven days of the week.

They train hard. They wish to become the next great champion. For Manat and the others, success here can give them better lives and a higher status in Thai society. Canadian coach Andy Thomson started the camp.

ANDY THOMSON, Thai Boxing Coach: Thai boxing offers the boys a chance at status…improve status in their community, the opportunity to earn some money, and most of them will have a dream of being a champion one day in Lumphini Stadium in Bangkok. It's an opportunity to open up their world.

NARRATOR: For Manat and the other boys, this is their chance to see more than their home village. It's a chance to make their family and friends proud. Manat is getting ready for his second fight which is tomorrow. Thai boxers have to be strong, but they not only train their bodies. They prepare their minds and the way they think about the fight. Modern *muay thai* is about learning to think and fight like a warrior. And it's about achieving personal goals.

MANAT, Thai Boxer: If I move on to bigger fights, one day I'll be a champion—a champion of Chiang Mai. I'll feel very proud and good. And I'll send the money I win to my parents.

NARRATOR: Manat's big night finally arrives. The fight is in a small town outside of Chiang Mai.

Manat goes into the ring for the 'Rama Muay', an ancient ceremony which focuses a fighter's strength and power. It helps him to get ready for the fight. After the ceremony, the fight begins.

THOMSON: The judges are looking for good, clean shot technique—both offensive and defensive. They are looking for the boxer who is in control of the fight.

NARRATOR: Manat fights hard, but for him, tonight is not the night. He doesn't win. Unfortunately, the boy Manat fought was taller, heavier, and more experienced than him. But even with these disadvantages, Manat did very well. He may have lost the fight, but his coaches now definitely believe that he can be a winner.

THOMSON: Manat's fight was very good. He fought really well. Good attitude . . . a good heart . . . very good heart. Even though he's not happy, he'll be all right tomorrow. He'll be back fighting again—no problem.

NARRATOR: Manat did not win tonight, but this was only one step in the long process of making a Thai boxing champion!

UNIT 12

VIDEO JOURNAL *MONARCH BUTTERFLIES*

NARRATOR: Every year's migration of North America's monarch butterflies is one of the great spectacles of nature.

Each year, up to 300 million monarchs travel more than 2,000 miles from northern America and Canada to a remote forest two hundred miles west of Mexico City.

But they are as fragile as they are beautiful.

Sudden changes in their environment can mean disaster.

A January 2002 rainstorm followed with freezing temperatures killed as many as 250 million butterflies, almost eighty percent of the population in the *El Rosario* butterfly sanctuary—just one of six sanctuaries in the area.

Their bodies covered the forest floor, giving off an unusual odor.

Mike Quinn is a Texas biologist with Monarch Watch—an organization based out of the University of Kansas.

He thinks logging, which happens more and more in these reserves, may have contributed to the death of the butterflies.

QUINN, Biologist: Logging is right up to the edge of the colony and logging opens up the forest and lets in the cold air and freezes penetrate into the forest whereas an intact forest acts as both an umbrella and as a blanket and that will severely protect the Monarchs.

NARRATOR: In the last 20 years, logging, mostly illegal, has destroyed nearly half the forests the monarchs need in this region.

The Mexican government, along with the World Wildlife Fund, has started efforts to preserve what is left. They offer to pay landowners to not cut trees.

But the money is very limited: 18 dollars for every cubic meter of loggable wood—not nearly as much money as they can make logging.

The 2002 storm wasn't the first to hit the monarch population, nor will it likely be the last.

For the moment, millions of the monarch butterflies still migrate each year.

UNIT 1 FRIENDS AND FAMILY

Lesson A

A. 2. He's Mr. Smith. 3. I'm Aisha. 4. You're Stefan. 5. They're Luis and Marta. 6. She's Noriko.

B. 1B. Fine. And you? 2A. Good morning. How are you? 2B. Fine thank you. And how are you? 3A. This is my friend Yong-Jun. 3B. Nice to meet you Yong-Jun. 3C. Nice to meet you too.

C. 2. My 3. Our 4. Their 5. Her 6. Your

Lesson B

A. 2. mother 3. brother 4. sister 5. grandfather 6. grandmother 7. husband 8. wife

B. 2. grandmother 3. mother 4. father 5. husband 6. sister 7. son

C. 1. am 2. is 3. are 4. are 5. is 6. are

Lesson C

A. 1. young 2. tall 3. married 4. handsome 5. old 6. short 7. pretty 8. single

B. Answers will vary.

C. 1A. your 1B. she, isn't 2A. are 2B. is, His, is, isn't, he's

D. Answers will vary.

Lesson D

B. 2. Jeff 3. Yuji 4. Sara and Emma 5. Hiroshi Yamada 6. Yuji and Aya

C. 1. Yes 2. No 3. No 4. Yes 5. No 6. Yes

Review

Across 1. my 4. her 5. is 7. grandfather 11. his 12. young

Down 1. married 2. brothers 3. their 6. not 7. good 8. are 9. family 10. how's

UNIT 2 JOBS AROUND THE WORLD

Lesson A

A. 2. She's a chef. 3. He's an engineer. 4. She's a banker. 5. She's an architect. 6. He's a teacher. 7. He's a doctor. 8. She's an artist.

B. 2. They aren't old. 3. She isn't an architect. 4. You're not a teacher. 5. We're not tall. 6. It isn't interesting.

C. 2. an 3. a 4. a 5. a 6. a 7. an 8. a

D. 2. They're good. 3. He's 23. 4. Yes, he is.

Lesson B

A. Written answers will vary. 2. How old are you? 3. Are you married? 4. What do you do? 5. Is your job interesting?

B. 2. How old are you? 3. Are you married? 4. What do you do? 5. Is your job interesting?

Lesson C

A. 2. It's in China. 3. It's in Chile. 4. It's in Korea. 5. It's in Japan. 6. It's in the USA (or United States of America) 7. It's in Brazil. 8. It's in Russia. 9. It's in Mexico. 10. It's in Argentina. 11. It's in Egypt.

B. 1. Asia 2. Europe 3. North America 4. South America 5. Africa 6. Australia

C. 1. you 2. from 3. Russia 4. Europe 5. Is 6. very

D. Answers will vary.

Lesson D

A. 1. T 2. T 3. F 4. T 5. T 6. T 7. F 8. F

B. Answers will vary.

Review

Across 2. boring 3. country 4. Korea 6. Europe 8. continent 9. Argentina 11. China 12. small 13. driver

Down 1. South America 5. wet 7. old 10. an 11. cold

UNIT 3 HOUSES AND APARTMENTS

Lesson A

A. 1. stairs 2. bedroom 3. kitchen 4. closet 5. dining room 6. garage 7. living room 8. bathroom

B. 1. There are 2. there is 3. Are there 4. there are 5. is there 6. is there 7. there isn't 8. there is

C. Answers will vary.

Lesson B

A. 2. There are three closets in my house. 3. There are two bathrooms in her house. 4. There are two fireplaces in their house. 5. There are three windows in my bedroom.

B. 1. Answers will vary. 2. Answers will vary.

C. 1. email address, write to 2. Jim and, and I, live very, this school 3. hurricanes are, worst type, type of, of extreme 4. learn at, least ten, ten new, new words, words every 5. think Cassie, will invite

Lesson C

A. 2. armchair 3. coffee table 4. TV 5. bed 6. bookcase 7. lamp 8. table 9. chair 10. stove 11. refrigerator 12. microwave

B. 2. next to 3. on 4. in 5. on 6. next to 7. on 8. in

C. Answers will vary.

Lesson D

A. Yoshi's bedroom: 3, 4, 6; Jessie's bedroom: 2, 3, 4, 5, 6

B. Answers will vary.

C. Answers will vary.

Review

Across 3. in 5. next to 6. aren't 7. garage 8. are 9. kitchen 10. is 11. bedroom 12. there

Down 1. house 2. on 3. isn't 4. bookcase 6. apartment

UNIT 4 POSSESSIONS

Lesson A

A. 1. book 2. notebook 3. dictionary 4. ring 5. necklace 6. wallet 7. bag 8. keys 9. watch 10. glasses 11. handbag 12. pen

B. 2. Is that your dictionary? 3. Are those your books? 4. Are these your glasses? 5. Is that your bookbag? 6. Is this your wallet? 7. Are those your notebooks? 8. Is this your watch?

C. 2. Francisco's 3. Paul's 4. Paul's 5. Francisco's 6. Jennie's

Lesson B

A. 2. That is Anita's car. 3. These are Martin's glasses. 4. This is Anita's handbag. 5. This is Martin's book. 6. This is Anita's wallet. 7. That is Martin's house.

B. 1. Answers will vary. 2. Answers will vary.

C. Long e sound like sheep: he's, he, she, three, we. Short i sound like ship: it, his, this, isn't.

Lesson C

A. 1. ipod 2. iPhone 3. car audio 4. CD player 5. camcorder 6. laptop 7. cell phone 8. DVD player 9. electronic dictionary

B. Answers will vary.

C. 1. Do you 2. Yes, I do 3. you have 4. has 5. Do you have 6. I don't 7. have 8. have

Lesson D

B. 1. T 2. T 3. F 4. T 5. F 6. F

C. My special possession is a watch. It's very big and old. It's gold. It's special because it's my grandfather's watch and it's 100 years old.

Review

Across 1. do 6. aren't 7. wallet 9. possessions 10. No 11. cheap 13. Yes

Down 1. dictionary 2. player 3. laptop 4. have 5. Does 8. isn't 12. has

UNIT 5 DAILY ACTIVITIES

Lesson A

A. 2. It's eleven. 3. It's seven thirty. 4. It's a quarter past nine. 5. It's two thirty. 6. Answers will vary.

B. Answers will vary.

C. 1. every 2. at 3. in 4. on 5. at

D. 2. takes 3. go to 4. has 5. finishes 6. go 7. takes

Lesson B

A. 2. Monday 3. Tuesday 4. Wednesday 5. Thursday 6. Friday 7. Saturday

B. 3. What time does he start work? He starts work at eleven o'clock. 4. What time does he eat lunch? He eats lunch at four o'clock. 5. What time does he finish work? He finishes work at nine o'clock. 6. What are their jobs? They are teachers. 7. What time do they get up? They get up at six-thirty. 8. What time do they start work? They start work at eight o'clock. 9. What time do they eat lunch? They eat lunch at twelve-thirty. 10. What time do they finish work? They finish work at four-thirty.

Lesson C

A. 1. d 2. b 3. f 4. c 5. a 6. e

B. Dennis and Susan: 2. Do they talk to people? Yes, they do. 3. Do they go to meetings? No, they don't.; Melisa: 1. Does she travel? No, she doesn't. 2. Does she talk to people? Yes, she does. Does she go to meetings? Yes, she does.

C. Answers will vary.

Lesson D

A. 3, 2, 1

B. 1. T 2. T 3. T 4. F 5. T

C. early, every, to, and, sometimes

D. Answers will vary.

Review

Across 2. at 3. talk to 5. take 6. What 9. sometimes 12. go 13. on

Down 1. meet 2. activities 4. on 7. have 8. fill out 10. o'clock 11. every

UNIT 6 GETTING THERE

Lesson A

A. 1. movie theater 2. restaurant 3. train station 4. library 5. bank 6. hotel 7. supermarket 8. park 9. museum 10. shopping mall 11. tourist office 12. post office

B. on, turn, walk, from, between

C. Answers will vary.

Lesson B

A. 1. Main Street 2. the Star of India Restaurant 3. do I 4. left 5. one block 6. Main Street and Lincoln Avenue 7. Thank

B. 1. Is there a bank 2. Long Avenue and King Street 3. go 4. two blocks 5. Mega Burgers

C. Answers will vary.

Lesson C

A. 1. bus 2. taxi 3. train 4. subway 5. rental car

B. 1. has to 2. has to 3. have to, don't have to 4. has to 5. doesn't have to 6. doesn't have to

C. Answers will vary.

Lesson D

A. 1. August 13 2. August 1 3. August 6 4. August 10 5. August 15 6. August 4

B. Answers will vary.

Review

Across 3.blocks 5. have 6. cheap 11. restaurant 12. cross 13. on 14. bank

Down 1. office 2. mall 4. shuttle 7. across 8. between 9. station 10. turn

UNIT 7 FREE TIME

Lesson A

A. 2. He's reading. 3. He's watching TV. 4. She's cooking. 5. He's listening to music. 6. She's playing the guitar.

B. 2. They're not going to the movies. 3. I'm not watching TV. 4. We're not going for a walk. 5. She's not listening to CD's. 6. You're not studying.

C. 2. What are they reading? 3. Where is he going? 4. What is she watching? 5. Where are you studying? 6. What is Lee cooking?

Lesson B

A. 2. What's Eric doing? He's taking a shower. 3. What are Joe and Tina doing? They're cooking dinner. 4. What's Julia doing? She's walking. 5. What's Mark doing? He's listening to music. 6. What are Sam and Connie doing? They're eating breakfast.

B. 1. d 2. a 3. e 4. b 5. c

C. Answers will vary.

Lesson C

A. 1. golf 2. swimming 3. tennis 4. ice skating 5. soccer 6. skiing 7. football 8. volleyball

B. Answers will vary.

C. Answers will vary.

D. can, can, can, Can you, can, can't, can't, Can you

Lesson D

A. 2. T 3. F, walk 4. T 5. F, eight 6. T

B. Answers will vary.

Review

Across 3. can't 5. listening 9. play 10. ice 11. watching 12. they can

Down 1. he is 2. they aren't 3. can 4. playing 6. I can't 7. going 8. where 11. what

UNIT 8 CLOTHES

Lesson A

A. 1. hat 2. coat 3. sweater 4. dress 5. shoes 6. jacket 7. shirt 8. pants

B. 1. red 2. white 3. black 4. brown 5. yellow 6. gray 7. green 8. blue

C. sweaters, Could, try, of course, small

D. Answers will vary.

Lesson B

A. 1. b 2. d 3. c 4. a

B. Answers will vary.

C. Answers will vary.

Lesson C

A. 2. purple 3. pink 4. orange 5. dark blue 6. beige 7. dark green 8. light blue

B. 1. t-shirt 2. socks 3. jeans 4. scarf 5. blouse

C. Answers will vary.

D. Answers will vary.

Lesson D

A. 1. f 2. e 3. a 4. b 5. c 6. d

B. waer-wear, pitures-pictures, buye-buy, winnter-winter, sweter-sweater

C. Answers will vary.

Review

Across 5. could you 9. course 10. try 11. assistant 12. light

Down 1. card 2. blouse 3. coat 4. dark 5. change 6. love 7. wearing 8. casual 13. hate

UNIT 9 EAT WELL

Lesson A

A. 1. cereal 2. eggs 3. fruit juice 4. steak 5. fish 6. pasta 7. chicken 8. salad 9. coffee 10. tea 11. chocolate cake 12. ice cream

B. 1. some 2. any 3. any 4. some 5. some 6. some 7. some 8. any

C. some, any, any, some

D. Answers will vary.

Lesson B

A. Answers will vary.

B. Answers will vary.

C. Answers will vary.

D. Answers will vary.

Lesson C

A. Uncountable nouns: some coffee, some tea, some rice, some juice
Countable nouns: apples, steak

B. Answers will vary.

C. 2. How much meat do you eat? 3. How many brothers and sisters does he have? 4. How much fruit does she eat? 5. How many hamburgers do you need? 6. How much ice cream do you have?

Lesson D

B. cake, ice cream—United States; pie—Russia; cake, pasta—Philippines; soup—Korea

C. I like my Birthday. My mother makes a great dinner with my favorite food. We eat steak and rice. She makes a chocolate cake. We sing Happy Birthday. We eat a lot of cake and ice cream.

D. Answers will vary.

Review

Across 3. juice 4. salad 5. meat 7. chocolate 11. some 12. fruit 13. many

Down 1. much 2. dessert 6. please 8. healthy 9. cream 10. menu 14. any

UNIT 10 HEALTH

Lesson A

A. 1. leg 2. head 3. ear 4. back 5. stomach 6. knee 7. face 8. hand 9. chest 10. finger 11. arm 12. foot

B. ☺: well, OK, great ☹: terrible, sick

C. 2. headache 3. fever 4. stomachache 5. backache

D. Answers will vary.

Lesson B

A. 1. toothache 2. cold 3. earache 4. measles 5. sore throat

B. 1. measles 2. cold 3. sore throat 4. toothache 5. earache

C. Doctor: How are you today?
Patient: I have a terrible stomach ache.
Doctor: Where does it hurt?
Patient: Right here.
Doctor: I need to examine you.

Lesson C

A. 1. go 2. see 3. take 4. lie 5. take 6. see

B. Answers will vary.

C. What should I do? You should go home. Should I go to English class? No you shouldn't. You should go to bed!

D. Answers will vary.

Lesson D

A. 1. F 2. F 3. T 4. T 5. F 6. T

B. should, shouldn't, shouldn't, should, should

C. Answers will vary.

Review

Across 1. flu 2. fingers 4. sore 6. examine 7. should 8. hurts 9. matter 10. shouldn't

Down 1. fever 2. feel 3. stomachache 5. great 6. ears 7. symptom

UNIT 11 MAKING PLANS

Lesson A

A. 1. e 2. b 3. a 4. c 5. f 6. d

B. 1. He's going to travel. He's going to the movies. 2. What is Mary going to do this weekend? She's going to have a family meal. She isn't going to travel. She isn't going to the movies. 3. What are Mr. and Mrs. Kim going to do this weekend? They are going to have a family meal. They are going to travel. They aren't going to the movies. 4. Answers will vary.

Lesson B

A. 2. sing Norwegian songs. 3. She is going to walk around the city with Norwegian flags. 4. it's a Norwegian summer holiday, Jonsok. 5. She's going to make a big fire and sing all night. 6. She isn't going to go to bed. 7. is a Norwegian winter holiday, Christmas. 8. She is going to make special cookies and cakes. 9. She is going to give presents to her family and friends.

B. Answers will vary.

Lesson C

A. 2. medicine 3. law 4. psychology 5. music 6. nursing

B. what would you like to do; Would you like to work; I wouldn't; Would you like to be; wouldn't; Where would you like to work?; would you like to work; would

C. Answers will vary.

Lesson D

A. piano teacher; architect; doctor; actor

B. I would like to travel in Europe. I want to visit France, England, Spain, and Germany. I need a lot of money. I'm going to get a weekend job and I'm going to work every Saturday and every Sunday. I'm going to save all my money. Then, I'm going to make plans for my trip. I would like to go to Europe next summer.

C. Answers will vary.

Review

Across 2. am going to 6. is going to 8. would like to 10. musician 12. medicine 13. holiday

Down 1. go 2. anniversary 3. wouldn't 4. meal 5. lawyer 7. out 9. have 11. the

UNIT 12 MIGRATIONS

Lesson A

. 1. leave 2. arrive 3. go, stay 4. return 5. come 6. move

. 1. lived 2. went 3. arrived 4. came 5. moved 6. stayed 7. returned 8. left

. 2. She went to Melbourne. She didn't go to Sydney. 3. She moved to Canberra. She didn't move to Perth. 4. She stayed in an apartment. She didn't stay in a hotel. 5. She returned to her home country. She didn't return to Australia.

. 2. Why did they move to a new house? 3. When did he leave his hometown? 4. Where did she live in Europe? 5. Why did they go to a restaurant? 6. Where did we stay?

Lesson B

. 2. two thousand and six 3. nineteen eighty-seven 4. two thousand and one 5. Answers will vary. 6. Answers will vary.

. Reporter: When did you arrive; Javier: came, didn't know, went; Reporter: Why did you leave; Javier: left, didn't have; Reporter: Where did you live?; Javier: lived; Reporter: When did you return; Javier: didn't return, returned, stayed

Lesson C

A. 1. have 2. pack 3. sell 4. buy 5. get 6. close 7. pack

B. 2. Did he get money from the bank? Yes, he did. 3. Did he go to the supermarket? No, he didn't. 4. Did he call David? Yes, he did. 5. Did he check e-mail? No, he didn't.

C. Answers will vary.

Lesson D

B. New York, stores, Washington D.C., White, shopping, Miami, beach, presents

C. Answers will vary.

Review

Across 2. came 3. had 8. moved 10. nineteen ninety 11. bought 12. left 13. did you 14. stayed

Down 1. passport 4. account 5. farewell 6. arrived 7. went 9. didn't live

Reasons for Writing

The Writing Program reinforce and complements the lessons in the Student Book. Writing gives students a chance to reflect on the English they've learned and to develop an indispensable academic skill.

The Writing Syllabus

The Writing Activities help students to develop all the building blocks of good writing: words, logical connectors, sentences, transitions, paragraphs, and short essays. As students progress through the levels of the **World English** series, the Writing Activities progress from the word and sentence level to the paragraph and composition level, allowing students to master the basics before they're asked to do more complex writing tasks.

The Writing Activities help students move from sentences to paragraphs as they show relationships between ideas and add detail and precision to their writing with descriptive adjectives.

Writing from Models vs. Process Writing

When students are provided with writing models–examples of completed writing tasks–they have a clear idea of what is expected from them as well as a model on which to base their own writing. Such models give students confidence and a sense of direction and can be found at all levels of the Writing Worksheets.

On the other hand, writers must also learn the writing process. They must generate ideas, plan their writing, perform the writing task, then polish their writing by revising and editing. The Writing Worksheets support process writing by providing activities to stimulate thinking, useful topics and vocabulary, graphic organizers for planning, and opportunities for students to share and refine their writing.

Ways to Use the Writing Program

In general, the Writing Activities are designed to be used after the class has covered all or most of a unit in the Student Book. The Writing Activities often contain grammar, vocabulary, and ideas from the units, which give students solid linguistic and conceptual ground to stand on.

On the other hand, it's not necessary to complete the Lesson D Writing task in the Student Book before using the Writing Activity for that unit. The worksheets complement the writing lessons in the Student Book, but can be used independently.

- **In-Class Discussion**

  Discussion is an important way to stimulate thinking and to help students generate ideas they can use in their own writing. When an activity contains a preliminary matching or listing activity, for example, ask students to share and explain their answers. Ask specific questions about the writing models in order to check comprehension and to elicit opinions about the topics. And be sure to take advantage of opportunities for students to discuss their writing with you and their classmates.

- **Homework**

  Most of the Writing Activities are appropriate for self-study as long as follow-up discussion and feedback are provided later.

- **Vocabulary Practice**

  Many of the Writing Activities contain target vocabulary from the corresponding unit in the Student Book. Ask students to locate vocabulary from the unit in the writing models, or check comprehension by asking students to explain vocabulary words in the context of the worksheet.

- **Grammar Reinforcement**

  Many of the Writing Activities require the use of grammar points found in the Student Book units, and using the grammar in context supports real language acquisition.

- **Pronunciation Practice**

  Although oral skills are not the focus of the Writing Activities, you can do choral repetition of the word lists in the worksheets or use the writing models to practice pronunciation points from the Student Book. Students can also do read-alouds of their finished writing in pairs or small groups while the teacher monitors their pronunciation.

- **Personalization**

  When students complete unfinished sentences, paragraphs, and essays, or when they do less controlled original writing, they bring their personal thoughts and experiences into the classroom and take ownership of the writing task as well as the language they are learning.

- **Real Communication**

  Since the real-world purpose of writing is to communicate, be sure to respond not only to linguistic and technical aspects of student writing, but also to students' ideas. Make comments and ask questions that show genuine interest, either in class or when you collect and give written feedback on the worksheets.

	Writing Tasks	Language Focus
Unit 1 Describe Your Family	• Use *be* in a conversation. • Draw and describe family members.	*Hi, my name is Michael.* *This is Toby. He is my brother.*
Unit 2 Describe a Country	• Answer questions about yourself. • Write sentences about countries.	*No, I'm not a doctor.* *Brazil is a large country.*
Unit 3 Describe a Room	• Finish sentences about a house and an apartment. • Write sentences about a room.	*There are three bedrooms in my house.* *There is a lamp on the table.*
Unit 4 A Short Story	• Finish sentences about possessions. • Write questions with *have*. • Finish sentences in a story.	*There is a watch in the purse.* *Does Hanna have keys in her purse?*
Unit 5 Daily Schedule	• Write sentences about a person's schedule. • Write sentences about one's own daily routine.	*Jillian gets up at 7:30 every morning.* *I do homework at 6:30 every evening.*
Unit 6 Museum Tour	• Answer questions with *have to*. • Finish a paragraph about a tour.	*Do you have to arrive before 9:00 a.m.?* *No, you don't.* *Our tour started at 11:00.*
Unit 7 Showing Contrasts	• Write sentences about what's happening now. • Show contrasts with *but*.	*Right now, people are playing sports outside.* *Anita can't swim, but Peter can.*
Unit 8 Likes and Dislikes	• Write sentences about what people are wearing. • Write opinions about clothes and colors.	*My brother is wearing brown pants and a white shirt.* *I like pink and yellow.*
Unit 9 Restaurant Conversation	• Answer questions about favorite foods. • Use *and* to connect ideas in a conversation.	*I like mangos and strawberries.* *Could I have spaghetti and meatballs?*
Unit 10 Letters of Advice	• Give advice to people with health problems using *should* and *should not*.	*I have a terrible toothache.* *What should I do?* *You should see a dentist.*
Unit 11 Letter to a Millionaire	• Write answers to questions about your plans for the future. • Write a letter about your wishes for the future.	*I'm going to go shopping tomorrow.* *I would like to travel to Asia.*
Unit 12 Past Timeline	• Write sentences about past events.	*Kayo got her passport in 1998.*

Photocopiable © 2010 Heinle, Cengage Learning

UNIT 1 FRIENDS AND FAMILY
DESCRIBE YOUR FAMILY

A. Read the conversation. Complete the conversation with *is*, *am*, or *are*.

Michael: Hi, my name _____ Michael.

Anna: Hi, Michael. Nice to meet you. I _____ Anna.

Michael: Nice to meet you, too. _____ you in my English class?

Anna: Yes, I am. We _____ in the same math class, too.

Michael: That's great!

✔ Practice the conversation with a partner.

B. Write about your family members. Draw pictures then fill in the blanks. Use real names and words from the boxes.

Example:

This is ___Toby___. He is my _brother_.

He is _young_ with _straight black_ hair.

family members	adjectives	hair types
grandmother grandfather sister brother mother father daughter son	tall short handsome pretty	curly wavy straight brown red black blond

This is _____. He/She is my _____.

He/She is _____ with _____ hair.

This is _____. He/She is my _____.

He/She is _____ with _____ hair.

This is _____. He/She is my _____.

He/She is _____ with _____ hair.

✔ Show your pictures to a classmate. Say the sentences about your family members.

UNIT 2 JOBS AROUND THE WORLD

DESCRIBE A COUNTRY

A. Write answers to the questions that are true for you. Use *I'm* or *I'm not*.

Example: Are you a doctor? <u>Yes, I'm a doctor.</u> or <u>No, I'm not a doctor.</u>

Questions	Answers
1. Are you from Brazil?	
2. Are you a student?	
3. Are you an artist?	
4. Are you married?	
5. Are you from a small country?	
6. Are you an interesting person?	

✔ Ask and answer the questions with a partner.

B. Finish each sentence with an adjective from the box. There may be more than one correct answer.

> hot large dry small wet cold

1. Japan is a _____ country.
2. The United Kingdom is a _____ country.
3. Chile is a _____ country.
4. Korea is a _____ country.
5. The United States is a _____ country.
6. Russia is a _____ country.

C. Read about Brazil.

> Brazil is a large country. It's in South America. Brasilia is in Brazil. It's the capital city.

✔ Write a similar paragraph about Argentina.

UNIT 3 HOUSES AND APARTMENTS

DESCRIBE A ROOM

A. Read about a house. Complete the paragraph with words from the box.

is   sofas   next to   armchair   are

There _____ three bedrooms in my house. There _____ a big yard, too.

There are two _____ in the living room, and there is one _____. The kitchen

is _____ the living room.

B. Read about an apartment. Complete the paragraph with words from the box.

microwave   are   is   small   lamps

I live in a _____ apartment. There is a refrigerator and a _____ in the kitchen.

There _____ a table next to the bed. There are two _____ in the apartment.

C. Draw one room in your house or apartment. Then write sentences about the room.
Use *there is/there are* and some of the words in the boxes.

in   on   under   next to

table   bed   bookcase   stove   refrigerator   lamp   TV   sofa   chair

_____

_____

_____

_____

_____

_____

_____

_____

✓ Show your picture to a partner. Say your sentences.

UNIT 4 MY THINGS
A SHORT STORY

A. Read about Hanna's purse. Complete the paragraph with *there is* or *there are*.

Hanna has many things in her purse. _____ keys to her apartment. _____ glasses because Hanna doesn't see well. _____ a watch in the purse, too.

✓ Read about Bill's backpack. Complete the paragraph with *there is* or *there are*.

Bill has many things in his backpack. _____ pens and a notebook for class. _____ a book in the backpack, too. _____ a cell phone in the backpack because Bill likes to call his friends.

✓ Write questions with *have*.

1. Hanna / keys? _Does Hanna have keys in her purse?_ _____
2. Hanna / cell phone? _____
3. Hanna / glasses? _____
4. Bill / book? _____
5. Bill / wallet? _____
6. Bill / pens? _____

✓ Ask and answer the questions with a partner.

B. Read the story. Complete the paragraph with words from the box.

have	keys	we	there	wallet	are	is

Bill doesn't remember things. Hanna remembers everything. This morning, Bill asked Hanna, "Where are my _____?" So Hanna said, "_____ your keys on the coffee table?" But there were no keys on the coffee table. Then Bill asked Hanna, "Do you _____ my wallet?" And Hanna said, "No, I don't. _____ your wallet in the bedroom?" But _____ was no wallet in the bedroom. Finally, Bill asked Hanna, "Do _____ have any eggs? I'm hungry!" Bill opened the refrigerator. In the refrigerator, there were some eggs, and some keys, and Bill's _____! So Hanna asked Bill, "Why are your keys and your wallet in the refrigerator?" And Bill said, "I don't remember."

UNIT 5 DAILY ACTIVITIES

DAILY SCHEDULE

A. Look at Jillian's schedule.

Monday	Tuesday	Wednesday	Thursday	Friday
7:30 get up	7:30 get up	7:30 get up	7:30 get up	7:30 get up
9:00 start work	9:00 start work	9:00 start work	9:00 start work	9:00 start work
12:30 eat lunch	12:30 eat lunch	12:30 eat lunch	12:30 eat lunch	12:30 eat lunch
	3:00 finish work		3:00 finish work	
5:00 finish work		5:00 finish work		5:00 finish work
11:00 go to bed	11:00 go to bed	11:00 go to bed	11:00 go to bed	11:00 go to bed

✓Use the words below to write sentences about Jillian's schedule.

1. get up / every morning _Jillian gets up at 7:30 every morning._

2. start work / every day _____

3. eat lunch / every day _____

4. finish work / Tuesdays and Thursdays _____

5. finish work / Mondays, Wednesdays, and Fridays _____

6. go to bed / every night _____

✓Compare your sentences with a partner.

B. What do you do every day? Fill in the schedule with your information.

Monday	Tuesday	Wednesday	Thursday	Friday

✓Write sentences about your schedule.

1. _____   4. _____

2. _____   5. _____

3. _____   6. _____

✓Say your sentences to a partner.

UNIT 6 GETTING THERE
MUSEUM TOUR

A. Read about a tour.

> ### Homes of the Hollywood Stars
> - Tours every day from 10:00 a.m. until 4:00 p.m.
> - Tickets: $14 for adults and $9 for seniors over 65 years old
> - No children under 12 years old
> - Bus transportation to the stars' homes
> - No cameras inside the homes

✓ Write answers to the questions.

1. Do you have to arrive before 9:00 a.m.? _No, you don't._

2. Do you have to arrive before 4:00 p.m.? _____

3. Do you have to pay $20 for the tour? _____

4. Do you have to be 12 years old or older? _____

5. Do you have to walk to the stars' homes? _____

6. Do you have to leave your camera on the bus? _____

✓ Ask and answer the questions with a partner.

B. Read the paragraph. Complete the paragraph with words from the box.

> for   to   afternoon   at   a   across

> ### My Tour of the Most Famous Homes in Hollywood
>
> Last week, I went on a very interesting tour. Our tour started _____ 11:00 in the morning. I'm only 35 years old, so I had to pay $14 _____ my ticket. We took _____ bus to the homes of famous Hollywood stars. I really liked Jackie Chan's home. It was huge! And it was _____ the street from the home of Marilyn Monroe! The tour ended at 1:30 in the _____. There was one bad thing about the tour. You have _____ leave your camera on the bus when you go inside the homes, so I don't have any pictures.

UNIT 7 FREE TIME
SHOWING CONTRASTS

A. What's happening right now? Make a check ✔ next to those things.

___ It's raining.	___ People are playing sports outside.
___ I'm doing a worksheet.	___ I'm sitting in a chair.
___ The sun is shining.	___ Someone is cooking.
___ I'm listening to music.	___ I'm talking on the telephone.
___ My teacher is working.	___ I'm studying English.

✔ Write sentences about what is happening or what is not happening.

1. _Right now, I'm doing a worksheet._
2. _It's not raining at the moment._
3. _____
4. _____
5. _____
6. _____
7. _____
8. _____

✔ You can connect two short sentences with *but*. Writers do this to show a contrast (very different meanings).

Example: Right now, people are playing sports outside, but I'm sitting in a chair.

B. These people have different abilities. There is a check ✔ next to things each person can do.

Anita		Peter	
✔ draw	✔ play the guitar	draw	play the guitar
✔ play golf	cook	play golf	✔ cook
ski	swim	✔ ski	✔ swim

✔ Write sentences with *but*.

Examples: Anita can play the guitar, but Peter can't.
Anita can't swim, but Peter can.

1. _____ 4. _____
2. _____ 5. _____
3. _____ 6. _____

UNIT 8 CLOTHES

LIKES AND DISLIKES

A. What are you wearing? What are other people wearing? Write sentences with words from the boxes.

shirt	pants	skirt	shoes	sweater	jacket	coat	
tie	hat	jeans	scarf	blouse	socks	T-shirt	dress

red	(dark/light) blue	yellow	(dark/light) green	orange	white	
brown	black	grey	purple	beige	pink	

1. _My brother is wearing brown pants and a white shirt._____

2. _I am wearing_____

3. _____

4. _____

5. _____

6. _____

✔ Say your sentences to a partner.

B. What do you like to wear? Write words for clothes in the columns.

clothes I love	clothes I like	clothes I dislike	clothes I hate

✔ Now complete the paragraph below. Use the plural form (*dresses, shoes*, etc.).

I have some strong opinions about clothes. For example, I like _____

and _____. And I really love _____. On the other hand, I dislike

_____ and _____. And I really hate _____. They're

the worst!

C. Which colors do you like and dislike? Write sentences about your opinions.

_____

_____

_____

_____

UNIT 9 EAT WELL
RESTAURANT CONVERSATION

A. What are your favorites? Complete with answers that are true for you.

Q.	A.
1. What are your favorite fruits?	1. I like _____ and _____.
2. What are your favorite vegetables?	2. I like _____ and _____.
3. What are your favorite drinks?	3. I like _____ and _____.
4. What are your favorite breakfast foods?	4. I like _____ and _____.
5. What are your favorite desserts?	5. I like _____ and _____.

✓ Ask and answer the questions with a partner.

B. Writers use the word *and* to connect two or more ideas.

Two ideas: My favorite fruits are <u>mangos and strawberries</u>.

Three ideas: Could I have <u>soup, salad, and fish</u>?

Four ideas: We need to buy <u>hot dogs, soda, ice cream, and cake</u>.

✓ Look at the commas (,) in the sentences above.

C. Complete the sentences in the conversation. Use your own ideas.

Larry: This looks like a nice restaurant.

Paula: It is nice. The food is good, too.

Larry: What should I have?

Paula: Well, the (*2 ideas*) _____ are both very good.

Waiter: Are you ready to order?

Paula: Yes, could I have (*3 ideas*) _____ ?

Waiter: No problem. And for you sir?

Larry: Could I have (*2 ideas*) _____ ?

Waiter: Very good. Anything else?

Larry: Well, I'll probably want dessert later. Do you have any desserts?

Waiter: Yes, we have (*4 ideas*) _____ .

Larry: Those sound good. I'll decide after I eat.

Waiter: Very good. Thank you.

Larry & Paula: Thank you.

UNIT 10 HEALTH

LETTERS OF ADVICE

A. Read about Chelsea's health problems.

> Dear Dr. Millham,
>
> My name is Chelsea. I have a terrible toothache. My mouth is very red inside, and I might have a fever, too. What should I do?

✓ Now read the doctor's letter to Chelsea.

> Dear Chelsea,
>
> You should take an aspirin. That will help the toothache and the fever. Then, you should see a dentist. You shouldn't wait. See a dentist today.

✓ Write a similar letter to each person below.

> Dear Dr. Millham,
>
> My name is Ryan. I think I have a cold. I'm coughing and coughing, and I also have a fever. What should I do?

> _____
>
> _____
>
> _____

> Dear Dr. Millham,
>
> My name is Lucinda. Everything hurts today! I have a bad headache. I have a backache, too. What should I do?

> _____
>
> _____
>
> _____

> Dear Dr. Millham,
>
> My name is Mi Young. I don't feel very well. Nothing hurts, but I'm very tired. What should I do?

> _____
>
> _____
>
> _____

UNIT 11 MAKING PLANS

LETTER TO A MILLIONAIRE

A. Write answers to the questions. What are your plans?

Q.	A.
1. What are you going to do tomorrow?	1. <u>I'm going to</u> _____.
2. What are you going to do next week?	2. _____.
3. What are you going to do next month?	3. _____.
4. What are you going to do next year?	4. _____.

✓Ask and answer the questions with a partner.

B. Read the letter. Why does the writer use *would like*?

> Dear Mom and Dad,
>
> Can you believe it? My birthday party is going to be next weekend! Thank you for having a party for me. If you don't mind, I would like to bring my girlfriend Clare to the party. She's really nice, and I think you're going to like her. I would also like Mom to make her special lemon cake. (Would you do that, Mom?) It's my favorite!
>
> See you soon,
>
> Mitch

C. What are your wishes for your future? On the back of this paper, write several things you would like to do in your life:

Example: I would like to travel to Asia.

✓Imagine this: There is a very rich person. This person wants to make someone's wishes come true! Write a letter to him or her about things you would like to do. (If you're lucky, the millionaire might decide to pay for everything!)

> Dear Millionaire,
>
> There are several things I would like to do in my life. First, I would like to _____
> _____
> _____
> _____
> _____
> _____ Thank you for reading my letter.
>
> Sincerely,
>
> _____

UNIT 12 MIGRATIONS
PAST TIMELINE

A. Look at the dates and events on the timeline.

Kayo's Years in Australia

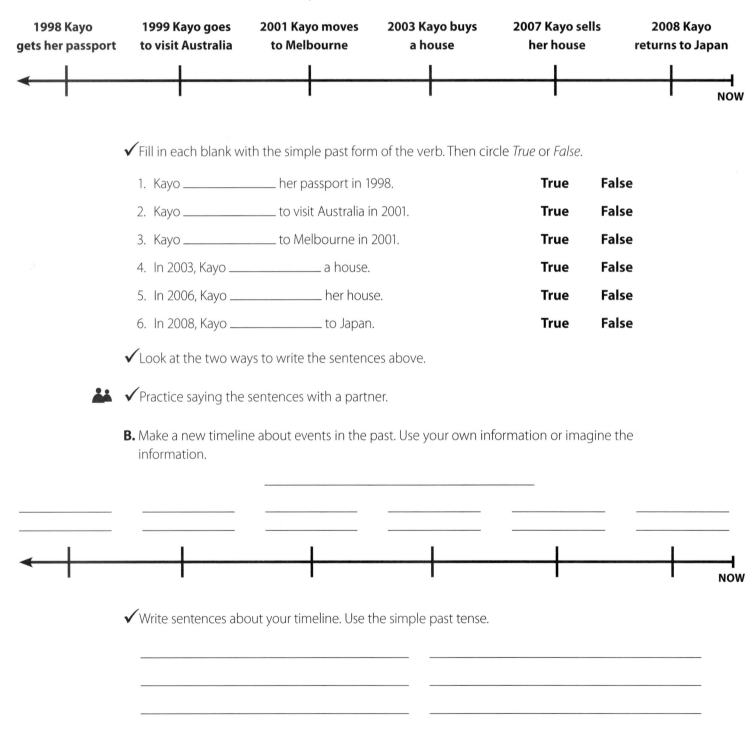

| 1998 Kayo gets her passport | 1999 Kayo goes to visit Australia | 2001 Kayo moves to Melbourne | 2003 Kayo buys a house | 2007 Kayo sells her house | 2008 Kayo returns to Japan |

NOW

✓ Fill in each blank with the simple past form of the verb. Then circle *True* or *False*.

1. Kayo _____ her passport in 1998.   **True**   **False**

2. Kayo _____ to visit Australia in 2001.   **True**   **False**

3. Kayo _____ to Melbourne in 2001.   **True**   **False**

4. In 2003, Kayo _____ a house.   **True**   **False**

5. In 2006, Kayo _____ her house.   **True**   **False**

6. In 2008, Kayo _____ to Japan.   **True**   **False**

✓ Look at the two ways to write the sentences above.

✓ Practice saying the sentences with a partner.

B. Make a new timeline about events in the past. Use your own information or imagine the information.

_____

_____   _____   _____   _____   _____   _____
_____   _____   _____   _____   _____   _____

NOW

✓ Write sentences about your timeline. Use the simple past tense.

_____   _____

_____   _____

_____   _____

✓ Show your timeline to a partner and say your sentences.

	Goals	Language Focus
UNIT 1 Friends and Family	• Describe a person	*She/He's young, with straight _____ hair.* *His/Her name is _____.*
UNIT 2 Jobs Around the World	• Asking for and giving personal information • Talking about jobs • Talking about countries	*What's your name? How old are you?* *Where are you from?*
UNIT 3 Houses and Apartments	• Describing a house	*What's in the big bedroom?* *There are two beds.*
Unit 4 Possessions	• Talking about the personal possessions of others	*These earrings look cool.* *She already has earrings. What about these sunglasses?* *They're ugly! Look at this desk lamp...*
UNIT 5 Daily Activities	• Asking and answering questions about work activities	*What time do you start work?* *What time do you finish work?*
UNIT 6 Getting There	• Ask for and give directions	*You are in the _____. Cross _____ Avenue.* *Walk two blocks and _____. Turn left/right and _____.*
UNIT 7 Free Time	• Talk about abilities	*Can you speak _____?* *Can you play the piano?*
UNIT 8 Clothes	• Describing peoples clothes	*He's wearing _____. What's his name?* *How do you spell it?*
UNIT 9 Eat Well	• Planning a dinner	*Could we have some soda, please?* *How many bottles do you want?*
UNIT 10 Health	• Describing symptoms and illnesses; giving advice	*What's the matter?* *You should...*
UNIT 11 Making Plans	• Express wishes and plans	*He would like to...* *She's going to...*
UNIT 12 Migrations	• Talking about people moving from place to place	*When did he leave _____?* *How long _____?* *Where did he live in _____?*

UNIT 1 FRIENDS AND FAMILY

Describe a person. Your partner says the name.

> **Student A:** He's young, with straight black hair.
> **Student B:** His name is Jason.

UNIT 2 JOBS AROUND THE WORLD

Student A

 Ask and answer questions to fill in the information.

Name:		Rafael
Age:		48
Single/Married:		married
Country:		Argentina
City:		Buenos Aires
Job:		teacher
Interesting/boring		interesting

Student B

 Ask and answer questions to fill in the information.

Name:	Maya	
Age:	30	
Single/Married:	married	
Country:	Russia	
City:	Moscow	
Job:	banker	
Interesting/boring	boring	

UNIT 3 HOUSES AND APARTMENTS

Student A

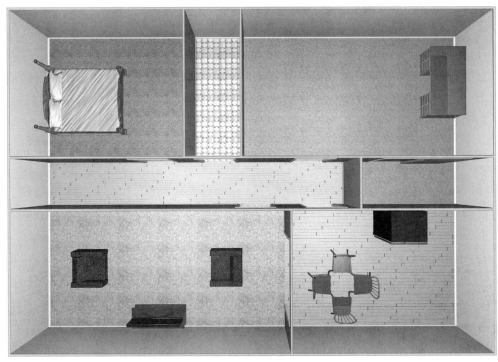 Talk to your partner. Ask and answer questions to complete the drawing.

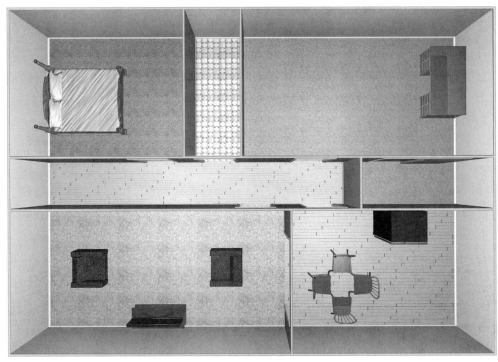

- -

Student B

Talk to your partner. Ask and answer questions to complete the drawing.

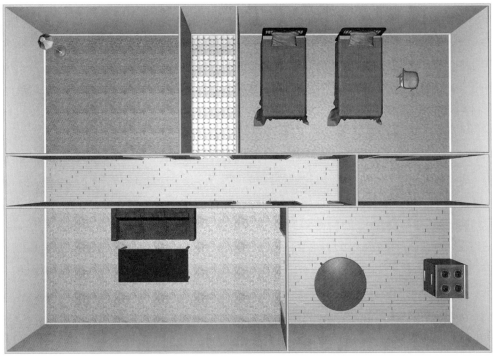

Photocopiable © 2010 Heinle, Cengage Learning

UNIT 4 POSSESSIONS

1. Your teacher will give you the names of two classmates. Look at the Web page and choose a present for each person.

1. Name:	Present:
2. Name:	Present:

2. Tell the class about the presents.

Communication Activity   T-197

UNIT 5 DAILY ACTIVITIES

Student A

Ask and answer questions to fill in the information. Are these good jobs?

Name:	Nathan	
Job:		baker
Get up:	4:00 p.m.	
Start work:	10:00 p.m.	
Have lunch:		8:15 a.m.
Finish work:	4:30 a.m.	
Go to bed:		6:30 p.m.

- -

Student B

Ask and answer questions to fill in the information. Are these good jobs?

Name:		Amanda
Job:	radio announcer	
Get up:		2:00 a.m.
Start work:		3:00 a.m.
Have lunch:	1:45 a.m.	
Finish work:		11:30 a.m.
Go to bed:	9:00 a.m.	

UNIT 6 GETTING THERE

 Look at the map. Ask your partner for directions to these places.

Student A
1. the tourist office
2. the art museum
3. Beijing Restaurant

Student B
1. the train station
2. the post office
3. Burger World

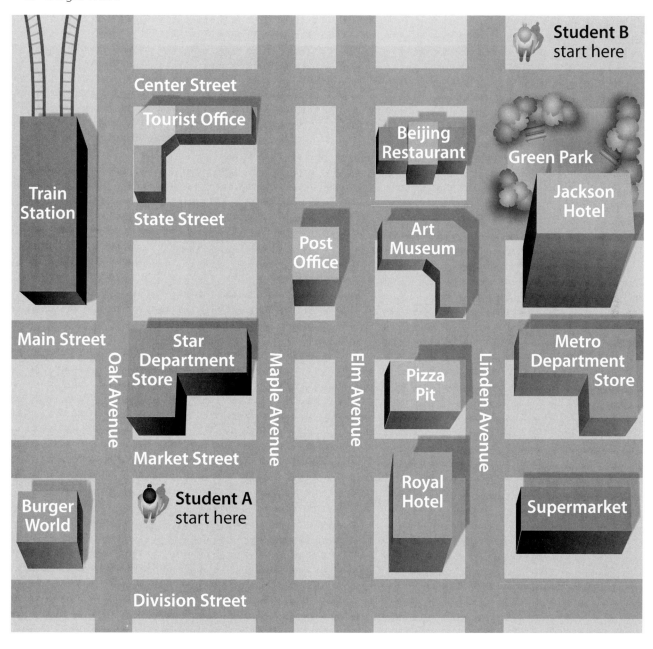

UNIT 7 FREE TIME

Ask and answer questions. Find a classmate who can do these things. Write the name.

Who can . . .	Name
1. speak two languages	
2. cook _____ (food)	
3. ice skate	
4. play the piano	
5. draw	
6. swim	
7. play _____ (sport)	
8. run fast	
9. play the guitar	
10. sing	

UNIT 8 CLOTHES

Student A

Listen to your partner's descriptions. Write the missing names.

He's wearing _____.

What's his name?

How do you spell it?

Student B

Listen to your partner's descriptions. Write the missing names.

He's wearing _____.

What's his name?

How do you spell it?

Photocopiable © 2010 Heinle, Cengage Learning

Communication Activity   T-201

UNIT 9 EAT WELL

You and your group are planning a dinner for a special day.

1. Choose a special day: _____

2. Write the menu here.

   Foods: _____

   _____

   _____

   _____

   _____

   _____

3. Write the drinks here.

   Drinks: _____

   _____

   _____

4. What time does your dinner start? What time does it end?

   _____

5. What clothes do people wear for your dinner?

   _____

6. Now tell the class about your dinner.

UNIT 10 HEALTH

Make conversations. Give advice to these people

1. He feels tired all the time.
2. She feels nervous about the test.
3. He can't sleep.
4. She has a very bad cold.
5. He can't understand his English class.

UNIT 11 MAKING PLANS

He would like to . . .

She's going to . . .

Look at the pictures. Talk about each person's goals and plans. Use your ideas.

Photocopiable © 2010 Heinle, Cengage Learning

UNIT 12 MIGRATIONS

Student A

 1. Ask and answer questions to fill in the information.

 2. With your partner, decide which person has a more interesting life.

Name:	Samuel	Ray
Born in:		1980
Home country:		The Philippines
Left his home country:		1999
Destination:		Australian College of Medicine and Science (Australia)
Migrated to:		Saudi Arabia (2002)
Moved to:		Riyadh, to work in a hospital as an x-ray technician

- -

Student B

1. Ask and answer questions to fill in the information.

2. With your partner, decide which person has a more interesting life.

Name:	Samuel	Ray
Born in:	1970	
Home country:	Nigeria (Africa)	
Left his home country:	1990	
Destination:	Oxford University (U.K.)	
Migrated to:	Canada (1996)	
Moved to:	Vancouver, to work in a bank	